PSYCHOANALYSIS AS A HUMAN SCIENCE: BEYOND FOUNDATIONALISM

. . .

PSYCHOANALYSIS AS A HUMAN SCIENCE: BEYOND FOUNDATIONALISM

...

BHARGAVI V DAVAR

·

PARAMESHWAR R BHAT

SAGE PUBLICATIONS
NEW DELHI/THOUSAND OAKS/LONDON

First published in 1995 by

Sage Publications India Pvt Ltd
M–32, Greater Kailash Market I
New Delhi 110 048

Sage Publications inc
2455 Teller Road
Thousand Oaks, California 91320

Sage Publications Ltd
6 Bonhill Street
London EC2A 4PU

Published by Tejeshwar Singh for Sage Publications India Pvt Ltd, Phototypeset by Pagewell Photosetters, Pondicherry, and printed at Print Perfect New Delhi.

Library of Congress Cataloging-in-Publication Data

Davar, Bhargavi V., 1962–
    Psychoanalysis as a human science: beyond foundationalism / Bhargavi V. Davar, Parameshwar R. Bhat.
        p.   cm.
    Includes bibliographical references and index.
        1. Psychoanalysis—Philosophy. I. Bhat, Parameshwar R., 1951–   II. Title.
[DNLM: 1. Psychoanalytic Theory. 2. Psychoanalytic Therapy. 3. Philosophy.
4. Cognition.   WM 460 D245p 1995]
BF175.D365   150.19′5′01—dc20   1995   94–39606
DNLM/DLC
for Library of Congress

ISBN: 0–8039–9196–7 (US-Hb)
        0–8039–9197–5 (US-Pb)

        81–7036–424–8 (India-Hb)
        81–7036–425–6 (India-Pb)

CONTENTS

...

ACKNOWLEDGEMENT

...

Work on this book was made possible by the grant of a Research Assistantship at the Department of Humanities and Social Sciences, Indian Institute of Technology, Bombay, for which the author is very grateful.

B.V.D

1

CRITICAL NORMATIVE PHILOSOPHY AND PSYCHOANALYSIS

■ ■ ■

I

This book addresses what is now popularly known as the 'foundations of psychoanalysis', an issue which pertains to philosophical discussions and evaluations regarding the status of this theory of psychopathology as scientific knowledge. This is essentially an epistemological problem relating to how we know what we claim to know about human behaviour. At the background of this epistemological issue is the traditionally posed philosophical debate of making a distinction between valid knowledge on the one hand, and belief, opinion and propaganda, on the other hand. However, for the purpose of this book, we assume simply that epistemology has to do only with the network of problems that arise in the context of *scientific* theories such as psychoanalysis and we are not concerned with the traditional philosophical debate as such. We are concerned with the current meta-scientific debate on what science is, how it differs from non-science, and where psychoanalysis falls within our scheme of things. There is, of course, some relation between the traditional debate on the epistemology of demarcating knowledge from opinion and the meta-scientific attempt of demarcating science from non-science. The latter may be viewed as a special case of the former, and specifically involves consideration of what scientists, as a social group which concedes certain normative standards, do when they do 'science', rather than what people in general do, when they claim to 'know'. In this book, we are concerned with the claims of psychoanalysis to the status of scientific knowledge.

The epistemological issue of the foundations of sciences, particularly human and social sciences, has assumed much importance in contemporary thinking. Philosophy has proved itself to be capable of raising pertinent issues about evolving criteria for accepting a certain proposed theory of human reality as 'valid' among many available and competing theories. Often this strong programme of staunchly rejecting philosophically 'invalid' theories is not always possible and it may also not be possible to specify the exact status of the theory. Even if foundational discussions do not always include a strong programme of eliminating some theories outright, they do try to assign the roles or functions of different scientific theories about human reality, with respect to a particular set of issues that concerns related communities. For example, the question of the evolution of the human race is plausibly explained by the Lamarckian, the Darwinian, the genetic and the Biblical theories. Foundational attempts would provide the involved research communities with philosophical criteria to decide which, if any, of these competing theories offer sound information about human evolution; or at any rate, what function, if any, these different theories serve in enhancing our understanding about human development. The philosophical focus on the foundations of a human science then is really a concern with a network of typically epistemological problems about deciding the philosophical viability of a proposed theory about some aspect or aspects of human reality and the way it enhances our understanding about this reality. Though the foundations issue has been raised in all sciences, it has been particularly fertile in the social sciences because the structure of these sciences are seemingly amorphous; concurrence on crucial issues has been hard to obtain; theoretical fecundity is often not supported by empirical facts; available facts are often unrelated to theory; etc. These and other interesting problems make it possible for philosophy to contribute to the evolution of social sciences.

This book is mainly concerned with the foundational evaluations of psychoanalysis. The aim of these evaluations in general has been to formulate stringent philosophical criteria on the basis of which psychoanalysis can be excluded from the realm of knowledge. The foundational issue is related to the traditional philosophical debate about demarcation, i.e., which theory, of the available theories, is justified in being used for human purposes and how it is possible to separate good theories from bad theories. The problem of demarcation is a typically philosophical problem, and enumerates the reasons for separating good theories from bad theories. Foundational ventures examine these reasons to determine which of the available theories are philosophically appealing on the basis of these reasons. The problem of demarcation and the foundational issue are often worked together in the decision regarding the claim of any theory to the status of knowledge. Sometimes it is argued that true theories, or theories which add to our knowledge about the world are scientific, and others are only metaphysical: they also make claims about the world, some or none of which may be true, even though many may believe them for various psychological, social or cultural reasons.

The philosophical demarcation of knowledge systems into good theories and bad theories about reality can be done on the basis of varying interests and norms. A fine example is the demarcation effected by philosophical assessments of psychoanalysis, leading to the negative conclusion that the theory must be excluded from the domain of knowledge. Psychoanalytic criticism[1] primarily has a *philosophical* genesis, originating either in the meta-scientific tradition inspired by Popper and his followers, or in the humanistic construals of phenomenology and existentialism. In the Popperian tradition, the philosophical demarcation is epistemological-normative, with the aim of separating scientific theories from pseudo-scientific ones by specifying the criteria of what constitutes science. In the existentialist tradition, the demarcation is ethical-normative, demanding exclusion of theories which are *dehumanising* from the realm of knowledge by specifying what 'humanism' is and describing the ethico-social commitments of science to society. The Popperian critique questions the scientificity of the theory on the grounds of the theory's negligible empirical support. The humanistic critique refuses consideration of the theory as it supposedly devalues human existence and upholds scientism. Present-day psychoanalytic criticism is inspired by one or the other of these philosophical traditions with entirely different demarcation criteria. Together, these two critical discourses lead to the often talked about 'crisis' (for example, Edelson, 1989) in psychoanalysis.

These two schools of philosophy, of course, have had an enduring animus on important philosophical issues relating to knowledge and

[1] The phrase 'psychoanalytic criticism' refers to any philosophical criticism of psychoanalytic theory. This book concerns particularly the western and the continental trends of such criticism.

the kind of commitments it must make to human interests. It is important to question whether the purely philosophical aporia around which the debate between positivism and hermeneutics has been centred has not altogether compromised the methodology of the science that they have critically examined; and whether the so-called 'crisis' imputed to the discipline of psychoanalysis reflects not so much the status of the theory in question, but rather the status of normative philosophy itself in its relation to social sciences, a project which to date appears to be confounded by its own internal politics. It will be seen that the history of philosophy, the philosophical vocabulary in which the foundational debate has progressed and the politics of this debate has not allowed a critical philosophy of science to grapple with conceptual and methodological developments in psychoanalysis and psychotherapy in general.

Of course, we do not claim that the foundational debate and the issues it raises for a human science are really non-issues and they can be explained away as historical accidents caused by philosophical dog-gedness. The philosophical exchanges have indeed been prolific in generating issues pertinent to a philosophy of social science—of doing social science in a reasonably sound way and of using such knowledge for the benefit of society. However, in bringing these philosophical issues to bear on the evaluation of the epistemological status of psychoanalysis, philosophical thought has not caught up with the science in question. Thought on 'science' and the possibility of its being committed to humanism has gone beyond the presuppositions upon which the philosophical critiques of psychoanalysis have been based. The philosophical deconstructions of the psychoanalytic theory by Popper and the empirical tradition as well as by the humanistic tradition, must themselves be deconstructed. Only this will lead to the possibility of providing different philosophical principles under which the psychoanalytic science might be organised, both epistemologically and ethically. It is possible to show, as we shall attempt to, that the ongoing psychoanalytic research programme can be brought under general epistemological principles which do not necessarily contravene humanistic ideals, contrary to what the critical traditions together claim.

II

Prima facie, the strikingly different claims by empiricism and hermeneutics about common philosophical issues lead to the impression that we are dealing with completely incommensurate theories of philosophy. Guided by a natural scepticism about the incommensurability of theories, we suggest that there is indeed a common epistemology underlying both these philosophies which we designate and describe as 'foundationalist'. We claim that both empiricism and hermeneutics have some common philosophical assumptions about the nature of knowledge and how knowledge is to be acquired. For the sake of simplicity and clarity, we have termed this set of assumptions as 'foundationalist'. Foundationalism is really a philosophical worldview, with metaphysical, epistemological and methodological implications. It is a theory of philosophy, guiding the decisions one may make regarding what is knowledge, when true claims have obtained and how true claims can be obtained.

Metaphysically, foundationalism implies the position that a certain kind of 'reality', such as a physical object or the self, as such is knowable in *guaranteed* ways and that the human mind does not distort such knowledge. The issue here is the place of the mind in the construction of knowledge, another conventional philosophical problem. According to foundationalism, cognition has no role in knowledge and valid knowledge obtains in a pure and objective form. For the foundationalists, knowledge is justified only when the mind is assumed to be a *tabula rasa* on which objects leave their trace. It is true that for the empiricists the primary object of knowledge is the physical object and for the humanists, it is the self. But both the traditions share the same assumptions about the nature of the relation between mind and knowledge, as will be seen later.

Epistemologically, this guarantee of cognitive self-evidence is assured for foundationalists by granting some criteria as privileged and as epistemically prior in the construction of knowledge systems. Of the possible criteria which determine the nature of cognitive claims, some, often one, such as sense data, observation or intuition, is given a privilege over all the others. This criterion need not even be of a definable character and does not require any further justification, but is simply posited as the self-evident basis or the pre-theoretic determinant which presides over knowledge. Margolis (1986) has referred to this stance in epistemology as a position which grants a cognitive transparency to the mind.[2] Tripplett (1990), in his taxonomic review of foundationalism, has noted its essential tenet: 'Basic propositions form a limited set of epistemically privileged propositions. They are privileged in that they are self-justified, or, in other formulations, noninferentially or immediately justified' (p. 96). The possibility of such uncorrupted self-evidence would predesign both the philosophical commitments regarding what counts as knowledge as well as that knowledge itself. Conclusions regarding an adequate epistemology as well as decisions regarding a good theory are both derived from the postulated fundamental axioms. Thus, for example, a prioritisation of 'observation' in logical positivism served as the basis not only for the subsequent epistemology of science, that is, of what an epistemology must rationally advocate as the ideal of science, but also as the scale against which a likely item striving for this status, such as psychoanalysis, must match up.

We claim that both the post-positivistic as well as the phenomenological critiques of psychoanalysis rest upon such a foundationalist philosophy. Other than being epistemologically and metaphysically foundationalist in the above senses, these critical traditions are also philosophically foundationalist in prioritising one *domain* of philosophy over others. The Popperian critiques refuse the status of knowledge to theories unless certain epistemological standards, particularly relating to 'truth' are met, whatever be the ethical/metaphysical consequences of these theories for human praxis. Inversely, continental thought disallows theories to be dehumanising, even though epistemological laxity is tolerable and recommended. Among the foundationalist assumptions that we question is the one about this prioritisation of the domains of philosophy. The issue before a philosophy of social science is to determine the balance which should obtain between epistemology,

---

[2] According to J. Margolis (1986),

> By the transparency thesis is meant all doctrines, however attenuated or variable, by which one holds that there is a determinate match or adequation between the cognizable properties of the real world and the cognizing powers of the human mind such that the *distributed* truths of science or of other disciplines inquiries may be assured that the inquiring mind does not, by its very effort, distort or alter or fail to grasp the world's independent (cognizable) structure: the world, or key parts of it, are in this sense cognitively transparent to the mind (p. xvi).

For more ideas on foundationalism and its implications for praxis, see Haller (1988).

metaphysics and ethics for the optimum functioning of the science and the place of demarcation in human praxis. Philosophy raises questions about what reality is, how to know it and what are the legitimate uses of such knowledge. These are related questions, requiring an integration of the domains of philosophy rather than their prioritisation.

The charge of foundationalism is not always to be construed negatively, as an intellectual tool with which to destroy philosophical systems. Even though in current philosophy foundationalism is accursed, our position does not claim that foundationalist arguments are unconditionally misguided. If an attempt at knowing how to acquire knowledge and the actual process of acquiring such knowledge has to be initiated at all, it must be done by prioritising a few or even one genetic metaphysical concept or an epistemological criterion over others and providing an intellectual place to begin. This is a cognitive *a priori*, given the limitations and possibilities of human attention and understanding. Every system of knowledge is 'foundational' in this sense. In Freud's intellectual history, for example, the cognitive concept of 'repression' took priority and, in fact, guided further conceptual development. However, philosophical problems become irresoluble when a theory dogmatically refuses to depart from its own genetic discourse; and when it fails to examine its metaphysics against normative considerations about what knowledge is, against its own capacity to realise these norms and its competence *vis-à-vis* rival theories of reality on crucial research problems.

'Foundationalism', or the need to show knowledge as being about some fundamental entities of reality and determined by a single important criterion of cognition, has presided over philosophy in the history of thought. Both the metaphysical and epistemological forms of foundationalism have a prodigious history in philosophical thought. Plato's theory of forms, Aristotle's causal theory, Leibniz's theory of monads, Lock's theory of experience and Hegel's historical *Geist* sought to provide the irrefragable ontological ground for knowledge. Different philosophical systems such as idealism, empiricism, naive realism, existentialism and logical positivism have sought to provide indubitable criteria of knowledge. Critiques of foundationalism are also very much part of the philosophical history beginning with Socrates, who was perhaps the first 'anti-foundationalist'. Hume, Peirce and Nietzsche have also been vocal in their objections to any fundamentalist attempt at founding knowledge.

What makes the foundationalist debate even more interesting is the multidisciplinary nature of modern attempts to answer it. As a philosophical enterprise, foundationalism has had a purely speculative history, depending very little on empirical psychology and other human sciences. Foundationalism, as a philosophical world-view, has been guided predominantly by purely abstract considerations. Philosophy itself is assigned a sacrosanct place, as the shelter within which comprehensive knowledge and, in fact, all human social praxis may be subsumed. However, it is recognised that the articulation of philosophically adequate responses to the question about the possibility of knowledge would be difficult unless the historical, linguistic, psychological and socio-cultural boundaries of human life are clearly understood. Modern discussions on the foundations of knowledge therefore often transgress purely philosophical limits entering into fresh pastures such as science of cognition, studies on human language, culture, history and social negotiations. This trend in general philosophy and in the philosophy of science is a renewal of the association with Immanuel Kant who tried to build philosophy on a human cognitive basis rather than on pure speculation. The trend also reaffirms some loyalty to Ludwig Wittgenstein who advocated that philosophy should simply articulate the rules which may apply to human social praxes. Modern philosophy appears to be redefining its own status with respect to sciences in general, limiting its task to providing rationalities for the sciences and also drawing important lessons from them on the nature of being human.

The two foundationalist traditions of psychoanalytic criticism show some similarity on the question of the philosophical features of a theory claiming to be knowledge. Foundationalism, in whatever form it is manifested, argues for the unitariness of knowledge systems and of the capacity of human beings to provide this unitary rationality: this is the claim that a theory is sound only if it satisfies a single criterion of knowledge, provides a single interpretation and adopts a single method. This is clearly a remnant of the positivistic legacy which emphasised the philosophical possibility of the unity of knowledge. In its excesses, the thesis of the unity of knowledge is that *all* knowledge is finally reducible to physical laws, or laws as defined by physics.

Many academic and administrative problems about knowledge, the world and human beings would be solved if we could obtain this state of rational union among our theories. Indeed, all human enterprise to attain knowledge is presided over by this philosophical utopia. The problem is how realistic this ideal is, and how far the formal nature of theories and the nature of human cognition on the basis of which theories are constructed will allow for the fulfilment of this ideal. Foundationalism has not given due consideration to these cognitive questions—of the active role human cognition plays in constructing knowledge—in their assessments of psychoanalysis, making their evaluations of psycho-analysis as well as the philosophical foundations of their evaluations unrealistic.

Foundationalism makes the assumptions that all interpretations of a theory are reducible to a single one and all theories relating to a particular domain are reducible to a single one. The assumption is a nostalgic yearning for reality, based on the belief that if a single rationality can be obtained on which all knowledge can be built, then this knowledge cannot but be a true metaphysical picture of the world. However, foundationalism is wrong in its claim that a general scientific theory, like Freud's psychoanalysis, is reducible to a single interpretative or theoretic possibility. It may be *desirable* to do so, and prospectively, all theories may even strive towards this ideal state of scientific theories. Usually we define an interpretation of a scientific theory as an empirical delimitation of a finite set of formally related and logically consistent concepts. But the logic, history and sociology of knowledge instructs us that no interpretation of a general theory is sufficient in itself. Gödel pointed one that no formal interpretation can be logically complete, and consequently, this renders its metaphysics and methodo-logy incomplete too. Wittgenstein initially believed that logic gives a picture of the world, but logic presents abstract *forms* as pictures of the world. Many forms are possible, allowing for many metaphysical possibilities. In one sense, logic overdetermines the world. At the same time, it also underdetermines the world, for no system of logic is philosophically complete. Logic describes too much or too little about the world and the metaphysical unity that foundationalism seeks from logic is not realistic. It is this logical incompleteness that motivates us who use these formal systems to look for philosophical *alternatives*, either by way of better metaphysical interpretations or better theories. It is a sociological truism that theories do not exist in isolation of other theories. The sociology of knowledge, that is, the study of growth of knowledge in society through a period of time, indicates that scientific theories are not *sui generis*. They are not generated out of themselves but grow out of interaction with other theories. The scientific growth of a theory is the outcome of an often unmeasured organic flux in which several competing theories participate. When metaphysically and logically complete theories are in principle impossible, the better option for an epistemology of science may be to recognise and account for the possibility of different scientific interpretations and their mutual interaction. Such an epistemology will contribute towards the theoretical and methodological evolution of science and will provide standards to measure their relative viability on common research questions. Working out the *comparability* between scientific theories is a more reasonable goal of epistemology rather than assessing the possibility of the unity of knowledge. This is particularly applicable to the social sciences. It is erroneous to claim as foundationalism does, that once a single interpretation and a single method is prescribed and adopted, a theory can go on without the benefit of critical interactions with related theories. It is this discursiveness between related theories on common research problems and our measurement of the degree of their performance that leads to a useful notion of the 'progress' of knowledge. This is an affirmation of the possibility and the advantages of a pluralistic epistemology for science. Later, this view of science will be termed the 'socio-cognitive' view of science. This view derives from an understanding that knowledge is possible because the human intellect is cognitive, and human beings can be scientific because of their natural, psychological constitution. The socio-cognitive view of science tries to comprehensively include the normative, philosophical dimension; the natural, psychological dimension; and the social dimension of knowledge.

By implication, the socio-cognitive view of science upholds the position that philosophy is itself interdisciplinary and that any evaluation of scientific theory must recognise this. This view of science raises several questions such as the relation between philosophy and scientific praxis, the place of philosophy with respect to science, and what it means to evaluate a science. We claim that the logical structure of the meta-level evaluation of a science and science itself must be more or less logically comparable for the normative inquiry to be meaningful in any way to the method of science in question. A relevant philosophy of science would acknowledge and begin from the inherent potential of growth in a scientific theory and would carry forward the core theoretical premises, goals and methods of the science. Foundationalism as a philosophical position about scientific theories supposes that philosophy supersedes and dictates to science in its prescription of norms. We find, on the contrary, that philosophy when divorced from scientific praxis, may fail to keep pace with the development of the science in question and then the normative enterprise itself might be anachronistic. This has happened in the case of psychoanalysis, where philosophy has simply failed to keep pace with the developments of the science.

III

Even though a common epistemology underlies both the post-positivistic and hermeneutic philosophical critiques of psychoanalysis, the radical difference between the two traditions must also be highlighted. The terminology 'external' and 'internal' foundationalism is devised in order to maintain this difference. One could, of course, have tried to understand the philosophical differences between these two schools of thought by using the traditional philosophical vocabulary and debates centred around the subject–object, idealism–empiricism, man–machine, cause–intention and other such conceptual polarities. However, by doing this, it would have been difficult to make discussions pertinent to psychoanalytic methodology in particular, and social science research in general. Philosophical debates are important for social science research, but they are not equally important. We need to focus on the methodologically significant debates which will contribute specifically to the progress of the science in question rather than on issues merely of philosophical interest. The terms, 'external' and 'internal' foundationalism give us an edge over traditional dichotomies in understanding and characterising the critical traditions in the light of their critical contribution to psychoanalysis and the nature and goals of this science.

The difference in the empiricistic and humanistic meta-scientific views of psychoanalysis relates particularly to issues of 'truth', 'meaning', 'observation' and 'explanation'. The external foundationalist critiques suggest that validation of psychoanalytic hypotheses will have to be done in artificially arranged experimental settings to conduct crucial experiments. In particular Karl Popper's and Adolf Grünbaum's critiques of psychoanalysis fall in line with this view of science. In this perspective observation and experiment have crucial roles to play. This comes close to the 'received view' stance of logical-positivism that knowing truth exhausts the epistemological goals of scientific theories and knowing such truth can only be accomplished by the standard, external and atemporal norms of an empiricistic meta-science. The notion of 'meaning' does not have any independent status in the

epistemology of science, but is simply identical to empirical significance, or the interpretation that a statement takes on through empirical
evidence. The philosophy of external foundationalism depends, for its
success, on the exaltation of the role of observation statements in the
sciences to the status of being immediately justified. The underlying
goal of science is objectivity and the possibility of knowing reality as it
is.

The internal foundationalist philosophy of hermeneutics and existentialism finds all this unpalatable. Based on an intuitivist epistemology,
this tradition refutes practically all possibility of an external validation
of psychoanalytic theory and anchors the determination of 'truth'
problematically within the clinic. The claim is that truth is constructed in
the course of the interpersonal transactions taking place within the
confines of the clinic. The internal foundationalist tradition of psychoanalytic criticism either makes the notion of truth redundant, or
reduces it to the notion of personal meaning, or the value a person
attaches to himself and the world. For the humanists, the norm which
allows meaning/truth to be possible is of an ethical or political nature.
According to this tradition, the goal of science, particularly a human
science, is not realism but ought to be humanism, where an ontological
discourse of the 'self' is accorded primacy. In an attempt to resolve the
problem of an inhuman engulfment of the psychoanalysed subject by
the science, the tradition attributes in an *a priori* way to the subject,
notions of self-understanding, freedom and equality and the possibility
of an intimate participation in and even knowledge of his own illness.
'Validation' of psychoanalysis, for the humanists, is possible from
within the narrative or dialogic space available between the psychoanalyst's authority and the patient's freedom. For them, the question of
truth is decided by resolving the question of power.

It is important to take note of and appreciate the humanistic common
concern on which both the critiques seem to apparently rest. Despite
what is claimed by the tradition, humanism is not the prerogative of
the continental humanistic tradition alone. This concern is strong in
the post-positivistic critical tradition also, in its ethical implications for
psychoanalysis and psychotherapy in general. The crucial problem in
psychotherapy is the real possibility of the psychoanalytic alliance
turning into a structure of appropriation by social authority, whether
such an authority is the psychotherapeutic institution, society or the
family. This raises a number of interesting questions in the realm of

psychotherapeutic ethics, such as the issue of forced interventions, the use of psychotropic drugs and hospitalisation. The demarcation interests of the philosophical traditions in question are both equally important in resolving the ethical issue of using psychotherapy in society. The resolution of this issue involves making not only an epistemological demarcation about when true knowledge has been obtained, but also an ethical distinction between when knowledge has been judiciously used and when it has not been used in the interests of the analysed subject. It is clear that two aspects need to be specified to resolve the ethical problem of the use of the knowledge to society: *what* 'knowledge' is and *how* it has been used. Only these two aspects together, the epistemological and the ethical, can really resolve the problem of appropriation of the psychoanalysed subject. In this sense, both the post-positivistic and the humanistic preoccupations are important. The post-positivistic tradition emphasises epistemological stringency so,that a common reservoir of knowledge about human nature becomes possible and everybody has public access to this knowledge. Knowledge, from this point of view, is universal *and* impartial. A critic of this bias may claim: after all, the psychoanalyst may be wrong in what he *thinks* he knows and may merely be imposing his own value structures on the psychoanalysed subject; so he must seek evidence through empirical research conducted outside of the clinic. The humanist agrees: indeed, psychotherapy is an institution with its own power structures; the psychoanalysed subject must have the freedom to speak within the clinical space. The humanist is concerned with the judicious *administration* of knowledge and not with its formation. But the two traditions fallaciously prioritise one domain of philosophy over the other, when addressing the general question of knowledge and human interests. Any humanistic consideration of knowledge, of using knowledge for enhancing the quality of human (psychological) life, will have to answer both the questions about the successful *formation* of knowledge and the effective *administration* of knowledge. The formation of knowledge relates to epistemology and the provision of norms. The administration of knowledge relates to the social organisation of this knowledge through societal institutions and making legislation for its judicious use. These reflections indicate at once, our critical stance with respect to the foundationalist philosophical traditions in question and our affirmation of both their programmes as inherently valuable.

This volume, as evident from the discussion so far, is a general essay on the philosophy of social science and tries to understand the science–society interphase. It seeks clarity on issues pertinent to our knowledge of human beings, of *what* makes humans know what they know about themselves and others, and *how* they use the knowledge thus acquired to further human ecological interests. Two kinds of philosophical disciplines are involved in this interphase, reflected in the unresolved but not irresoluble difference between external and internal foundationalism: these are the disciplines of epistemology and of ethics. The former articulates those acontextual and abstract, philosophical norms which sciences need to conform to in order to be a 'science' and the latter determines the place of science in society, by providing us with norms for assessing the impact of science on humans, for easing the integration of science with culture and tradition, for devising socially appropriate technologies, etc. This volume pertains particularly to the mental health sciences, and hopes to contribute to the evolving field of the philosophy of psychiatry. Psychoanalysis is used as a case study in order to illustrate how a philosophy of psychiatry is possible and how philosophy can contribute to the growth of the science.

IV

The aim to deconstruct the philosophical assumptions of contemporary psychoanalytic criticism is in some ways a subversion of the usual normative interest which often inspires such criticism. From our perspective, this subversion is important for it has significant implications for the kinds of things that philosophers can henceforth say and do about psychoanalysis. It is this programmatic subversion which allows us to work out the fundamental premises of an epistemology suited for psychoanalytic science. Of course, it must be cautioned that psychoanalysis does not require a separate or unique epistemology different from other natural and social sciences. We do not subscribe to the thesis that a social scientific rationality is radically different from a natural scientific rationality. However, any philosophy of science which denies this radical difference must still be universal enough to be able to accommodate the different sciences. Traditional philosophy of science, in its account and conception of what science is, in its choice of examples, in its historico-contextual analyses of paradigmatic science, has been singularly naturo-centric, though superficially it claims universality. Most discussions on the philosophy of science thus tend strongly towards physics, with a cursory remark that the philosophy itself is universal and equally applicable to the other sciences. Avoiding both these excesses, we want a universal view of science that will not necessarily exclude psychoanalysis from its domain as pseudo-scientific.

In the context of psychoanalysis, orthodox formulations of foundational issues have always been posed in terms of whether the theory is 'science' or 'art'. The subsequent approach to resolve this issue has been for philosophers to choose among different norms, what appears to them to be the most rational and philosophically defensible. According to Von Eckhardt (1982), the critical challenges to psychoanalytic theory 'in the past twenty years have taken the following form: Premise A: To be scientific, something must have a certain property N. Premise B: Psychoanalysis does not have property N. Therefore, psychoanalysis is not scientific' (p. 140). These efforts have reduced practical problems in different sciences to linguistic problems about refining and clarifying the way the word 'science' is or is not to be used, and which, if any, of the sciences can be identified as exemplifying the usage. The demarcation problem in philosophy, essentially a methodological problem, is reduced to a linguistic problem about the right use of the word 'science'. The methodology of science and the interesting philosophical problems therein are subsequently disregarded. It is, of course, important to solve linguistic puzzles and to attain clarity on usage of terms but, if in the process, the very relevance of raising the issue is lost one must question the exercise. The question whether psychoanalysis is a 'science' or not is an important one only when it is formulated as a *cognitive* issue and not as a linguistic puzzle. When raised as a cognitive issue, one wants to know whether *synthetic knowledge* pertaining to the human mind, such as the theory claims, is possible and how it can be made philosophically acceptable. The Kantian question of the possibility of synthetic knowledge is equally applicable to the science of the mind. Verbal or logical adjustments made in classifying psychoanalysis do not help one to gain insights into the possibility of knowledge about the functioning of the human mind.

A purely normative evaluation of a science may be of some interest to philosophers but would be of very little significance to social scientists and as such makes little contribution towards advancing the methodology of science. In the syllogism pointed out by Von Eckhardt, philosophers can change (and *have* repeatedly changed) the content of Premise A, by substituting for different properties for N, and advancing different definitions of 'science' and different evaluations of a theory. In the history of philosophy of science, different essential properties have been attributed to 'science'. Property N could be deductive completeness, falsifiability, inductive support, historical rationality, social consensus, etc. There is an open-endedness to the normative exercise which is perhaps due not so much to the fecundity of a philosopher to substitute for property N, but to the nature of the task itself. Just as scientific theories change and are superseded, so also philosophical norms and perspectives about what science is change and are superseded. The discursive limits which philosophers claim apply to sciences are applicable to philosophy as well. The history of the philosophy of science has highlighted that unitary rationalities provided to science have been riddled with as many internal inconsistencies, paradoxes and contradictions as the scientific theories which they address. Cushing (1990) has defended the claim that 'there are no invariant (ahistorical, atemporal) characteristics of science that distinguish it from nonscience' (p. 178). He has argued that the science–meta-science distinction is a false one and that the so-called meta-scientific 'norms' have been abstracted from particular and often only successful instances of scientific praxis. The rules of science, according to him, are networked with science in such a way that both science and the philosophy of science evolve together and change in time. All these current critical reflections on the historical vicissitudes of meta-science fundamentally question the hitherto ahistorical and universalised attempts by philosophers of science in evaluating the scientific status of a theory. They must be construed not as a historical thesis about science but rather as a cognitive thesis about the essential interaction of the science–meta-science relationship which the philosophy of science must take note of.

The postulation of norms is of course not totally dispensable in meta-scientific considerations. Knowledge in our post-modern world is governed by social institutions and their political and administrative imperatives. Our capacity to make judicious decisions regarding the use of a scientific theory for society depends on the potentiality of that theory to conform to certain standards of rationality. The line between 'rationality' and 'irrationality' is drawn for human social agency by positing philosophical norms. However, the problem arises when philosophy exaggerates its own importance with respect to the pragmatics of science. In psychiatry, for example, philosophical normative considerations about rationality and irrationality are often only remotely connected with the kinds of theoretical and practical problems that clinicians deal with. And this being the case, the very relevance of the normative enterprise is often questioned by clinicians (Macklin, 1983).

Any inquiry which begins with the purpose of making a normative 'assessment' inevitably carries within it, as a hidden premise, the very judgment which it seeks to establish. According to Von Eckhardt (1982),

> (I)t is appropriate to raise the question of the scientific status of psychoanalysis, or to challenge this status, only if there is, at least, some *prima facie* presumption in favour of its being scientific. In contrast, one would not raise the question of the scientific status of, say, Shakespeare's 'Romeo and Juliet' (p. 141).

Begging the question is inherent to all normative attempts that search for a unitary rationality underpinning the different sciences. This circularity is not intrinsically problematic, for any evaluative comparison between two items *presupposes* that the family resemblance theory is true: this is the philosophical intuition that two items are comparable because they are tokens of a particular type and are both denoted by some common attributes. Comparability presupposes that the things being compared have some properties in common. It is only an intuition that psychoanalysis is perhaps more comparable with the sciences than with the arts that makes it even possible to ask explicit questions about the theory's scientific status. In asking this question one grants so much that the theory is a *likely*, even if not exactly exemplary, candidate for assigning the status of a science.

The debate between 'science' and 'art' itself has been historically determined and has definite *philosophical*, rather than methodological or pragmatic, significance. Even though ordinarily we can easily pick out disciplines or objects such as a Picasso or an industrial boiler, as falling naturally into the one or the other category, philosophical history has problematised the science or art question. For the concerned research community in psychotherapy working with these philosophical debates, however, necessitates taking positions about the significance and the place of these debates *vis-à-vis* their practical constraints and requirements. The demarcation issue *per se* does not interest the research and the practicing community. Often, and naturally so, the community perceives itself as doing science. Mental health and the science of the mind contribute to global human development;

contemporary society and its politics recognise it as such. Even though psychoanalysts are sometimes tempted to decry the status of their theory as science, in practice psychoanalysis is recognisably aligned within the larger framework of science. The psychological and psychiatric discourses relate themselves naturally to questions that psychoanalysis raises about the mind and mental illness and the integration of the mentally ill into social units. In practice, then, the status of psychoanalysis as a science is more or less assumed, and correctly so, even though philosophical debates about its status continue to date.

V

Psychoanalytic criticism has been active almost since the time of Freud, and has become virulently so since Popper, as will be seen later. As the practitioners of psychoanalysis themselves have taken these critical philosophical traditions seriously the evolution of modern psychoanalytic research and practice has been considerably guided and influenced by these philosophical critiques. The influence of philosophical criticism on social sciences has carried forward the philosophical assumptions of foundationalism into the fold of psychoanalytic pragmatics. Psychoanalytic pragmatics include both the components of therapy as well as research in the discipline of psychoanalysis. Specifying the exact relation between therapy and research has been of some concern to thinkers and practitioners in the area. Current thinking on psychoanalysis recognises that it is important to sustain the distinction between therapy and research. It is rightly argued that the normative considerations which preside over therapy are not the same as those which guide research. This distinction is perhaps comparable to the distinction often made between clinical practice and medical research in organic medicine, or between applied science and pure science in the natural sciences, though the issues involved are not very clearly enunciated in the field of psychotherapy. There is indeed a close interaction between the frontline research and its application in the clinic, but it is widely recognised that there can be no sound rationality for collapsing the difference altogether. Referral to pragmatics in psychoanalysis may thus be made either in the therapeutic context or in the research context and often, in the course of discussions, it may be crucial to make the context explicit.

The attempted grounding of psychoanalysis in two widely different philosophical contexts has simply inducted the conflict between the contexts into psychoanalysis as well. The so-called inner 'crisis' of psychoanalysis is perhaps the reflection of a crisis in the philosophies which have addressed the issue of science. Pragmatics in psychoanalysis specially in terms of therapy has allowed itself to be moulded after the foundationalist philosophies adhered to by the critical traditions. In other words, answers to specific methodological debates such as whether justification of psychoanalytic claims is possible within the clinical set-up has been shaped by the particular philosophical position that the practitioner endorses. The well-entrenched response to this methodological problem was initiated by David Rapaport in the sixties. He has posited a clear distinction between the so-called Freudian 'clinical theory' and 'meta-psychology', a distinction which has been debated ever since and known as the 'Great Meta-psychology Debate' in psychoanalytic literature (Wallerstein, 1986a, p. 417). Meta psychology is the abstract, formal theory of psychology that Freud proposed in order to explain certain types of abnormal behaviour. The clinical theory is the phenomenal manifestation of the meta-psychological theory in the clinic. A host of thinkers associated with this movement, such as Holt, Home, Rycroft, Klauber, Gill, Klein, Schafer and Spence (for a review of literature, see Wallerstein, 1986a; Holt, 1985; Eagle, 1984) have argued contentiously that the meta-psychology that Freud proposed must be weeded out, and that only the clinical theory must be retained. Among the various arguments advanced to show the redundancy of meta-psychology (Holt, 1985) the notable are: that the general theory has not been integrated into therapy; that concepts are ill-defined, diffused, self-contradictory, metaphorical and often reified; that the theory is based upon an outdated physiology, anatomy and early evolutionary biology; that the instinctual theory represents a dehumanised view of man; and finally, that it rests upon philosophically weak foundations. To overcome these difficulties it was proposed that a purely clinical theory be constructed. The clinical theory is alleged to be observationally 'pure' and supposedly restricts itself only to clinical presentations.

Those who celebrate what Holt has designated as the 'death' of meta-psychology can be grouped into different categories, leaning philosophically towards one or the other side of the schism between internal and external foundationalism. There are those who stress the epistemological need to clearly formalise and objectively study clinical interactions, and those who decry epistemology altogether and argue simply in favour of humanly satisfying interpersonal relationships between the analyst and analysand. For the former, human beings, as they are seen in the clinic, are objects of knowledge and can be known like other objects of the world, through natural, causal laws. The epistemology assumed by the empiricistic clinicians is a theory of human behaviour based on causal laws that allows us to know and predict the behaviour of the analysed subjects in the clinic. For the humanists however, human subjects are not at all reducible to such causal principles as is commonly accepted by a meta-science. Special epistemological terminology in terms of an introspective and intentional self has to be devised based on the recognition of the essential in-effability of human reality. An object, as in the physical sciences, is believed to be effable, but not so in the case of humans. The subjects of therapy are not objects but 'selves' and a 'self' is a radically distinct philosophical entity from an object. There is supposed to be an irreconcilable difference in the kinds of things that can be studied and a philosophy of social science must *a priori* grant this difference. Human subjects can only be understood through dialogue in the clinic and theories about subjects are only narratives constructed meaningfully for both the analyst and analysand, making no claim on truth or reality.

Regardless of the philosophical differences, the main purpose of clinical theorists is to do away with the abstract and theoretical framework known as 'meta-psychology' which Freud had evolved to explain abnormal behaviour in favour of a purely clinical theory. This shift from the general Freudian theory to a clinical theory by psychoanalysts carries the full import of foundationalism. Whether in the positivistic variants or in the humanistic variants, philosophically, this shift of attention from meta-psychology to the clinical theory endorses the claim that the analysand as the object of the analyst's knowledge can be known as such, through pure observation within the clinical setting.

It is precisely this claim, that psychoanalytic laws can be validated within the clinic which has become the bone of contention between the critics and the practitioners. For critics like Grünbaum and Eagle, validation of psychoanalysis is an epistemological question relating to research and it is incorrect to raise it in the context of the clinic which is therapy-oriented. Those who argue for the adequacy of the clinical case study method of validation, however, claim that the individual undergoing therapy is an adequate sample from which general laws about human behaviour can be derived. They claim that the pursuit of cure in no way detracts from the research possibilities of the clinic. The case study method is widely adopted by psychoanalysts. They believe that this method is rigorous enough and if some thumb rules are conscientiously adopted documentation of case studies can be an effective way of accumulating knowledge. In one sense, this is an old problem facing the philosophy of social sciences, about whether the study of human beings implies acquiring deep understanding into a single case, or whether it is about formulating universal laws by abstracting from many cases, the perennial problem of induction.

In another sense, there is an important difference between this general problem and the problem as it has been posed in psychotherapy, a difference which makes the general problem pertinent to psychotherapeutic research. In psychotherapy, the problem is not only about formulating general laws from a single case, but also about the possibility of using therapeutic success as proof for the validity of these laws. Any attempt at validating a general law from a case study will have to indicate the standards or the rationality of claiming that a particular case study instantiates a law. These decisions cannot be arbitrary and based upon personal taste, but rather, will have to be based upon an informed rationality. Stating these norms explicitly will enable us to evaluate whether a law has been 'true' of particular instances, failed in others, and to be generally aware of the empirical limits of the law in question. Even in case studies, it is argued, some conception of induction is inevitable, because it is always possible to generalise and derive a law from a case and to apply it to other cases. Orthodox psychoanalysts have been using the notion of therapeutic success as the standard for their case studies and subsequent judgment about the truth value of a psychoanalytic law. That is, if a therapy has been successful, then the laws which have been assumed in order to accomplish this are treated by clinicians as valid. Philosophically, a pragmatic theory of truth is assumed in this inference: that if something *works* by making the assumption 'a', then the assumption is true by virtue of it having worked. If the patient is 'cured' by making some assumptions about cognition, then the cure is because of the truth of these assumptions. It is this inference, from the success of therapy to the truth of the theory, which the critics are quick to reject as logically fallacious for reasons which will be discussed later. Since the case study method allows for faulty inferences, these critics claim that this method should be given up in favour of extra-clinical, artificially simulated and controlled epidemiological, comparative and cognitive studies on mental illness.

These specific debates on methods in the general problem of validation of psychotherapy are naturally linked to the issue of the place of measurement in sciences in general, and the role played by instruments in limiting the attainability of 'truth' in systems of science, particularly social science. The role of instruments in experiment, validation and arriving at evidence is a well debated issue today in the philosophy of natural sciences. In social sciences there is no place for sophisticated instrumentation though an analogous place may be granted to the analytical methods used by social scientists. The different methods of analysis in social sciences may be conceived of as tools by which we understand social and human reality.

Philosophically, several ideas are implied by the word 'tool', *à la* Martin Heidegger and the subsequent philosophy of technology that he inspired. A tool is a means to an end and its function is determined solely by its use. It has a range of applications and uses but there is a limit to this range of uses. For example, a hammer may be used to hammer a nail, to break stones, to drive a wedge, to break glass, to commit murder, but not surely to climb a tree, to cross a river, to take a photograph or to fly a kite.

A method in science has a similar purpose, serving as a means to achieve the pragmatic ends of a scientific theory. One of the important functions of a philosophy of science is to indicate 'appropriate' and 'inappropriate' methodological tools available in sciences. Methodological tools in the social sciences can be invented or improvised, depending upon human needs, socio-culture perceptions and contexts. An efficient methodological tool makes a scientific theory *pragmatic*. The use of a theory in human praxis solely rests on its applicability. A theory becomes pragmatic because of the intervention of tools between the theory and the world. It is possible to apply a theory to the world because the steps to accomplish this application are worked out methodologically. This application depends on the specification of method. Formal theories are given empirical meaning in terms of phenomena and their interrelationships as they are captured through the perceptual, numerical and other tools of analyses. If there is no method by which a theory can be applied to the world, the presumed semantic relation of a scientific theory to the world would not exist.

A method is not an end in itself but a means by which the larger goal of science, what we call its 'reality commitment', is achieved. Philosophically, any science is committed to the reality of the world. Scientific realism is an inevitable goal of all natural and social sciences. What is at stake in the methodological discussions between the psychoanalytic clinicians and the philosophical critics is the capacity of the methods under debate to satisfy the larger, realistic goals of the science. At the bottom of the methodological discussions is the question whether justifying psychoanalytic claims in the clinic gives a true theory of psychology, a universal theory of man and abnormal cognition; or whether it is only an idiosyncratic picture, determined largely by the individual outlook of the practising analyst and the analysand.

This discussion indicates that philosophical foundationalism has clear implications for the methodological debates on both psycho-analytic therapy and research. The problematisation of the philosophical foundations of psychoanalysis calls into question the praxis in very specific ways. Any response to the philosophical critiques which aims to undo the 'crisis' in psychoanalysis needs to address these methodo-logical issues also. It will have to make explicit the philosophical features of a clinical interaction and whether these allow for the possibility of validation of the theory's cognitive claims. An under-standing of the essential nature of psychoanalysis as a psychopatho-logical theory of the mind is required and also an understanding of what the epistemological commitments of the theory must be, in order that it does not fall short of the usual normative standards of a science. Such an attempt needs to understand the nature of the psychotherapist's work in the clinic and the assumptions upon which any therapy in general, and psychoanalytic therapy in particular, is based. Reflections on all these questions will eventually comprise a response to the foundations issue with respect to psychoanalysis.

The extensive documentation of case studies made available by Freud makes him a good choice for our understanding of the essential nature of the theory and its use in therapy. However, given modern developments in psychoanalysis, this choice is not the only one nor even, perhaps, the best one. Philosophical critics such as Habermas and Grünbaum have chosen to focus singularly on Freud for various reasons including that his documentation is extensive and meticulous, modern psychoanalysis evolved from his general theory, modern psy-choanalysis is too fragmented and his is the *only* correct model of psychoanalysis. The false assumption the critics make is that with Freud vanquished philosophically, the followers of Freud will fall too.

These rationalisations of choosing Freud as the target of philosophical criticism allow the critics the liberty of ignoring or taking lightly the prodigious efforts of post-Freudians in shaping the evolution of the discipline. There is a certain sense in which foundational questions must be *contemporary*, and must grant the possibility that modernity may have cleared up at least some of the illusions of a visionary founder. As purely philosophical exercises, as attempts to understand Freudian humanism, the logic of his discoveries, the ideological underpinnings of his science, the philosophy of his theory, the socio-cultural determination of his theory, the founder's psychohistory, and so on, such dependence on Freud's texts would be warranted. These issues, interesting as they are, are researched not in order to verify the 'truth' of the theory but rather to understand Freud's place and role in the subsequent evolution of the discipline itself and psychotherapy in general. From this historicist's perspective, Freud was an intellectual medium through which psychotherapeutic thought was carried forward, on a par with a Galileo or a Newton. But any understanding of the science, especially an epistemological assessment of the science, will also have to consider contemporary psychoanalytic praxis and not *only* how Freud practised. It is important to take into account how the discipline has responded to questions related to both the epistemological viability of the theory as well as its commitment to humanism. This response from the discipline has involved some thinking about the epistemological norms which any human science, including psychoanalysis, must commit itself to.

VI

Two things need to be done in foundational ventures in the context of the science in question. First, a relook at Freud's works and examine what he wanted his theory and his therapy to be; and second, a review of the way in which modern, therapeutically active and useful interpretations of psychoanalysis have critically evolved from Freudian psychoanalysis. In general terms, this involves an inquiry into the viability of Freudian philosophy and psychology in the contemporary venture to understand mental illness through scientific procedure. It is an attempt to understand what Freud's theory of psychology essentially is.

Addressing the methodological debate first, it is important to ask whether meta-psychology is a redundant vestige or whether it is an indispensable part of the theory. We claim, contrary to the clinical theorists, that it is not philosophically possible for a psychodynamic theory like psychoanalysis to be divested of its meta-psychology. According to Freud, meta-psychology had to perform several functions in his general theory of psychology (Holt, 1981a). More important, he wanted it to be a general explanatory theory of abnormal cognition. His psychological theory depended on the distinction between conscious and unconscious mental states. Meta-psychology was to be the formal theory which would capture the difference between conscious and unconscious states of the mind. However, the ontological form which he gave meta-psychology changed from the initial to the later stages of his intellectual evolution, from a purely physicalistic causal interpretation to a more psychological, although still causal, interpretation.

Freud wanted meta-psychology to encompass 'the theoretical assumptions on which a psychoanalytic system could be founded' (Freud, S.E., Vol. 14, p. 222). Meta-psychology was to present a second level perspective of what his psychology was to be like. On the basis of his 'meta-psychology', Freud tried to formulate a theory of abnormal cognition. It is true that the norms he provided for this theory were somewhat limited epistemologically, particularly his rejection of empirical cognitive research and his unshaken predeliction for verifying the truth of his hypotheses based solely upon clinical findings. Yet, he made no claims that his theory described the phenomena presented before him in the clinic in purely observational terms.

A cognitive theory like psychoanalysis cannot be 'clinical' in the true sense. The clinic itself is only a setting where various extra-clinical factors are played out. These factors may be of the nature of historical contexts, theoretical discussions, technical developments, etc. Freud made several non-clinical assumptions about the nature of the human mind and behaviour. His fundamental assumption was that the mind always works rationally. Even abnormal behaviour is in some sense rational in so far as scientists can organise such behaviour through laws. For Freud, though the mind was complex and structured at different levels of consciousness, all action, whether normal or abnormal, was caused. Freud believed that meta-psychology addressed the overall personality of man rather than the particular symptoms presented in the clinic. As will be seen later, the history of psychoanalysis highlights the fact that Freud's approach to the treatment of his patients, his proto-model of psychoanalysis, was nothing but the application of considerations derived from outside the clinic, particularly medical debates concerning the nature of hypnosis and hysteria.

Wittgenstein may have said that psychoanalytic practice is possible only because the clinicians pre-reflectively apply the cognitive rules provided by the theory. Philosophically, the very notion of 'practice' implies rule following of this sort. Rule following requires prior understanding and competence in the use of the vocabulary of the theory in question (Johannessen, 1990). The rules of the theory are cognitive in nature, giving knowledge about objects, rather than how something can be done. Scientific rules are related to 'what' questions, rather than to 'how' questions. Therapy in the clinic presupposes the rules given by the general theory. This general theory is derived from research conducted extra-clinically, satisfying the epistemological norms of scientific procedure rather than the therapeutic imperatives that hold sway in the clinic. It is for this reason that the epistemological validation of the cognitive claims of the theory cannot be done in the clinic. For the same reason, the clinical theory is not adequate in itself and depends, for its realisation, on meta-psychology.

We understand Freudian psychoanalysis as being essentially a *cognitive* theory of human behaviour. Perspectivising Freudian psychoanalysis thus allows us to leave behind the philosophically dubious 'foundations' of the science suggested by both kinds of foundationalism. It opens up the possibility of providing a fresh direction to the foundation question using modern thinking on the philosophy of science, mind and language. There is increasing recognition of the interdependence between psychology and epistemology. The important question which is raised today is whether the natural cognitive limits to knowledge make objective knowledge and realism impossible in the sciences; and also, whether the cognitive sciences are not themselves bound by epistemological norms. These questions necessitate an examination of the relation between mind and knowledge and the relevance of this relation for a philosophy of the science of mind like psychoanalysis. The foundations that we provide for psychoanalysis may be designated 'cognitivist', for the epistemology is derived largely from responses made to these epistemological issues in the growing field of cognitive science. The cognitivist foundation of psychoanalysis emphasises at least three requisites of scientific psychological theories: the interdisciplinary nature of research; the theoretical delimitation or demarcating the explanatory scope of the theory; and the build up of a vast empirical pool on which the theory is to be based. This science is, as mentioned earlier, socio-cognitive in nature, particularly requiring the possibility of comparably relating to other kindred theories of cognition.

This perspectivisation of psychoanalysis on a cognitivist foundation has several implications for the science. The very *possibility* of this perspectivisation presupposes that the assumptions of cognitive science and psychoanalysis are comparable.[3] Psychoanalysis views abnormal behaviour not as a *behavioural* problem but as a *cognitive* problem. In any cognitive science, human behaviour is not an unrelated sequence of overt physical or physiological action generated by a 'mentally' inert biological organism, as it is for the behaviourists. It is rather the observable effects of psychologically active states of an organic system engaged in the task of being in the world through the acquisition and processing of information. The mind is not a *tabula rasa*, as the foundationalists have conceived it, but has an active role to play in the constitution of knowledge and action. The mind is structured as an organic system and observed behaviour is the output of specifiable functions that it performs. In understanding the purely psychological nature of the mind, the machine analogy is useful though it has its limitations. Human action is the result of the mind working with or processing information about itself and its surroundings through cognitive grids. The processing of information is possible because the mind can work with symbols, the patterning of which may be called representations. Based on the implications of this view of the mind, we can understand the network of relations that individuals are involved in, such as the self–self, self–other and self–object relations. 'Abnormal' cognition, according to this cognitive view of human behaviour, is subsumed under the general category of human cognition, as a special type of cognition.

Philosophically, the cognitivist foundation we want to provide psychoanalysis is based on the Kantian–Wittgensteinian stand on epistemology that knowledge unmediated by human symbolic praxis is impossible. The human mind, because of its competence to work at different levels with these symbols, mediates our efforts to understand all kinds of objects, including ourselves, through representations. That knowledge is possible because of the mind does not however make knowledge idealistic. The mediation of cognitive symbols in our efforts to know is not a denial of realism. The range of representations that can possibly be constructed by the mind is determined by reality itself. Scientific theories are the result of human cognition and are constrained

<hr />

[3] These ideas were discussed briefly in V. Bhargavi and P.R. Bhat, 'The Epistemic Comparability of Psychoanalysis and Cognitive Science', paper presented at a thematic session of the *XVth International Congress of Psychology*, Brussels, Belgium, 19–24 July 1992.

by formal and empirical norms. Our approach to reality is determined by these theories. However, the force of reality limits these theories. This Kantian synthetic viewpoint of knowledge, retaining both the empirical and cognitive components of knowledge, flavoured by the Wittgensteinian thesis about the rule governed behaviour of human action, forms the essential basis of realism that underpins any cognitive science. The sticky philosophical problem here is how realism is possible in psychology. For, the mind is not tangible like a physical object, leading many philosophers to dismiss all talk of the mind as linguistic jargon. The possibility of realism in psychology is an issue which will be dealt with in detail later.

The claim that psychoanalysis rests on a cognitivist foundation is a meta-level claim about the philosophical nature of psychoanalysis. Classical psychoanalysis has, since Freud, led to better, empirically grounded, synthetic and domain specific *models* of psychodynamic psychotherapy. The cognitivist perspectivisation is essentially not about salvaging the general Freudian theory, for this will involve, among other things, a formal and comparative analysis of the theory in the light of current empirical research in the field. This is a task beyond the scope of this work. The perspectivisation is rather a philosophical one, related to the epistemological nature of psychoanalysis and the specification of philosophical conditions which show the psychopathological theory as philosophically acceptable.

A cognitivist epistemology for psychoanalysis would necessitate an examination of the psychological theory and the Freudian enterprise in a certain way. Any cognitive science presupposes a psychological thesis that the mind relates in certain ways to different objects or units of organisation. What we perceive as objects is the result of the active organisation by the mind using various categories of understanding, such as colour, shape, time and space. Ordering of inputs from the world using some general principles results in our cognition of objects. Objects are representations of the mind; the mind relates to the world through representations. Objects are not unitary but are related both among themselves and with respect to the subject. The aim of epistemology is to provide norms for making these object relations computable. Object relations, fundamentally a cognitive concept, is a definitive psychoanalytic concept as well.

A theory of psychology like psychoanalysis tells us how we are capable of ordering objects in different ways. Psychoanalysis claims that 'objects' are of two kinds—those we represent to ourselves as existing in 'reality' and those we represent to ourselves as 'imaginary' (Edelson, 1989). All objects are representations that the subject's intentions take on, but among these objects, distinctions are necessary for explaining rationality. The distinction that we make to ourselves, that some objects are 'real' and some are 'imagined', lies at the base of our rationality. Psychoanalysis attributes to the normal human mind the capacity to make a distinction between real and imagined objects. An irrational mind fails to make this distinction.

In the case of both philosophy and psychology, the question of rationality and irrationality is an important one. Philosophy is concerned with making rationality possible through formal means. In psychology, rationality is a natural state of being and irrationality requires special attention and explanation. A psychopathological theory explains irrationality. Both rational and irrational experiences are human experiences, resulting from the same set of specifiable cognitive functions. Though the entire range of cognitive states and functions are the same in all human beings, yet the irrational experiences are a result of some aberration or the other of cognitive functions.

The demarcation problem which has attracted the attention of thinkers like Karl Popper and Adolf Grünbaum is at a deeper level, the same as the problem of providing a logical basis for making a cognitive distinction between 'rationality' and 'irrationality'. The demarcation problem reveals a concern with when scientists have made rational choices and when they have not. An epistemology gives us some criteria to effect this distinction, psychology tells us what it is in the nature of our cognition which allows us to make this distinction, and a theory of psychopathology indicates both what happens when we fail to make this distinction and how to restore this function when it is lacking in some human beings. Psychoanalysis is one such theory which claims that the mind can relate to objects at the levels of both the conscious and unconscious mental states. Distinctions are possible among these different states, such as wishing, dreaming and thinking. Formal semantics specifies how these states actually relate to overt behaviour, both normal and abnormal, through causal laws. The theory stipulates various processes of agency to the mental states defined by the theory, assuming *a priori* that abnormal behaviour, like the so-called normal behaviour, also serves a role in the larger organisation of the human being. These processes are said to be causal and the theory is essentially a causal theory of human behaviour. There are, of course, philosophical problems regarding how mental causality is possible; however, the practical details of these processes and their links with behaviour have been worked out to some extent. In order to obviate the philosophical problem, various conditions are made binding on the nature of causal laws. It is argued, for example, that the causal law would capture structural identity between the posited mental states and processes on the one hand and overt behaviour on the other (Edelson, 1986b). These causal laws, because they connect clinical observation with the theory in clearly specified logical steps, make extra-clinical empirical research possible; they connect the theory to clinical observation.

The specific advantage of perspectivisation of psychoanalysis is that it throws up possibilities of resolving the problems of theoretical delimitation of psychoanalysis. The problem of theoretical delimitation is related to the question whether psychoanalysis is a general theory of psychopathology or whether it is only a small part of the wider discipline of psychopathology. These problems have appeared recurrently in literature and have strengthened the virulence of the psychoanalytic critical tradition (for pertinent discussions on this problem, see Rangell, 1988; Wallerstein, 1988, 1990). The traditional adherence of practitioners to the former position has led to the impossibility of specifying what the theory *leaves out* of its explanatory scope, which, as Popper points out, is an important part of all scientific theorising. This is particularly a problem when there is not sufficient empirical warrant for the theory for assuming such universal scope. The critiques, particularly the Popperian and hermeneutic, often depend upon facile simplifications and generalisations of Freud's theory, reflecting only the theory's own problematic claim to such generality. There is a growing need to resist the claim to generality of psychoanalytic theory and to view it as a small part of the psychopathological discipline by orienting the general theory in terms of domain specific interpretations. Our re-orientation of the foundations of psychoanalysis to a cognitivist epistemology changes the focus of the science from being an autonomous theory of man and integrates it into the stream of mental health sciences. From our perspective, psychoanalysis is interdisciplinary in nature and is concerned with common issues of cognition and abnormal behaviour, along with such other disciplines of psychopathology, neuroanatomy, development studies and animal behaviour studies.

VII

The idea of science defended by the external foundationalists, Popper and Grünbaum, comes very close to what has been called the 'justific-ationist' view of science in literature (Lakatos, 1976). Any justificationist position assumes that there is a psychologically decisive and self-evident, or 'natural' difference between the theoretical and observational statements of a science. Lakatos has designated this assumption as the 'naturalistic doctrine of observation'. Another assumption common to all justificationist positions is that if a statement fits the criteria stipulated for it to be termed as 'observational', such a statement is also 'true'. This is known as the 'doctrine of observational proof'. Philosophically, these two assumptions are closely linked to the problems of truth and demarcation and demand a number of things from a science. All statements of a scientific theory are grouped into either theoretical statements or observational statements. Further, all theoretical statements can be logically reduced to observational statements. Once all observational statements have been verified through experimentation, we have a true scientific theory. Any scientific theory has to pass through these two processes, that is, reduction of all theoretical statements into observational statements; and second, the experimentation process. Any theory which does not permit this is unscientific. As will be seen later, both the external foundationalists, Popper and Grünbaum, fall within this justificationist perspective of science.

The epistemological problem that the justificationists seek to resolve pertains to the nature of 'truth'. Traditionally, in philosophy, truth is viewed as a logical property, deducible from the logical structure of the propositions of a scientific theory. If a statement, say, 'all ravens are black' is expressed in its logical form, then all the possible truth values that it can take on can be immediately known, irrespective of the actual colour of ravens in the world. The logical formatting of a proposition is what enables us to know whether it is possible for any particular statement to take on one of the values of 'true' and 'false'. Logic gives us the possibilities of truth of statements. To arrive at a decision regarding the truth of any proposition, the proposition must be logically well formed. The structure of truth is propositional in nature. However, the most that this view of truth guarantees is that any statement expressed in its logical form is capable of taking on values of truth. The actual truth or falsity of the proposition, or the 'proof' of the proposition, cannot be logically derived or inferred from this. Such proof can be arrived at only through the extra-logical means (Lakatos, 1976, p. 207). This is what Lakatos meant when he said that logic can 'transmit' truth, but cannot 'establish' truth. As will be discussed later, experiment is the scientific way to know truth and experiment lies at the basis of the realism of sciences.

For Popper, empiricism is essentially a conflict between theory and experiment and the conflict decides whether a given proposition is capable of being disproved by the experiment. 'Proof', such as demanded by the inductivists and the neo-inductive probabilists, cannot be given, for inductively, all theories are equally unprovable and improbable. Disproof is possible by virtue of the logical nature of propositions and a honest science aims at disproof. Empiricism should specify which, of all states of affairs, is *prohibited* by a theory and the truth value of a proposition is decided by its refutability. The goal of science, according to this view, is to formally encode these prohibited states of affairs and test for disproof, so that only those propositions which have survived disproof fall within the scope of a theory. This set of propositions would be 'scientific' and the others would be 'pseudo-scientific'.

Grünbaum, like Popper, has insisted on the need to maintain the conclusivity of experiment in sciences and the need for demarcation of theories into science and metaphysics. However, for him, the possibility of empiricism lies in induction and not in falsifiability. Popper, according to Grünbaum, misunderstood induction and his critique of psychoanalysis is therefore faulty. For Grünbaum, psychoanalysis is not a science, but for reasons other than those cited by Popper. Psychoanalysis is not an inductive science and therefore, it is not a science at all. Grünbaum's 'neo-justificationist' critique of psychoanalysis is inductivist and probabilistic.

The justificationist basis on which the external foundationalist critique of psychoanalysis rests is often called the 'simple' model of science. The simple model of science 'represents science as based on induction and the hypothetico-deductive method through the sequence: observation, hypothesis, prediction, confirmation, leading upward to TRUTH' (Cushing, 1990, p. 181). For Popper, of course, the method of science is deduction and the sequence that science must follow is: observation, hypothesis, prediction, falsification, leading to falsity. The simple model of science assumes that 'truth' is at the top of the epistemological priorities of a science. The model assumes that once truth is known then nothing else needs to be done in science and that knowing truth is the ultimate goal of a scientific theory. Another assumption made by the simple model is that there is complete parity between what is 'true', what is 'known' and what is 'real', that is, there is complete equivalence between truth, knowledge, and reality. If a basic set of observational propositions has been predicted as 'true' of a particular scientific theory, then this set is also at once metaphysical, giving the ontological structure of the world. Knowledge is not mediated by cognitive constraints, according to justificationism, but is immediate. The goal of science, according to this view, is to arrive at this knowledge, and once the complete set of proven observational statements is obtained, questions relating to the validity of such knowledge may be laid to rest. According to justificationism, a scientific theory is validated solely on the basis of its own merits, that is, on the basis of how well it performs with respect to empirical reduction and experimental assessment. Further, a true scientific theory is validated in isolation of other theories and interaction with other theories is neither possible nor desirable. This justificationist view of science is foundationalist in the way that has been described earlier.

It can be noted that the philosophical distinction between 'validation' and 'verification' is being collapsed in the foundationalist's simple perspective of a science. This is an important distinction which has significant implications for a meta-science. According to Popper and Grünbaum, the primary occupation of a science is supposedly the assignment of truth values to basic statements, thus making it possible to verify or refute them. This is a very atomistic perspective of science, a view which designates as 'scientific' only those set of statements to which such values can be assigned. According to these thinkers, if all statements of a theory are verified as either true or false, the theory is validated epistemologically. Even though this view of truth and verification as being the fundamental goals of science is questionable, an important point in the justificationist's view must however be retained by a meta-science. Empiricism, from the perspective of the simple model of science, guarantees the possibility of making decisions regarding the truth of experiential statements. If a decision regarding the truth of a statement can be made at all, it is because of empiricist, experimental considerations. But it guarantees only this much and scientific praxis involves much more than simply assigning truth values to basic statements. The validation of a theory or the philosophical rationale for designating a theory as 'scientific', is not completed by exhausting the process of verification. Validation has to do with the entire rationality of the science, its logical form, its metaphysical content, its historical background, its goals and methods and its relative comparability to other theories; in short, the entire socio-cognitive discourse committed to some general conditions of rationality by a community. Science, as noted earlier, has a social, cognitive as well as a normative dimension. The notion of validation is associated with ideas like scientific convention, linguistic agreement and holism in science, whereas, verification is associated with the notion of operationalism, induction and causality.

Another problem with the simple model is its neglect of notions of meaning and explanation in its treatment of science. Within the Popperian and the Grünbaumian perspectives, meaning is not spoken of at all. The notion of meaning carries the epistemological goals of a science beyond the assignment of truth to observational statements. A theory in science is general and abstract, involving notions of meaning and use, competence and performance. These are not empirical notions but are linguistic in nature. A theory, like a rule, recommends the use of its key concepts in certain definite ways. It is only this rule-like nature of a theory that makes verification possible. A theory works like an analytical proposition, or what one may call in the language of Wittgenstein, grammatically. A theory provides the rules for the application of certain concepts, and is employed by the research community. Verification involves the application of a particular rule to specific instances using certain procedures. The validation of a scientific theory does not depend on the verification of one or two applications of the theory, but verification itself is made possible because of the theory. It is well recognised that not only psychoanalysis, psychology and biology would fail to satisfy the meta-science proposed by the foundationalists but also the paradigmatic natural sciences such as physics and chemistry.

Two general notions are pertinent to any contemporary discussion on the nature of sciences, natural or human. These are the notions of a scientific 'domain' (Shapere, 1977, pp. 521–22) and of a 'research programme' (Lakatos, 1976). These notions are used naturally throughout this book. A domain refers to a related body of information or facts which comprises an area of investigation for the involved research community. The problem of anxiety neuroses, for example, is a domain. This body of information denotes the metaphysics—the structure or the essential nature of reality. The body of information may already be well established in the history of the science as part of normal science, as a set of hitherto unquestioned information about reality. However, subsequent scientific activity might occasion scientists to notice formal or material problems about this set of related information, giving forth a set of research problems for the science to solve. An important characteristic of a scientific domain is that there must be a single or a set of problems that research communities identify as important relating to this body of information; the science must also be able to specify the steps involved in solving these problems. The formal structure of the problems as well as the logic of the solution to these problems must be clear to the scientists. The entire range of activities that a scientific community undertakes in order to solve these problems may be termed as its 'research programme'.

There is a difference of emphasis and import in the two terms 'domain' and 'research programme'. The notion of 'domain' refers to the nature of the scientific theory, whereas 'research programme' refers to the activity of the scientific community working in specified domains. The concept of domain as conceived by Shapere provides an atemporal and logical view of what a scientific theory is, much in the same spirit as Popperian philosophy. This view shelves the historical, social and personal aspects of science and looks at it as a purely logically determined activity. It gives a cognitive view of science, of what an ideal science should be. The notion of 'research programme', however, looks at science primarily as *praxis*, as temporal and social praxis and emphasises the limitations of logic in capturing the essence of science as it evolves over time. Both these concepts, however, are helpful for an understanding of a science and they are used as supporting each other rather than as combative notions.

Both these views of science are holistic, viewing science as a social activity, as a set of events of which empiricism is only a small part. Research issues in a science are not necessarily restricted to problems of verification or observation. What may be at issue in a scientific theory is not just 'observations' which delimit the theory in the justificationist sense; but it could be an entire network of related problems, assumptions and methods, involving a whole range of activities, none of which may be presumed to be primary and all of which have separate philosophical rationalities. Progress in science, for example, from the medical to the psychological model of hysteria, may involve not only the testing of theoretical statements for empirical support, but also an examination of the theoretical, explanatory and methodological premises of the concerned theory. When the research community faces a problem in any science, it is not always solved by referral to observation. Often, a quest for strengthening the epistemological foundation of a particular science may be more than a request for empirical evidence.

The most rational choice before the scientific community may not always be the rejection of a scientific theory in favour of a 'better' theory, but finding a number of alternatives to the theory, any of which may have empirical support. The same so-called 'facts' or the metaphysics of the theory are placed before the scrutiny of scientific communities working in the same or related areas. In the case of the problem of hysteria, for example, hypnotists, medical men and neuro-anatomists were interested in the problem and offered alternative explanations of hysteria. A significant characteristic of this view of science is the magnitude of publicness it allows to 'science': the openness with which it invites related scientific communities to attempt different solutions to what is commonly understood as a problem. This view holds that science is not something which goes on exclusively within the canonical boundaries of a theory itself, but between competing theories, between related theories which critically question and vie with each other in order to improve our understanding of some reality. It is well known, for example, how problems that the classical Freudian theory formulated about hysteria were largely determined by the state-of-the-art research available at the time on neuro-anatomy. Freud himself acknowledged that he was forced to find alternative explanations only because the well used medical model had failed to provide him with a philosophically acceptable solution to the problem of hysteria.

This view of science has been called a 'pyramidal' view of scientific knowledge and growth. With respect to the question of the relation between theory and observation in the sciences, it stresses a top-down pyramidal structure, a descendence from the abstract theoretical statements to empirically bound statements. The simple view had visualised science merely as a bottomline arrangement of empirically close statements and the complete redundance of theoretical statements. In the pyramidal view of science, the empirical content is high at the lower end of the pyramid whereas at the top end of the pyramid, the theoretical content is high though at any level of the pyramid, the theoretical and empirical contents are mixed. The elaboration of this view of science depends on the rationality that one can provide to the notion of 'observation' and its place with respect to meaning, explanation and truth in the sciences. Observation is a cognitive concept and involves some understanding of the process of attention of a scientist. These issues will be discussed later.

Modern thought on cognition and on the nature of a cognitive theory instructs us that it is important to maintain a distinction between a 'theory' and a 'model', or between what Merton has called the 'abstract' theory and the 'concrete' theory. A general theory, such as Freud's meta-psychology or Newton's theory of gravitation, is abstract, philosophical and metaphorical. It is largely unwieldy because of its generality and its attempt to bring different kinds of phenomena within its explanatory scope. In this sense, Freudian meta-psychology does not exhibit curiously unscientific properties but only those properties of any general theory of science. The general theory, as proposed by the founder scientist, is usually not the result of compiling together repeatedly verified empirically warranted propositions but rather of discoveries revealed through some, even one, case studies. Freudian theory, as a general theory of abnormal cognition, is not a justified theory in the manner in which Freud presented it; but importantly, his main interest did not lie in justification. The question of empirical justification arises only when the general theory is *interpreted* as a 'model'. The interpretation of the general theory requires cognitive concepts associated with linguistic competence and performance: it involves choosing the 'core' conceptual relations from the general theory, giving it a logic and an aim, and applying it to a delimited and specific range of phenomena. In this sense, the various forms of 'clinical theories' may be considered as models of the general theory proposed by Freud. By the very nature of his task, Freud, as the founder of psychoanalysis, could not have provided empirical warrant of his general theory in the form that the modern empiricists demand. A survey of the developments since Freud shows that the models have been often successful in improvising their conventional methodologies and in garnering such warrant, not only from within the canon but also from external, related disciplines.

On the basis of all these reflections and an examination of some of their implications, we will attempt to provide a unifying scientific rationality to psychoanalysis. It will be seen that the research programme, by its commitment to the larger psychiatric movement, is doing science though the theoretical and methodological problems remain. Philosophers can and have, indeed, fruitfully addressed these debates. There are differences in the universe of discourses defined by the terms 'science' and 'scientific'. It makes no sense to ask whether a theory is a science or not, unless one makes the assumption, like the justificationists do, that a scientific theory is *sui generis* and self-validating. By virtue of its participation in a social, collective activity, as a member of a series of theories addressing the same or related problems, the status of a theory as a science is decided by the status assigned to this larger enterprise. Often, the decision to designate a group of theories as science is historically determined and the decision is seldom questioned, as in the case of physics. There is also an administrative or political motivation for designating groups of theories as science. The assignment of this status provides a convenient label or index for classifying knowledge and organising it. Such organisation is required if decisions regarding the promotion of research and the use of research for society have to be made.

Even though the question whether a theory is science or art can be asked in overarching and irrelevant ways, it does profit us to ask whether any decision, made in the conduct of a science, is 'scientific'. Though a science may be established, like physics, it is still possible to ask whether a particular decision taken by a physicist or a group of physicists is scientific or not. In raising this question about the scientific nature of decisions (and not theories), one is genuinely inquiring about the rational basis of that particular decision. Contrarily, contesting a particular decision by scientists does not bring into question the scientificity of the entire discipline within which the decision has been made. In fact, this questioning of certain decisions has the critical force to carry the science forward. In this sense, even if the empiricists' total claims of the 'unscientificity' of psychoanalysis may excusably be considered irrelevant to the science in question, their critical examination of the theoretical and methodological decisions of the discipline are likely to prove only useful for the development of the human science.

VIII

The humanistic charge of the internal foundationalists, that epistemological stringency calls into question the capacity of a science to be human, is the last question that will be addressed in this volume. For the internal foundationalists, psychoanalytic science is dehumanising because human beings are so different from one another that it is unethical to universalise about human behaviour. For the humanists, man cannot be bound by causal laws because consciousness is of an intentional nature, and creatively free. Any human science must take into account these features of being human. The knowledge that the psychoanalyst uses in the name of cure must be accepted by the patient as being in his own interest. The epistemological 'validity' of the theory depends on this.

The philosophical issue of humanism comprises a set of questions: whether providing norms for knowledge, truth and understanding detracts an inquiring mind from granting human, individual possibilities of creation, freedom and expression. And contrarily, whether granting freedom and creativity of self liberates human beings from rule following; whether by affirming a rationality regarding the knowledge we have about ourselves and fellow human beings, the range of possibilities of human agency is somehow restricted or constrained. We must examine the place and role of knowledge and epistemology with respect to social praxis, i.e., the place of epistemology with respect to individual ethics. In order to do this, we must examine how the humanistic tradition has conceived of this relation and finally, what humanism essentially means and the place it must be assigned in our social discourse. We must also know whether psychoanalysis is dehumanising and what a theory such as psychoanalysis must philosophically commit itself to in order to escape the humanistic charge. These questions will be discussed at a later stage.

For the moment it can be said that the continental critiques' use of the concept of humanism as an ethico-normative demarcation principle is questionable. These critiques aim to divide theories into those that are individually liberating and those that are dehumanising. The demarcation actually effected by the tradition is between science as a whole and art. The tradition not only claims that psychoanalysis is dehumanising, but also that *all* sciences are dehumanising, in sharp contrast to the arts, particularly poetry. The critique of science, as will be seen later, is accorded a central place in the internalist tradition and the psychoanalytic critique depends on this. The critique of science shows on the one hand a misunderstanding of what science is and on the other hand a naivete regarding the emancipatory possibilities of extra-scientific ventures. It can be argued that science provides valid knowledge about ourselves and what makes us evil and wicked at times. In a sense, science can liberate us from ourselves and our seemingly indomitable nature. It can also be said that non-scientific ventures, such as art or religion, are not always liberating. The question is more complex than the way in which it has been raised by the humanists.

The real question facing any sociology of science is which of the available technological possibilities relating to specific human problems is more humane than others and *not* which *theory* is human or otherwise. Just as one cannot ask about a general theory like Freudian psychoanalysis, whether it is a 'science' or not, this question too cannot be asked meaningfully. No theory of human beings would explicitly claim to be dehumanising. The ethical ideal of knowledge is enhancement of quality of human life and, hence, no theory would surrender this ideal except at the cost of its own fall from grace from social praxis. The principle of humanism is too general to permit a demarcation of good theories and bad theories.

Demarcation interests, whether ethico-normative or epistemologico-normative, fail in serving their purpose when normative issues are posed in such an all-embracing way. The philosophical problem of demarcation, of course, arises from a genuine need to organise knowledge into useful categories so that we know how to manage these in terms of extra-epistemological considerations such as the economic, ethical, sociological or political frameworks within which any society functions. Demarcation of knowledge systems into science and non-science, into good science and bad science, provides us with some guidelines as to the epistemological and ethical limits of these systems, as to how rational and human, sciences are. A knowledge of these limits allows us the possibility of strengthening the philosophical base of the systems, both epistemologically and ethically. There is no doubt that knowledge serves human interests. To this extent, as a pragmatic way of organising knowledge to suit our interests, we need reference to some principles of epistemological and ethical demarcation, however we may further wish to define and clarify these principles. We need to know both the cognitive limits of a theory which can be provided by epistemological demarcation, and the ethical limits of a theory, of when it can be put to bad use. But there are conditions which must be imposed on this demarcation venture itself. The concept of humanism, for example, is not a sufficiently stringent demarcation principle. No humanly conceived philosophy would fail the test if this principle is used. These reflections urge us to reconsider the meaning of humanism in sciences like psychoanalysis.

There are more specific problems involved in the humanistic charge, such as what 'causality' implies for a science and whether admitting causal laws implies forfeiting freedom. Kant recognised correctly that the nature of causality and freedom are raised in two different domains, the former in epistemology and the latter in ontology. The expectation that psychic reality becomes known to us through the articulation of causal laws reflects *our* ways of ordering things in the world. It reflects our cognitive capacity to understand the world we live in. The expectation is presupposed by every psychological science. The possibility of knowledge rests on certain conditions of rationality and the expectation that this rationality can, metaphorically, 'capture' reality in object laden terms. If we are able to speak at all about an object, whatever the nature of the object, it is because of our capacity to name, classify and describe the object, even if the object is the mind. But to claim this is not to subtract from the ontological possibilities of the object under study. Freud recognised, in many of his papers on methodology relating to the conduct of psychotherapy, that the voice of the subject is an enduring part of the process of therapy: its initiation, its movement and its culmination.

The scientific community makes an effort to understand the human subject by assigning to the subject the capacity to follow some rules. Social science is possible because of this assumption that human behaviour has some rationality and that we can know this rationality. In this sense, no radical peculiarity can be granted to the human subject on grounds of subjectivity, though a qualitative difference from the natural object may be granted. Human beings are different from natural objects, but not so radically different as to require a radically defined science. Philosophically, the formal nature of a 'science' and 'object' is the same, whatever the science. However, material differences in objects allows for different contents in the sciences. Hence human sciences are not formally different from natural sciences, though they may be materially different.

The notion of self does not necessarily require a unique individuation incapable of transcending particulars, as the humanistic critiques claim. Studies relating to the self indicate that not only methodologically, introspective approaches are not in any way superior to other kinds of approaches but also that there are cultural, genetic, biological, developmental and linguistic factors determining the self. These studies question not only the primary methodological assumption made by the humanistic tradition about the private self which ought to certify knowledge obtained in the clinic as valid. They also question the philosophical claim that the ineffable self is incapable of being subjected to rigorous study. Knowledge, and sufficiently thorough knowledge at that, about human beings is possible through rigorous and controlled research. It is important for us, as social beings, to know how our personalities which appear so indubitable and real to us, are determined to a large extent by factors, such as culture, history, language and biology, in ways beyond the reach of our natural, quotidian experience. This knowledge, of course, like any other knowledge, is limited by discursive and ideological constraints. However, this knowledge in the end may contribute to making us better, psychologically tranquil and self-realised human beings than any introspective knowledge which we may be deluded into thinking we have.

There are many ways in which we may see ourselves as human beings. Metaphorically speaking, we may see ourselves in a polished mirror, in a portrait, in a photograph, by inscribing our name on paper or wood, by looking into a bowl of water or polished metal, etc. Each of these methods gives us a view about ourselves in greater or lesser detail. Some may be more useful than others, some psychologically more satisfying than others, some more objective than others and so on. Priority need not be accorded to anyone method of knowing ourselves over others as the internal foundationalist traditions claim. The philosophically interesting issue here is whether a subject's intentions are at all computable or whether the private language argument should at times be considered true.

It is important to know where and how to raise the issue of humanism. Humanism is related to knowing when appropriation of the patient by the analyst is effected. Clearly, the issue of humanism is not raised in the domain of research, at least not in the same terms, but only in the domain of therapy. The question of humanism is not a cognitive issue nor is it an issue about knowledge; it is an ethical issue. Humanism does seek an answer to an important question: whether the political, administrative and moral imperatives of the psychotherapeutic community have in some way subverted the interests of the patient when he is undergoing treatment. Humanism concerns itself with providing norms for making a decision regarding when treatment has been based on the patient's complete acceptance and when treatment has fallen short of this ideal. The issue of humanism then cannot be about whether knowledge, in any form, undermines the quality of life, as the internalist traditions claim. If this was the case, a surgeon would be no better than an aimless assassin of humans.

Humanism is essentially concerned with the *use* of knowledge and this use is decided by us, not by theories. We can justifiably accuse our fellow human beings, particularly politicians, who decide the ways knowledge must be used, of dehumanising life, but not theories. In this sense, we can critically examine whether the political, social and moral commitments of the psychoanalytic community in particular and the mental health institutions in general are humanistic. We can ask whether, given our present knowledge about human beings and their teleological possibilities, the organisation of such knowledge by administrative bodies is committed to the enhancement of life or not. These are important issues in the sociology of psychiatry which are fruitfully addressed again and again. But even this addressal is presided over in terms of research questions and their competent execution; in other words, by epistemological concerns and not simply by values. In order to address specifically humanistic queries in the realm of mental health, we need research skills and sensitivity to normative issues about what is good research. The humanists' insistence on critical social science should be recognised, but not their prioritisation of politics and ethics over epistemology. Critical praxis, if it must serve humanism, would involve understanding and working with both epistemology and ethics. The humanistic organisation of institutions of mental illness depends upon the productive use of both.

2

Evidence, Truth and Psychoanalysis

• • •

I

Karl Popper's indictment of psychoanalysis seems to have triggered off an entire research programme in the philosophy of psychiatry, a consequence which Popper perhaps did not intend. For Popper, psychoanalysis served only as an example of a pseudo-science. It came at the end of his discussion on what it means for a theory to fall short of a type which could be designated 'science'. Psychoanalysis, according to Popper, was a token of a 'pesudo-science' along with Marxism and the Darwinian theory of evolutionary biology. Psychoanalysis was not even worthy of being a case study for his general preoccupation with the nature of a science. By using psychoanalysis as an example, Popper was not *asking* anything about the status of the theory as a science, but rather, assuming many things about this status. Philosophically speaking, while examples instantiate the type, their choice is also determined by the type. A circularity is inevitable in all choice of examples.

It is significant that Popper's almost passing reference to the theory has been exalted to the position of a central problematic in critical philosophy. However, Popper's own philosophical consideration of psychoanalysis may be described only as casual, rather than critical. Popper's choice of psychoanalytic theory as an example of a pseudo-science was important for drawing what he thought was a well defined contrast between a rationally acceptable and an unacceptable theory of science, between paradigms of science and pseudo-science. The philosophical context which demanded this critical re-examination was logical-positivism, with its inductivist principle of demarcation, a standard unacceptable to Popper.

Popper, viewed induction[1] in science primarily as an Aristotelian/ Baconian idea fundamentally based upon the Socratic notion of 'mid-wifery' or 'maieutic'. Understood in this way, it is a notion which claims the possibility of a 'true reading of the book of Nature' devoid of cognitive or interpretative latitude. The infallibility this position grants to human cognition, particularly the primacy it accords to sensory experience, is repugnant to Popper. Popper fully agreed with David Hume, for whom, induction could not circumvent the logical problem: no formal steps will allow us to infer that all experiences which are possible in all possible worlds will be of the same logical order as a finite experienced set. No universal law about the sequences of events can be obtained from particular instances, except by a non-logical leap. A general law is of a logical, atemporal order of our understanding whereas particular events are synthetic and obtain in the temporal order of our experiences. Induction, according to both Popper and Hume, is logically unjustifiable.

According to Popper, Hume was essentially right in his objection to induction as being logically unjustifiable. But Hume made the mistake of believing that a science could not do without induction. For him, induction is psychologically compelling even if not logically justifiable. Therefore, Hume justified induction in science on psychological grounds. He provided a psychological theory of habit based upon the notion of repetition to justify the use of induction in science. However, this putative 'justification' only generates fresh problems, both as a theory of psychology as well as logically. Psychologically, the genesis of habit is not always repetition, contrary to what Hume assumed it to be. Habit is a form of human practice and often is the result of tacit but conscious knowledge rather than automated and unconscious condition-ing. For example, acts of riding a bicycle or typing may look mechanical and repetitive but could only be the result of premeditated and conscious ways of relating to the world. According to Popper, this is why the human agency, even of the nature of habit, is not like a machine simulation!

Logically, a notion of habit which is based on the notion of repetition leads to an infinite regress. The notion of 'repetition', on which Hume seemed to depend so heavily, is possible because of one's discernment

---

[1] The sections here were developed from Popper, 1965, pp. 3–65.

of the 'sameness' or 'similarity' between two or more events. Of a set of events, it must be possible for the perceiver to identify two events in a manner which permits him to say that the event has been repeated. To make this judgment however, a view from outside the sequence of events would be necessary. To say that two (or more) events are the same and therefore have been repeated, the perceiver will need to have external cognitive criteria about sameness. In other words, there must be a cognition to discern sameness before one can identify repetition. Hume attempted to explain repetition, but he could not accomplish this without a theory of cognition. But granting a cognitive dimension to the possibility of repetition would ruin the chances of the psychological theory of habit that he had proposed. The only other option that Hume had was to explain cognition itself through earlier repetitions, committing the philosophical fallacy of an infinite regress.

In Popper's view similarity of events, which is at the base of our inductive expectation, is perceived not because of earlier repetitions of experiences. Rather, repetition is possible because we can perceive similarities. According to Popper,

> . . . similarity-for-us is the product of a response involving interpretations . . . and anticipations or expectations . . . . It is therefore impossible to explain anticipations, or expectations, as resulting from many repetitions, as suggested by Hume. For even the first repetition-for-us must be based upon similarity-for-us, and therefore upon expectations—precisely the kind of thing we wished to explain (1965, p. 45).

It is hard for us to resist a comparison with Wittgenstein, who said in his *Philosophical Investigations*: 'Before I judge that two images which I have are the same, I must recognize them as the same' (1974a, § 378). Cognition of similarities comes before recognition of repetition. Popper was one of the early initiates into the *cognitive* view of knowledge and science, as evident from these reflections and others which will be discussed in the following.

The option before Hume, according to Popper, was to give up the idea that induction is indispensable for science or advocate induction at the cost of its logical unjustifiability. The latter is a thoroughly irrational strategy as far as Popper is concerned. Hume chose to be irrational by not giving up induction in science. Popper has boldly, and somewhat problematically, claimed that induction is *not* required for a science. Even though Popper has rejected induction, he has appreciated the need of a science for *regularities*. In Popper's view, Hume incorrectly thought that induction is a psychological *a priori*. For Popper, not induction, but the expectation to find regularities in the world around us, is a psychological *a priori*. This cognitive expectation is a natural, almost instinctive or genetic, but certainly a constitutional part of being human. Moreover, Popper believed that it is a logical *a priori* for the expectation that regularities exist in the world is prior to and presupposes any attempt to observe. Instructions issued to a person to record observations will have to necessarily be accompanied by providing a frame of reference which articulates *expected* regularities. A scientific theory provides this frame of reference.

According to Popper, induction is one of the many ways of arriving at regularities and there are ways which are more rational and philosophically sound than induction. Induction cannot still answer the Humean problem, of justifying the transtemporal leap from existential statements to universal laws. The claim that an event (or a necessary sequence of events, in the case of claims for inductive causality) has happened in the past and therefore, it will always occur in the future cannot be offered as a justification of induction, because this claim itself has been arrived at inductively. From the earlier, repeated successes of judgment regarding events no 'cognitive guarantees' covering all future instances can be offered. Induction can be justified only inductively, leading to a circularity of thought. Therefore, any advocate of induction, like Hume himself, would have to settle for something less than rationality. 'Rationality', according to Popper, means the traditional, logical deductive rationality.

A philosophy of induction depends primarily on confirmations or a criterion of verifiability. Attempts to verify depend on prior suppositions of what must be verified and how, and in order to stipulate these, it is necessary to fall back upon the theory. The theory which is supposed to be under test, itself imposes constraints on the outcomes of the verification. A verification cannot begin on a *tabula rasa*; but when theoretical conditions are imposed upon the verification, it can no longer be called pure verification. This is the paradox facing a philosophy of induction, in fact all attempts at verifiability, according to Popper. An inductive justification of a hypothesis, then, cannot be a true reading from the book of nature as a Baconian science assumes, but rather, only a cognition of nature through the methodological tools of a science.

From our own perspective, Popper's emphasis on the cognitive dimension to science is important and a scientific epistemology will attempt to retain this, even if it rejects other aspects of Popperian philosophy. Popper has recognised that a meta-science requires some cognitive criterion for determining those scientific statements which are true and those which are false. Applying a theory to the world depends, as noted earlier, on our being able to make this distinction. Knowledge, including observation, is a cognitive activity and for this reason, a theory of science based on the uncorrupt nature of observation or verification is an impossibility. However, this rejection of the possibility of pure observation does not mean that scepticism is the only philosophical option, but rather that we must continue to search for an alternative method which does not imitate the errors of induction. Methodology is the most important part of a philosophy of science; it should provide guaranteed ways of arriving at knowledge, as opposed to belief, opinion and mere propaganda. A philosophy should tell us when true knowledge has been obtained. The demarcation problem, which Popper placed at the very centre of philosophy, is related to making these cognitive distinctions and a demarcation principle would have served its purpose if it allows a science to make these distinctions.

In Popper's view, induction as a demarcation principle fails to make it possible for a science to do this because of a problem that it faces: whatever the nature of the theory, confirming instances could be easily found. This is because of a fundamental limitation of logical systems, pointed out quite early in philosophical thought by Rudolph Carnap. Statements can be logically related and the associated notions of truth and confirmation can be carried across these logically related, logically equivalent, statements. Consider the classic example of the black raven: even a white handkerchief can be viewed as a confirming instance of the statement 'All ravens are black'. This is because a white handkerchief confirms its logically equivalent statement, 'All non-black things are not ravens'. As there are an infinite number of white things, they would all confirm the universal law that all ravens are black. A theory of induction depends upon verification, but there is no logical control on confirmations.

According to Popper, any theory could be shown with the facility to exhibit the confirmatory criterion given by the inductive principle. Between competing theories, it would be impossible to say which one is closer to reality, or is true, because all of them impose their own conditions upon observation and thus give a distorted view of reality. Given the terms of the theory, Popper feared that each of these ways would emerge as 'true'. About the same phenomenon, many 'truths' could be formulated, each consistent with its own foundational theory. A theory contains more than just observational statements. The experiential reduction, that is, conversion of all theoretical statements into observational statements, at the basis of a theory of induction is not possible, according to Popper: no scientific statement can be strictly reduced to sensory experience. Insofar as any attempt to decide the truth is linked with mediation of experimental and other non-theoretic methodological considerations, the notion of 'truth' underscoring a philosophy of induction is an inadequate epistemological notion. Conclusivity or unequivocal decisions about the status of scientific statements claiming to be knowledge is not possible with an experiential notion of truth.

In Popper's view, inductive empiricism is questionable because it allows many 'truths', even conflicting truths, to co-exist. Any scientific theory includes non-observational statements as well. Given this, there can be two mutually exclusive theories with all true observational consequences such that a non-observational statement and its negation would belong to the two theories, both of which are true: implying that both the non-observational statement and its negation are true (Friedman, 1985, p. 148). According to Popper, the impossibility of arriving at truth is not because of lack of sophistication in instrumentation or other psychological limitations of the inquirer, but because of the very terms of the philosophy of induction, which seem to defy all logic. An inductive philosophy is, in principle, flawed and makes knowledge impossible. Truth itself, along with verifiability and induction, is an inherently problematic notion which a meta-science can well dispense with. The epistemological ideal of science and knowledge is to arrive at a set of unequivocal and universal statements, fully supported by facts and unconditioned by the theory. Making epistemologically indubitable statements is the goal of science and the traditionally revered notions of truth and verifiability in the philosophy of science do not fulfil this ideal.

Even though Popper has viewed the notion of truth with dubiety, he has accepted that the notion of falsity is epistemologically more sound. According to him, the aim of any science is not to arrive at truth but to eliminate falsity. Even though adding a number of confirming instances can never justify the inference of the truth of a universal law, an instance *countering a proposed law* can justify the falsity of the law. A scientific law has the logical form of a tautology. A singular, existential statement countering the law can impose the required logical conditions on a universal statement, giving an idea about the generality of the statement as well as its explanatory scope. The notion of 'truth' was meant to do this but failed. The empirical significance of the law would be clearly delimited with a notion of falsification. Any attempt to test the empirical consequences of a theory would involve a search for *counter* instances, rather than confirming instances. Failure to find counter instances would render the law corroborated, and conversely, finding it would falsify the law. For example, the proposed law that 'all ravens are black' is refutable. It is possible to say what will have to occur for the law to be falsified. Actually finding a non-black raven would prove the law to be clearly false, whereas failure to find it would only provide greater corroboration for the generalisation, but the search for non-black ravens would continue.

A theory like psychoanalysis is pseudo-scientific, according to Popper, because it is unable to specify the conditions under which it would be false. Refutability and providing counter-instances for a law is not possible for this theory, according to Popper. It is one of those theories which is 'able to explain practically everything that happened within the fields to which they referred. The study of any of them seemed to have the effect of an intellectual conversion . . . . Once your eyes were thus opened, you saw confirming instances everywhere . . .' (1965, pp. 34–35). Psychoanalysis, in not being able to specify the conditions of refutability, is also unable to empirically delimit the explanatory scope of its laws. Popper believed that psychoanalysis is an empirically sterile theory. The analysis of imagined therapeutic interpretations from the Adlerian and classical Freudian points of view of the behaviour of two men towards a drowning child led Popper to conclude:

> I could not think of any human behaviour which could not be interpreted in terms of either theory. It was precisely this fact—that they always fitted, that they were always confirmed—which in the eyes of their admirers constituted the strongest argument in favour of these theories. It began to dawn on me that this apparent strength was in fact their weakness (1965, p. 35).

For Popper, the pre-scientific nature of psychoanalysis is often occluded from our philosophical vision because we have depended on a philosophy of verifiability and induction for our assessments. In providing innumerable confirmations, the theory is using an inherently flawed philosophy to pretend scientificity.

II

Popper is both right and wrong about the nature of induction on which his critique of psychoanalysis is based and in his judgment about the radical implications of his proposal for an alternative demarcation criterion for science. Popper's uncritical dependence on a Humean philosophy of induction allows him to discredit modern theoretical developments in induction. He assumed, like Hume, that induction has a deductive logical structure and is an inference and that induction is only Baconian and enumerative. Both these assumptions are questionable.

Popper has correctly recognised that no science can be strictly and completely reduced to observational statements and in doing this he pioneered a radical departure from the logical-positivistic philosophy of science. However, it appears that he has ignored the fact that no theory can be strictly reduced to its logical deductive or syllogistic form. Popper has rightly claimed that empirical significance does not exhaust a theory's meaning, but he erroneously believed that deductive logic can. In principle, as noted earlier, there are limitations to logical systems: logical deduction by itself cannot render a theory applicable to the world. The very rationale for devising a procedure different from deduction is to make such an empirically bound semantics possible in the sciences. There is an important difference between ampliative inferences and non-ampliative, or demonstrative inferences (Salmon, 1967, pp. 5–11; Cohen, 1989, pp. 1–2) which Popper has ignored. A demonstrative inference, typical of deductions, contains in its conclusion no more than what is stated in the premises. A deductive conclusion does not amplify upon the premises but only reiterates the linguistic possibilities of the premises. However, any empirical relation is obtained only by stating in the conclusion what is not already contained in the language of the premises. An inductive inference is ampliative in this sense. The conclusion goes beyond the form of the inference and makes commitments regarding the empirical contents of the inference. It must, of course, be possible to say when legitimate commitments have been made and when they have not been made. Popper has failed to appreciate that deductive logic can only give the *form* of theories and it is the *content* which matters in the context of relating the theory to the world. Logic can tell us, through a meta-language, whether the required conditions of rationality are adequately met by a theory. But if the formulation of an object language, or specifying the contents of the theory is to be possible at all, procedures must be devised which allow synthetic statements. These procedures cannot be purely deductive.

Like the traditional philosophers, Popper believed that truth was an ontological notion, not allowing the possibility of epistemological manipulation or analyses. He accorded a sacrosanct place to this notion in his logic and then found it too difficult to accept. The only truths that he allowed were tautological in form. But this is to empty the notion of truth of any significance that it might otherwise have for the science. Truth is important to science in an empirical but not in a logical sense. It is a cognitive concept, like observation, relating to *our* expectation that a theory refers to the world in the way we claim. It is well recognised by Bayesians, the most well defended section of probabilists today, that induction provides a philosophical standard for rational belief and in this induction is equally cognitive. Inductive methods in the sciences do not make ontological claims about the world but *cognitive claims about the reliability of our view of the world and how much of this view we can take to be objective*. It provides a statistical measurement or a degree of probability of how rational we are to believe in a particular claim. We are able to apply a scientific theory to the external world because we can provide such measurements of the satisfaction of a theory to our expectations of the world. Induction is a method of measurement of the probable competence of a theory to relate to the world. Thinkers in the area of probability and induction acknowledge that induction is a process of *estimation* of truth in the sciences (Rescher, 1980).

There is nothing pernicious about the so-called inductive 'leap', as Popper feared, for induction is a pragmatic method by which we arrive at these estimations of truth in science. It is an insidious leap only if it is incorrectly presumed, as Popper did, that induction should reveal the structure of a deduction. In current thinking on induction, there are epistemological conditions which limit the 'leaps' that can legitimately be made. There are good leaps as well as bad leaps, even in psychology, and a philosophy can specify these leaps. Popper believed that if traditional deductive logic is forsaken by a particular method no logic at all can be provided to the approach. But this is not true, as evident from the prodigious work currently in progress in the study of induction and probability (see, for example, Cohen, 1989; Grünbaum, 1976; Salmon, 1967, 1971). In incorrectly assuming it to be a deductive inference, Popper and Hume were demanding more of the method than it was capable of providing.

Definitively, any correct inference, whether deductive or inductive, is truth preserving, that is, true premises must lead to true conclusions. There are a few problems about the truth preserving nature of deductions, but in induction, the problem relates to the status of the truth of conclusions because of their ampliative nature. Popper and Hume rightly recognised that an inductive inference is open with respect to the truth of its conclusions; their truth does not necessarily follow from the truth of the premises. But it is in fact this problem, peculiar to induction, which makes empiricism possible and necessary in the sciences. As is obvious to everyone, the so-called 'truth' of a syllogism is in a way not a truth at all: it is a boring truth, a truth which has no further practical consequences even if it is stated explicitly. It does not add to our knowledge nor does it contribute to what is called *progress* in knowledge. We cannot know the truth of the conclusions from the premises in the case of an ampliative inference, but knowledge of the truth is important if we want to acquire knowledge of the world. If inductive knowledge is to be possible, we need to somehow know, in a philosophically redeemable way, the truth of the conclusions from the premises. On this depends the reliability of knowledge derived from the inference. In so far as the nature of the inference itself does not allow us to know the truth of the conclusion, we resort to the extra-logical method of experiment. The philosophical control that must be imposed on induction, then, is not and cannot be of a logical order. It is instead of an empirical, experimental order. We seek empirical warrant for scientific statements in order to restrict the ampliative scope of conclusions derived from true premises. The decision regarding the truth or falsity of conclusions is dependent on this restriction born of the experiment.

This non-deductive restriction of the ampliative scope of conclusions is philosophically redeemable and every correct inductive procedure is bound by this restriction. Popper's critique of induction may well be based on a 'caricature' of the procedure, because he does not believe that induction is conditioned by such epistemological restrictions, i.e., he does not believe that there can be a philosophical distinction between 'correct' and 'incorrect' inductive inferences, a distinction that every philosophically sensitive statistician is aware of. The epistemological control on induction has been termed 'declared consequence restriction' by Grünbaum (1979, p. 133). This condition *withholds* the decision about the truth value of a statement till after the required experiment has been carried out. In other words, this condition safeguards the truth-functional outcome of the observational consequences of a hypothesis and against the kind of epistemic contamination that Popper feared *until* these consequences have been experimentally tested for truth. The possibility of introducing epistemic controls on the procedural determination of truth limits the occasion on which truth claims can be made to only *after* such tests have been carried out. Experimentation in science, even social science, is sophisticated enough to make it possible to say that, of all testable statements, some will be 'true' and others 'false'. Popper was wrong in his objection to induction on the grounds that every hypothesis can be shown to be true if induction is used. Popper's concern that a law must have applications is correct, a false law would fail to apply and hence deserves to be condemned. However, even in induction, the epistemological restriction that a law must delimit a definite domain which it purports to explain, is clearly possible though the considerations and criteria are different.

In arguing for the falsifiability criterion, Popper wanted a cognitive method of demarcation, but he did not realise that induction is equally cognitive. Prediction and certainty, concepts associated with the objectivity of science, are cognitive ascriptions, of the rationality or the expected utility of making certain scientific claims. We predict a future course of events on the basis of natural laws. Generalisability in science, however we define it, is possible because of rule governed words and their extension. Natural laws are linguistic in nature, and are cognitive inventions: It is because of the nature of our mind and the nature of language that we have natural laws about the world and about ourselves. An extension of a word like 'gravitation' always falls within the scope of the rule and one imagines the future course of events, or make predictions, on the basis of this extension. In so far as our mind and language are limited, there are cognitive limits on the nature of prediction also, making induction and probability indispensable to science.

Popper attributed deductive features to inductive inference because he supposed, like the earlier logical-positivists, that science has a *logical* form rather than a *mathematical* form. Mormann (1991) has shown that it is the opposite case using, surprisingly, Husserl's philosophy of science. Science deals with objects and it is mathematics which is commensurate in general structure, aims and philosophical foundation with this aim of science and not logic. Ontology, or the formal study of objects and the possible relations between them, is the aim of mathematics and not logic. Mathematics offers ways of knowing what it means to say formally that, for example, two objects are the 'same'. Notions of identity, equality, unitariness, plurality, multiplicity, magnitude and permutations between objects, in short a formal ontology of objects, is possible because we can express them mathematically. Deductive logic has primarily a linguistic, propositional form and deals with syllogisms and inferences of thinking. This logic provides the general principles of thought, not in its empirical aspects but in its formal or universal aspects.

Popper's charge that justifying induction on the basis of its continued success is illegitimate is questionable. The scepticism about the impossibility of obtaining logical guarantees for the future based on past successes is unjustified. The 'guarantee' we look for from induction is not a logical guarantee, but rather a *cognitive* guarantee. This is involved in the very use of the notions of 'method' and 'success' in science. Philosophically, the notion of 'success' implies the perceived utility of a scientific method. A method in a science, as referred to earlier in the introduction, is a way of making a theory pragmatic, that is, of making it refer to the world. If success is not a reasonable parameter on the basis of which we can decide and justify the use of a method in science, then it is unclear what else can be. A method provides ways of approaching and intervening in the world and success is a measurement of the appropriateness of this aim of a method in science. Practice is justified by its success, though it is not and can never be deductively validated by its success. Theories can be thus 'validated' but not their methods. One can talk about the correctness and incorrectness of using a method, or its appropriateness or inappropriateness. Norms and measurements can be devised for defining these notions with respect to particular sciences. But these norms are not of a deductive form; they only offer probabilistic predictions about the expected utilities (Maher, 1990) of the method for that particular science.

For example, suppose a person wants to cut glass and uses the following implements: sulphuric acid, stone, orange juice, a saw blade or a pen-knife. If he finds out that he has not exactly achieved the results that he wanted with these 'tools', and if, further, he finds that diamond is able to cut glass, then he is reasonable in assuming that the method he is using is a 'valid' one. Taking the example further in line with the philosophical reflections above, the master craftsman may even be able to give a statistical form to the success and failure of each method used with respect to the expected utility that he has standardised. Of course, he can never prove his use of a particular method on the basis of its conformity to a syllogistic logic, but it would never occur to him to try either. And no doubt, he would be wasting his professional time if he did.

Popper has to admit, at the extreme, some form of inductivism into his meta-science, as he sometimes grudgingly acknowledges and as his critics have repeatedly noted. Popper's view poses some discomfiting paradoxes. By claiming that a science should try and prove the falsity of its hypotheses, he also claimed that sometimes a hypothesis *may be* omitted from the domain of knowledge as pseudo-scientific even though it is true! If so much is granted, hypothetically, it may well happen that we would have a collection of hypotheses which we know to be certainly false, but we would not know about another collection of hypotheses which is true (for a historical example, see Maher, 1990). It is not even as if Popper has thrown out the baby along with the bath water, but it is as if he has kept the bath water but thrown the baby out! The problem with Popper's meta-science is that it is a negative theory: it specifies when a theory is a pseudo-science. If a theory is not a science, one could find out by using Popper's criterion and falsifying it. A science is negatively defined as a theory which is as yet unfalsified. When all the pseudo-sciences have been weeded out, what we would have is a set of theories whose status is unspecifiable, because Popper's criterion can only tell us how to recognise a pseudo-science and not a science.

Another paradox confronting Popper is related to his objection to probabilities as providing a reasonable measurement of truth in science. It can be shown that the applicability of the falsifiability criterion of demarcation depends on the acceptance of some notion of probability. For showing this, we must closely examine Popper's stance that every theory is not only equally unprovable logically, but also equally improbable. According to Popper, every theory must test itself repeatedly for its falsity. For Popper, a theory which does not stand the test is to be superseded by one which does. Among the many theories vying for the status of a science, scientific communities are most rational when they choose an alternative which has withstood the test of falsifiability than one which has not. The demarcation principle that Popper has stipulated aims to provide ways by which to compute the *comparative* resilience of different theories to the test of refutability. The demarcation principle is then a principle by which different theories may be compared for degrees of resilience. It is clear that the practicability of Popper's demarcation principle depends on his acceptance of the *degrees* of success, or some probability measure, of the theories being compared.

Popper, of course, was correct in his objection to a philosophy of induction based upon the indubitable and primary nature of our sensory experience. The enumeration of observation statements is based on our cognitive, theoretical and normative competence in bringing statements together as being observationally relevant. To say what is empirically relevant for justification, we need at least the theory, statistical and instrumental tools, and perceptual skills. Popper was essentially correct in his emphasis on the cognitive dimension of all observation. He was right to seek a method which did not give such an overarching power of arbitration, on the question of demarcation, to sense experience. For Popper, logical-positivism was erroneously based on a psychology of observation, and what science required was a methodology of observation. Popper surely set a more stringent standard for a science of science.

Popper was, however, wrong to believe that induction was *not* cognitive, that induction did not fit his philosophical requirements of a sound scientific methodology and that there was a very significant difference in the demarcatory consequences of verifiability and falsifiability. Further, he was wrong to believe that the set of unscientific theories picked out by deduction and by induction are entirely different. The traditional notion of 'truth' and Popper's notion of 'verisimilitude' are analogous, as are his empirical criteria of falsifiability *vis-à-vis* verifiability. Ideally, an empirically sterile theory, such as Popper would expect from a pseudo-science, is not testable whether the method adopted is verification or falsification. For Grünbaum, the post-Popperian psychoanalytic critic, psychoanalysis is a case in point. According to Grünbaum, demonstrating how a theory can be verified is to have a better meta-science than showing how it can be falsified.

III

Adolf Grünbaum has argued that Popper's analysis of psychoanalysis and his assessment of its nature as a pseudo-scientific theory must be treated with suspicion, because first, the philosophical basis of his critique is unsound. Second, Popper has disregarded the very history and nature of psychoanalysis in his critique. Grünbaum has questioned Popper's indictment of psychoanalysis that it is irrefutable methodologically. According to Grünbaum, Freud appeared to have worked as if he believed in the falsifiability criterion, as evidenced, for example, by the collapse of the seduction etiology of hysteria in 1897 (Grünbaum, 1986, p. 221). Freud diagnosed that hysteria in women was brought on by early experiences of incestuous seductions. However, other sociological factors, such as the actual incidence of child abuse by fathers, contradicted his theory: Freud had evidence contrary to what his theory predicted, leading him to give up the theory. Another example that Grünbaum has cited is 'A *Case* of Paranoia *Running Counter* to the Psychoanalytic Theory of Disease'.[2] Here Freud explicitly recognised the need to abandon his theory that paranoia is caused by repressed homo-eroticism, if the case in question showed that paranoia is not invariable with homo-erotic attachments (Grünbaum, 1984, pp. 108–9). According to Grünbaum, these examples make it arguably clear that psychoanalysis is *scientific on the basis of Popper's demarcation criterion of falsifiability*. However, this consequence is simply false, for Grünbaum, because Popper's decision is based on a flawed philosophy of science. Induction, not as Popper understood it but in its modern sense, shows that the epistemological foundation of psychoanalysis is a pathetic shamble.

Grünbaum's intention of objecting to Popper's psychoanalytic critique is clear: Popper's demarcation criterion of falsifiability is not adequate to fundamentally question the basis of psychoanalysis. It faces the same problems that Popper charged of induction. The falsifiability criterion is at once too narrow and too broad. It allows an unscientific theory, like psychoanalysis, to appear scientific, whereas it disallows the possibility of determining the truth of even a simple case such as 'Man is mortal'. To satisfy the falsifiability criterion in this case, we must attempt to produce a man who never dies! Grünbaum has defended Freud's methodology as being more

---

[2] Emphasis added. The language Freud is using here could well be Popperian.

sophisticated than Popper has made it out to be, a view which, incidentally, has irked both committed Popperians and conservative anti-Freudians! According to Grünbaum, Popper's view of psychoanalysis is a 'misdiagnosis' and the real problem with the theory is the insufficiency of empirical, particularly inductive, warrant. If the theory had as much inductive warrant as Popper has claimed it has, it would rest on more secure epistemological foundations. It is precisely Freud's theory which lacks empirical warrant and thereby shows how wrong Popper was to disregard induction as a stringent criterion for demarcation. According to Grünbaum,

> it is ironic that Popper should have pointed to psychoanalytic theory as a prime illustration of his thesis that inductively countenanced confirmations can easily be found for nearly every theory, if we look for them . . . *it is precisely Freud's theory that furnishes poignant evidence that Popper has caricatured the inductivist tradition by his thesis of easy inductive confirmability of nearly every theory!* (1989a, p. 41).

According to Grünbaum, Popper had a naive notion of how induction works, particularly with respect to a psychotherapeutic system like psychoanalysis: because he incorrectly raised the question of scientificity of the theory within the context of the *clinic*. Popper's conclusion that induction has failed to discredit psychoanalysis is based on his analysis, if it may be called that at all, of imaginary *clinical* transactions between the patient and the therapist. However, in doing this, Popper used a wrong context for trying out the demarcation principle: Neither induction, nor deduction, nor any other metascientific demarcation criterion can make a valuable contribution to the judgment regarding the scientific nature of psychoanalysis, if the criterion is applied in the context of the clinic. The clinic is where the psychological theory is applied in therapy and raises questions related to the *use* of the science, rather than its validity. It is not the fault of induction that truth cannot be found within the confines of the clinic; rather, it is the fault of the therapists who believe that it can. By showing that correct inductive inferences cannot be made in the clinic, Popper fallaciously inferred that the error lies in the method of induction. He should have instead questioned the very attempt, traditionally entrenched in psychoanalysis since Freud's time, to examine hypotheses for their probative value within the clinic.

The clinic has the natural language setting required for ordinary communication, and is motivated by therapeutic goals. The issue of the validity of psychoanalysis is, however, to be determined by setting cognitive goals. Freedom of speech and expression of the interlocutors in a clinical setting is an expectation to be satisfied for the dialogue to proceed normally, without formal constraints. However, these stipulations support therapeutic goals rather than research goals. The clinical circumstances do not allow for the stringent formal conditions as usually prescribed for standard empirical sciences. To raise the issue of the validity of psychoanalysis in the clinic is just as fallacious as deciding the validity of a law of thermodynamics based on the working of a particular combustion engine. The clinical setting, in other words, is 'epistemically contaminated' in many ways and does not carry sufficient controls for deciding the truth or falsity of a hypothesis. Based on these crucial and essentially correct arguments, Grünbaum has offered a panacea that the validation of laws in psychoanalysis should be tested outside of the clinic, or 'extra-clinically'. In arguing for the corroboration of laws through these artificially arranged and controlled 'extra-clinical' studies, Grünbaum has taken a position with Eagle and others, against the possibility of determining the validity of causal hypotheses within the clinic. Popper erred in that he unreflectively granted what he should have questioned: that the validity of the theory could be obtained within the clinic. His evaluation of the theory and his rebuttal of a philosophy of induction are both problematised because of this unwarranted and rather naive assumption.

Popper, according to Grünbaum, also appears to have lost the essential nature of psychoanalytic theory as being synthetic and causal. For such a theory, principles of induction underlying statistical, specifically probabilistic, inferences are indispensable. These principles enable us to make synthetic evaluations among actions as being causally connected, co-incidental or accidental. By rejecting induction, Popper also rejected the possibility of formally capturing the essentially synthetic, causal nature of psychoanalytic theory. His misunderstanding stemmed from his expectation that a scientific theory must be logically deductive. He erroneously assumed the tautological or necessary *a priori* status of all scientific laws.

Grünbaum's critical method is very different from Popper's, particularly in terms of literacy in psychoanalytic thinking. He has cast some of the so-called central psychoanalytic hypotheses in a *necessarily causal* form to show how 'observable' conclusions can potentially be tested for truth by standard inductive procedures used in empirical psychology. A theory of psychology like psychoanalysis is easily broken down into its theoretical components and observable, testable consequences. The psychological theory would be philosophically sound in so far as it attains corroboration through these empirical tests. The comprehensive research outcome of these extra-clinical inductive studies would, Grünbaum has claimed, give us the validity of the theory as either true or false, and would put it on sound scientific footing. But in so far as such studies are not yet available, and no attempt is being made towards furthering such research, the theory rests as of now on 'spurious' foundations and is unscientific.

In order to explicate Grünbaum's critique more closely, we consider an example of his analysis of what he believed is the 'central thesis' of psychoanalysis: the 'Necessary Condition Thesis' or the 'NCT'. This analysis is typical of Grünbaum's critical approach to Freud's theory. The usual steps involved in this approach are: the recasting of a Freudian hypothesis into a necessarily causal form; the derivation of empirical conditions which will verify the thesis; and the conclusion that empirical warrant does not exist.

According to Grünbaum, Freud tried to erroneously include within the NCT thesis both a theory of therapy as well as a piece of psychoanalytic knowledge. Psychoneurotic patients were treated by Freud using the 'catharctic method', or a method involving the systematic uncovering of the patient's unconscious which Freud assumed, was causally linked to the symptoms. The recovery of the unconscious in turn removed the symptoms, leading to successful therapy. Through his clinical appraisals of successful therapy, Freud believed that valid psychoanalytic laws may be formulated about the causal psychic pathogens of the patient through analytic interpretation and that only valid hypotheses would lead to success. This entire network of assumptions linking therapeutic success and theoretic validity has been labelled by Grünbaum as the 'NCT'.

The NCT, according to Grünbaum, is a conjunct of two causally necessary premises, put succinctly as follows: 'only psychoanalytic interpretations that "tally with what is real" in the patient can mediate veridical insight, *and* such insight, in turn, is causally necessary for the successful alleviation of his neurosis' (1980, p. 321). On the basis of these presuppositions, Freud *ruled out* the possibility of his therapy being simply a suggestive technique, unlike hypnosis. The assumption that Freud made is that the patient simply does not acquiesce to *any* interpretation but only to *some*, namely, to those which 'tally' with what is real in him. This has been termed the 'tally argument' by Grünbaum. Only those interpretations which truly fit the patient's life context will have therapeutic value or will lead to successful therapy. Any other interpretation would be deemed irrelevant and would be eliminated from the therapy as 'false'. This is possible not through hypnosis, but only through psychoanalytic therapy. On the contrary, a successful therapy shows that the interpretations used by the analyst are true and valid. Thus, Freud concluded, from the NCT, that the success of therapy entailed the validity of the theory.

The NCT is crucial for Grünbaum in his aim to show that even though the psychoanalytic theory is so evidently amenable to the kind of validating inductive methodology which he has demanded from an empirical science, psychoanalysis has resisted such attempts. By conflating the therapeutic issue of the success of therapy with the epistemological issue of the validity of the theory, this typically Freudian argument incorrectly vindicates psychoanalytic theory as validated within the clinic. It erroneously brackets the need for standard empirical procedures of lab testing. The theory's claim for validity *turns on* its success, and yet it altogether dismisses the question of using treatment outcome studies to assess its own negligible merits compared to other therapies. The two premises of the NCT, the 'tally argument' and the therapy's success, are easily corroborated empirically by inductive, longitudinal studies using experimental controls and yet it was precisely this sort of corroboration that Freud appears to have dismissed in principle. This makes Freud open to Grünbaum's charge that his theory works by mere 'placebos'.

The charge of 'placebo', well documented in literature, refers to the diminution of epistemological considerations necessary for controlled experimental treatment of a theory being used in therapy, wrought by the patient's deferential acquiescence to the analyst's theoretic persuasions. The charge of placebo is that the therapeutic setting is designed in such a way that the patient is led on by the therapist to endorse the analyst's interpretations, much as a witness is led on by a clever lawyer in court. According to Grünbaum, there is a clear sanction for this in psychoanalysis in the notion of 'transference'. Transference is a process by which the patient cathartically overcomes his neuroses by imaginary identification of the therapist with the authority figures of his oedipal life. Freud's view, often explicated textually, that psychotherapy cannot proceed unless the patient commits himself to the personal authority of the analyst is seen by Grünbaum to be an exhortation of doctrinal allegiance by the patient. Viewed thus, 'cure' itself would be questionable. According to Grünbaum, the NCT cannot avoid the circularity entailed by the very implications of the so-called therapeutic process of transference. Freud inferred the validity of his interpretation by the patient's tally verdict. By using the notion of transference, he ensured that the patient endorsed the interpretation anyway and was 'cured'. The validity of the theory is assured by the very terms of the therapy. The NCT involves 'logically a viciously circular bootstrap operation', for this reason. Freud could have avoided this circularity by resorting to empirical research on outcome studies and other extra-clinical cognitive research. The theory's claim to scientific status and to valid knowledge of human behaviour hinges on its recognition of this research.

IV

Adolf Grünbaum's ambitious critique intends to question not only Freudian theory, but also *all* evolutes from that theory. In his view, the objection that he has raised against Freud is encompassing enough to be used as a weapon against all contemporary models of psychoanalysis. For Grünbaum, in so far as any model of psychoanalysis has not taken the question of empirical warrant into its own fold, no model of psychoanalysis can claim the status of valid knowledge or of a science.

Grünbaum's critique, quite influential in the current development of contemporary psychoanalytic criticism in the philosophy of science, is not unproblematic (for discussions of Grünbaum's critique, see Holt, 1985; Von Eckhardt, 1982; Wallerstein, 1986a). Incidentally, Grünbaum's critique suffers from the tension generated by his dual attempt to historically defend Freud against Popper as a sophisticated methodologist, and to epistemologically critique Freud. Philosophically viewing Grünbaum's overall aims, it may be noted that his historical aim is incommensurate with his epistemological aim. In his historical attempt to defend Freud against Popper, Grünbaum's concern is the historical contexts in which Freud proposed and gave up his hypotheses. Answering this involved bracketing the question concerning the empirically justified 'truth' of psychoanalytic hypotheses and focusing attention on the contextual development of Freud's ideas. He had to assume, like the historicists, that a scientific theory is a fluid, historically determined entity where problems of justifying theoretical laws empirically are not so primary to scientific praxis as seeing simply that the context demanded their postulation. A discovery, according to this view, has its own logic quite different from the logic of justification.

Contrarily, Grünbaum's epistemological critique addresses the question of the 'truth' of Freud's hypotheses. In answering this question, Grünbaum has shelved the contextuality of discovery. Instead, he has adopted the justificationist's meta-scientific rule that scientific epistemology is atemporal and universal, and conclusivity of empirical studies is the final arbiter on the question of knowledge. These two conflicting aims lead Grünbaum to hold two contradictory theses about Freud. On the one hand, he has dismissed Freud's hypotheses as being spurious, because of lack of empirical, inductive evidence. On the other hand, and in quite a contradictory way, he has noted: 'More generally, upon looking at the actual development of Freud's thought, one finds that, as a rule, his repeated modifications of his theories were *clearly motivated by evidence and hardly idiosyncratic or capricious*' (1979, p. 135).[3]

Ferguson (1985), Carveth (1987), Levy (1988) and Sachs (1989) among others, have provided a much needed though not sufficient, analysis of Grünbaum's critique of psychoanalysis, particularly in terms of both his exegetical claims and methodological recommendations. Levy, for example, has noted the 'serious misinterpretation of Freud' effected by Grünbaum, legitimately questioning the alleged centrality of the NCT thesis. According to Levy,

> 'an author wishes to attribute a central thesis to Freud, on the basis of which all of Freud's work (*and we might add, all of his followers' works*) is supposed to be flawed. But he claims that Freud only asserted this thesis in two places, neither of which seems to support the attribution very well. Granted the NCT sounds like the sort of thing many intelligent people suppose Freud to have meant, and possibly quite a few texts can be found in which he says things close to it. But if so much is to hinge on Freud's adherence to such a thesis, ought we not be supplied with a very high order of proof that Freud did actually adhere to it? (1988, p. 197).

Levy's astonishment is understandable. The claim to centrality which

---

[3] Emphasis added.

Grünbaum has attributed to the NCT in the entire psychoanalytic edifice demands at least that the thesis be linked with other theories of psychoanalysis. It is now well recognised that Freud's theory is not one 'theory', but rather a set of theories: a theory of dreams, a theory of instincts, an oedipal theory, a personality theory, etc. In other words, Freud's 'theory' is rather a scaffolding and is to be treated as a network of theories, as complex as any other general scientific theory. It is amazing to think that the epistemological validity of *all* these theories depends *centrally* upon the NCT. The least requirement that Grünbaum should have attended to for sustaining his claim is that the links between the NCT and the other theories be well defined. Grünbaum cannot claim that psychoanalysis as a grand theory is unscientific on the basis of the objectionable nature of the NCT. As noted earlier in the introduction, to ask whether the grand theory is scientific or not might well be a fruitless pursuit. Grünbaum might have been raising these questions about the classical 'model' of psychoanalysis: the model that currently claims for itself a status as the traditional model. But he has not made this addressal explicit and has failed to address the evolution and mutation of the classical model from Freud's theory. Grünbaum has claimed that his critique has fundamentally questioned the status of the entire psychoanalytic research programme. However, this claim needs elaborate proof, requiring an examination of evolving psychoanalytic models from Freud's time in the light of contemporary empirical research in the field. Other critics of Grünbaum such as Carveth, following different perspectives, reiterate that Grünbaum's reading of Freud is caricaturist.

Grünbaum's objection to both Popper and Freud was on their conflation of therapeutic issues with questions relating to justification of the theory. Ironically enough, Grünbaum has failed to appreciate that the NCT, allegedly the central thesis of psychoanalysis, is a therapeutic heuristic rather than a psychoanalytic law. The NCT is not the kind of concept on which one can base an argument, as Grünbaum has done, for the spurious or unscientific nature of psychoanalysis. The NCT is not even a 'law' of psychoanalysis capable of 'verification', much less the 'central' law. It is a concept associated with therapeutic discussions, such as the success and goals of therapy and one does not, except in error, associate the notion of verification with it. Grünbaum is perspicuous and far-sighted to point out the necessary requirement of separating therapy from the validation of the theory, of carefully segregating the theory from the therapy in his critique of Popper and

Freud, but lamentably, he has not himself strictly satisfied this all-important requirement.

Grünbaum has rightly objected to an inference such as the following, which he has imputed to Freud:

1. A particular therapy has been successful.
2. Only psychoanalysis can effect this success.
   Therefore, the theory is valid

For Grünbaum, this fallacious inference mixes up therapeutic issues of success with research issues of validity. However he has drawn the *same* kind of inference when he used Eysenck's behaviouristic studies to show the placebo nature of the theory on the basis of the *negligible* merits of psychoanalysis as a successful therapy. He inferred:

1. Psychoanalytic therapy is not successful.
2. Other therapies perform much better than psychoanalysis.
   Therefore, the *theory* is a placebo and is invalid.

Here Grünbaum repeated in reverse Freud's erroneous inference: from the lack of empirical support from behaviouristic success studies of therapy, he concluded the placebogenic nature of the theory. If Freud is to be charged of confusing a cognitive issue with a therapeutic issue, so is Grünbaum.

Of course, there is a cognitive claim hidden in the NCT, which may be labelled definitively psychoanalytic, and binding on all forms of psychoanalysis—this is the theory of repression. The NCT is a plausible therapeutic thesis because of the cognitive claim contained in it that analysis will bring to the fore the repressed unconscious. However, Grünbaum needs to examine the empirical support that exists and is growing for the theory of repression, to testify to the lack of empirical credibility of psychoanalytic theory. He would have done this if he had faithfully followed his own empirical leanings and his call for an 'extra-clinical' cure for psychoanalysis. The empirical tradition in psychoanalysis has a long history. He should have examined this history to see if the cognitive claim of the NCT, namely, the theory of repression is empirically justified or not. This requires more philosophical effort and methodological understanding than Grünbaum has granted psychoanalysis. Instead, in his critique of the so-called central psychoanalytic thesis, he has fallaciously introduced therapeutic notions, such as the clinical inference from success to validity, as cognitive claims.

This confusion between cognitive and pragmatic issues is discernible in Grünbaum's treatment of the notion of 'placebo'. The notion of 'placebo' is a therapeutic concept and not one associated with the epistemological foundations of the theory as Grünbaum assumes in the above argument. The notion has been used in two important senses in the available literature—epistemological and ethical. Discussions about placebo are often confusing because these senses are not always kept distinct, as they should be. In its epistemological sense, placebo refers to treatment factors other than those ascribed to a particular therapy in use, contributing to therapeutic change. A placebogenic cure has been effected if symptom relief has occurred not because of the factors attributable to the particular therapy being used but rather because of factors beyond the scope of the therapy over which the therapy can make no claim whatsoever. The cure effected has no ascribable causes within the given framework and fall outside of the therapy in clinical use. This is an important clarification that Grünbaum (1989b) had made, contributing in a significant way to a befuddled concept of placebo in medicine and psychiatry.

In this epistemological sense, the concept gives rise to a number of interesting research problems in psychotherapy. An epistemologically sound approach of a therapy to the problem of placebo would be to find stringent criteria relating the cognitive claims of the theory underpinning the therapy. This is really a specification of the treatment factors of a particular theory, of how cognitive states stand in causal relation to human behaviour. Under ideal conditions (Karazu, 1986), a therapy should be able to explicate the nature of its users and make predictions regarding the etiology, treatment and prognosis of the illness in question. A therapy should be illness specific and user specific and philosophical scrutiny should determine how these can be effected. Used in this sense, the charge that psychotherapy is a placebo is really an appeal for clarifying the *specificity* of psychoanalysis, an appeal which is legitimate and equally binding on all therapies.

Even though Grünbaum has made an important contribution by clarifying the notion of placebo in a meaningful way for psychotherapeutic research, in actual usage of the concept, he (see, for example, Grünbaum, 1983a, pp. 14, 18, 19, 21; 1984, p. 178; 1986, p. 223) has reverted to the ethical usage, thus making the same error that he attributes to others in the literature pertaining to the study of placebo. In its ethical usage, a placebo refers to the situation when a patient is coerced or persuaded into accepting the interpretations, analyses and solutions of the analyst. A placebo, in this sense, is equivalent to 'suggestion' and also to psychological coercion. It is no longer used within an epistemological context and raises the question of the judiciousness of the therapist in enforcing the knowledge which he has on the unsuspecting subject. In this second sense, the charge of placebo brings into question, not the theory as Grünbaum has assumed in the NCT, but the continuation of a specific therapy under a particular therapist that the patient had consented to. Grünbaum's conclusion that psychoanalysis is unscientific and placebogenic refers to the concept of 'placebo' in the second sense. Psychoanalysis fails to be epistemologically sound for Grünbaum, because in neglecting the question of empirical warrant, the therapy can only be a suggestive technique. Understanding Grünbaum's position in this way, as being an unjustifiably mixed notion of placebo, his conclusion can be faulted on two counts. First, it conflates an ethical issue with an epistemological one. In medical and psychiatric ethics, the question of the patient's consent *vis-à-vis* coercion is a well debated moral issue. It is not clear from Grünbaum's works how the philosophical consequences of this debate relates to the purely *epistemological* one of justification of the theory. By Grünbaum's own declarations in the context of his critiques of both Popper and Freud, such a conflation is unjustified. Second, even if we grant that Grünbaum is using the concept in his own, epistemologically refined sense, he could still be charged with the conflation of a therapeutic concept with a cognitive concept of empirical justification, a distinction which he himself rightly upholds as necessary and crucial for epistemological discussion. If, by his own criterion, validation of psychoanalysis is primarily decided by extra-clinical testing of its cognitive claims, Grünbaum's dependence on the placebogenic nature of the therapy for testifying to the unscientific nature of the theory is unwarranted and contradictory. He should have examined extra-clinical studies, such as they exist, in order to draw his epistemological conclusions. These reflections only further support our earlier claim that Grünbaum is as wrong as Freud was, to link the question of the unscientific nature of psychoanalysis with the placebo nature of the therapy.

The following question can be framed in order to make our charge more clear that Grünbaum has conflated an ethical issue with an epistemological issue: if all the so-called extra-clinical truths in psychoanalysis were known to us, would it solve the placebo problem? In the first, epistemologically defined sense, it would and it is important, as the community itself recognises, to pursue psychotherapeutic research which will fulfil this ideal. This research would make psychotherapies illness specific and ideally, user specific, ameliorating the well recognised problem of fragmentation in therapeutic praxes. However, in the second ethical sense in which Grünbaum uses it, the placebo problem cannot be solved. *Even if all the truths of psychoanalysis were known, that would still not be reason enough for the psychoanalyst to persuade the patient to accept his solutions.* Taking an analogous case from clinical medicine, we know, for example, all that requires to be known in order to perform a theoretically successful open heart surgery. However, in the domain of medical ethics, the mere availability of this knowledge does not necessarily override the question of the patient's consent to such surgery. The mere availability of knowledge does not excuse us from considering questions relating to its use on human beings. Similarly, the ethical problem of the subject's consent to a particular therapy would not be eliminated by the availability of true cognitive claims in psychotherapy. The moral issue in medical and psychiatric ethics is related to granting freedom to the consumers of these practices to accept or reject such practices; the ethical issue facing a subject or a user of therapeutic practice is not concerned with the truth or validation of knowledge, but the use of that knowledge to himself. Grünbaum's ostensibly epistemological, in fact, ethical conclusion of the placebogenic nature of psychoanalytic therapy has no bearing whatsoever on the question of validation.

Grünbaum's claim that Freud drew conclusions about the validity of the theory from the success of the therapy is itself questionable from a more philosophical point of view. In claiming this, Grünbaum might well be confusing the epistemological distinction between the *hypotheses* of the theory with the *interpretation* of particular experiences. Freud was indeed wrong, as Grünbaum has pointed out, to neglect empirical warrant for his theoretical presuppositions about the nature of cognition and its relation to abnormal behaviour. Because of this neglect, he had no way of finding out whether the hypotheses he was using in the clinic were true or not. The case study method, as Grünbaum has indicated, is indeed not suitable for the purpose of arriving at the truth of psychoanalytic hypotheses. But in his case studies, Freud could arguably justify the correctness of the *interpretation* that he was using from the success he obtained in the removal of symptoms using the theory.

If we strictly adhere to the research/therapy distinction, it will be clear that interpretation in the clinic and the laws of psychoanalysis are two different kinds of epistemological entities altogether. As Dilman (1984) has noted in a Wittgensteinian way, the generality of interpretation of dreams, for example, is not the same as the generality of a law of psychoanalysis about dreams. Both involve rule following, but the rules binding on them are of different types. An interpretation refers to the particular application of the methodological rule that a theory stipulates. A law is a conceptual relation existing between entities referred to by the theory. An interpretation is a matter of skill; a law is a matter of cognition. The former relates to the heuristics of practice; the latter to the science. The former is particular and contextual; the latter is universal and general. In the clinic, an interpretation definitively is in the context of the individuation of the patient and his specific psychohistory. The interpretation of dreams and associations depends on training and skill, purely praxaeological notions, and aims at 'taking the dream with the dreamer's associations and placing it in the context of his growing knowledge of the dreamer's particular life' (Dilman, 1984, p. 160). The difference between interpretation and a theoretical law is the difference between driving a car and knowing the laws of combustion. Or, it is the difference that has been often emphasised between cognitive and pragmatic issues. From the success of the therapy, Freud *was* entitled to infer the *correctness* of the interpretation: that is, the judgment that the interpretative rule he was using fitted the particular case in question. Of course, he needed independent methodological criteria for generalising even heuristic rules, but the clinical inference itself, from the success of the therapy to the correctness of the interpretation used in therapy, is not invalid. The justifiability of explanations in the clinic for praxis or interpretative force is possible on the basis of this kind of inference. It must be granted of course, that the criteria must stipulate when such an inference has been legitimate. Also, it is illegitimate, as Grünbaum has argued, to validate the *law* from the validity of the *interpretation*. But the philosophical point must be noted that decisions regarding the validity of scientific laws are not made the same way as decisions regarding the validity of interpretations. The clinical inference of the validity of the interpretation is correct in the NCT, but the cognitive inference of the validity of the law is incorrect. In entirely rejecting the NCT, Grünbaum has lost sight of an important epistemological aspect of therapy. If he had studiously carried forward the distinction between therapy and research, he might not have done this.

Grünbaum's indictment of Freud's spurious inference of the validity of the theory from the success of the therapy in fact correctly recognises a theoretical problem in psychoanalytic research. The problem is: what *is* to count as a successful therapy. There is often a circularity involved in responding to this problem: the theoretical foundations underscoring any therapy determine the criteria upon which 'success' can be evaluated. Each kind of therapy also carries prescriptions regarding what is to count as success or when a cure has been effected. This theoretical bias of therapies gives rise to the issue of the evaluation of different therapies, especially when they are all operating under different theoretical guises. The question is whether such a comparison is possible at all, and how comparison can be effected without adversely affecting the theoretical premises of a particular therapy.

Comparative studies of the sort Grünbaum has emphasised are important in judging relative successes, by assuming some common standard. However, the possibility of such comparability of successes of different therapies presupposes that their theoretical foundations are *known* to be compatible and comparable. But such knowledge is not fully available, raising doubts whether comparisons of successes have at all been made legitimately. There are two sides to the problem of determining the 'success' of therapies, only one of which Grünbaum has highlighted in his critique of psychoanalysis: that any therapy can claim its own success based strictly upon its internal rules. Grünbaum has neglected the other critical problem which, if he had considered at all, would have perhaps forced him to take a more moderate view of the scientific foundations of psychoanalysis: any comparative account determining the relative successes of different therapies must provide norms which are logically compatible with the therapies being compared. Grünbaum has taken for granted the behaviouristically defined notion of 'success' and has evaluated psychoanalysis against this notion. Grünbaum's notion derives largely from the works of behaviouristic treatment outcome studies of Eysenck. This school of thought defines success in operational terms, taking cure to be the disappearance of symptoms or symptom relief. Grünbaum has been faulted for taking Eysenck too seriously (see Ferguson, 1985, for a review of critical literature on Eysenck). Eysenck's method has been faulted for his having used too stringent criteria in his assessment of psychoanalytic theory. His studies are explicitly behaviouristic: this raises the problem of researcher's bias, particularly when any measurement of comparability between psychoanalysis and the behaviouristic underpinnings of his calculus is lacking. Grünbaum has not fully appreciated the entire implications of his dependence on the behaviouristically biased treatment outcome studies for his evaluation of psychoanalysis. Such a recognition could have productively involved him in other epistemological problems in the general domain of psychotherapeutic research. Instead, he has assumed and inducted many assumptions about the notion of 'success' uncritically for his evaluation. If this evaluation has to be taken seriously, he has to participate in the general therapeutic debate about success, which raises a host of epistemological problems.

The determination of therapeutic success and of the relative merits of different therapies is not as unproblematic as Grünbaum has assumed it to be. Particularly in the case of psychodynamic models such as psychoanalysis, one must cautiously treat a strictly behaviouristic identification of therapeutic success with symptom relief. Freud, the first psychodynamic psychiatrist, was unhappy with this identification for very specific reasons. Freud's disenchantment with hypnosis, for example, was based on the inability of the treatment to provide the causal principles which led to pathology. Even though hypnosis provided symptom relief, it left the question of the genesis of illness unanswered. In his 'Analysis Terminable and Interminable' (S.E., Vol. 23, pp. 216–53), Freud addressed the question of the relapse of illness, after therapy has been administered. The phenomenon of relapse illuminates the fact that psychological explanations which are assumed to be complete with the relief of symptoms do not go far enough in the explanation of psychopathology. Practically, an adequate explanation is required for the practitioner to decide when to terminate an analysis. A criterion such as symptom relief is not satisfactory if it leaves open the possibility of the relapse of illness. Any treatment cannot be thought of as complete if relapse occurs after its termination.

Freud's important contribution to the discussion on the success of therapy is his insistence that any psychopathological theory must also specify under what conditions a therapy can *fail*. It is imperative to provide explanations regarding the failure of a therapy if the therapy is to be viewed as adequate. A theory of success based upon symptom relief is bound to be limited, because mental illnesses do not always conform to the epistemologist's stringent ideals. Freud cautioned that defining the 'end' of analysis as a measure of the analyst's efforts to exert 'such a far-reaching influence on the patient that no further change could be expected to take place in him if his analysis were continued' (S.E., Vol. 23, p. 219) is too ambitious. A failure of analysis could be due to accidental factors, for example, when a trauma is not 'tamed by the ego'. It could also be a constitutional failure as when instinctual forces inexorably resist such taming. Psychoanalysis recognises the fact that not all of a person's instinctual life is available to the analyst and that instincts are not overtly manifested but must be inferred from behaviour. The analyst hence suffers from all the limitations of human cognitive fallibility. The lengthy nature of the psycho analytic contract, of course, was for Freud a practical entailment of the difficulty inherent to the realm in laying bare the entire cognitive map of the patient's instinctual life.

The success of a therapy is inherently problematic, requiring mutlidimensional analyses. This would involve discussions about constructing an adequate psychotherapeutic nosology taking into account different causal possibilities of instinctual presentations. The pluralistic shift in diagnoses of mental illness already well established in psychotherapy, or the view that mental illnesses are to be seen as falling along a continuum rather than as discrete disorders, entails a recognition of a range of possible causal explanations of mental illness. The behaviouristic model of success assumes, rather, a linear causal chain of a single symptom <=> single cause. The use of induction with respect to success outcomes which Grünbaum has recommended is constituted in such a manner that it requires a causal relation between cognitive claims of the theory and symptomatology to be tested only in very small packages involving theoretic reduction into bi-conditionals. Only by adopting arbitrary scissoring techniques from within the explanatory model can the grand theory be adapted as a model that will suit such inductive methods. Freud, repelled by this reductionist idea of symptom relief, cautioned thus:

(Their) expectations clearly presuppose a number of things which are not precisely self-evident. They assume, firstly, that there really is a possibility of disposing off an instinctual conflict . . . definitively and for all time; secondly, that while we are treating someone for one instinctual conflict we can, as it were, inoculate him against the possibility of any other such conflicts; and thirdly, that we have the power, for purposes of prophylaxis, to stir up a pathogenic conflict of this sort which is not betraying itself at the time by any indications, and that it is wise to do so (S.E., Vol. 23, p. 223).

Another factor which confounds behaviouristic evaluations of the success of a therapy is the 'non-specific' nature of disorders (Ferguson, 1985). The individuated patterns of symptoms in different persons may not have more than a family resemblance to an ideal definition of, say 'neurosis'. The term neurosis may refer to unidentical symptomatic patterns in different individuals. Ferguson has discussed the implications of this problem in psychotherapeutic research in the context of evaluating Grünbaum's demand for comparative outcome studies. Ferguson has noted that a 'depression', for example,

> can be mild or severe, situational or chronic; it can be a transitory phase in a manic-depressive psychosis . . .; it can occur at the anniversary of some painful event . . .; it can have all sorts of concomitant somatic complications which may be of more immediate urgency than any subjective feelings of misery, e.g. anorexia, insomnia, or drug addiction. The point is that the word 'depressive', can mean so many things and is related to so many intrapsychic as well as situational factors in the person's life that to compare percentages of large groups of these people without discrimination is practically meaningless (1985, p. 335).

Ferguson has pointed out that a comparison of groups, as in Eysenck's works, on the basis of a certain typified kind of illness has its limitations. Attempting to bring this group together under the name of an illness as though the name is a rigid designator will inevitably lead to treating symptoms as if they were the illness, with no evolutionary, aetiological or relational bases (for a similar objection, see Carveth, 1987). This model of illness, other than being incompatible with the nature of psychodynamic theories of therapy such as psychoanalysis, cannot but lead to a choice of criteria for the analysis of data which are too stringent.

Grünbaum's charge of psychoanalysis as placebogenic is based on the so-called 'fact' that there is no empirical evidence to show that therapeutic success is greater than the rate of spontaneous remissions for particular disorders, such as psychoneuroses. Incidents of spontaneous remissions are an embarrassment to all forms of therapies, and not just pschoanalysis. A 'spontaneous remission' occurs when symptoms are removed *without* therapeutic intervention. Eysenck has noted that the phenomenon of spontaneous remission is the 'most clear-cut' fact in the entire history of neurotic illnesses, a form of mental illness that psychoanalysis definitively addresses itself to. If a large number of neurotics can be relieved of their symptoms without psychoanalytic intervention, it follows, at least for the sceptics, that psychoanalysis can make no claim to being therapeutic even in those cases where it has intervened. In other words, psychoanalysis cannot provide adequate criteria for deciding when success has occurred because of the treatment factors it claims for itself, and when success has occurred as it were gratuitously. So long as such criteria are lacking, according to the critics, aetiological hypotheses cannot be differentiated from mere placebos.

It is, however, too early to dismiss the validity of psychoanalysis on the grounds of the phenomenon of spontaneous remissions. (We need not stress the fact that Grünbaum has brought in yet another therapy related notion for concluding an epistemological issue.) Freud's rationale in looking for the failure of therapy, of the scientist's fallibility and the complexity of mental life, could be applied to the problem of spontaneous remission also. No therapist has ever claimed that mental illness cannot be resolved unless therapeutic intervention in the classical sense takes place. In so far as individual, social, developmental, biological, genetic and cognitive factors are involved in the aetiology and the resolution of illness, it is entirely plausible for an illness to be resolved without therapy. This does not make the therapy redundant, nor the treatment a placebo. Far less does it render a psychopathological theory unscientific! A migraine can disappear without medical intervention, but no one has even claimed the redundance of medicine or its overall nature as quackery because of this fact. Nor can anyone claim that the disappearance of migraine is entirely gratuitous and an explanation need not be rendered about the genesis and treatment, or the gratuitous disappearance of migraine.

The notion of spontaneous remission, at least as Eysenck has used it, is a behaviouristic concept related to symptom relief and not a cognitive concept. Definite measurements regarding what would constitute spontaneous remissions are lacking. This is especially true of disorder patterns that recur or have a cyclic symptomatology. Ferguson has pointed out that in cases like manic depression, the illness pattern is cyclic: there are periods when the symptoms are overt, and periods when the symptoms seem non-existent. By any comparative study, those periods when the symptoms are not manifest would be considered, erroneously of course, as having 'spontaneously remitted'.

Comparative studies in the area of psychotherapy in general are teeming with many such interesting problems exposing the inherent methodological limitations. There are also other problems of, for instance, duplicating symptomatology with the same intensity and affective impact in neutral conditions (Edelson, 1986a). This fact that any study of cognitive processes must take into account the individual variability in functioning, is also recognised by researchers in cognitive science. To ensure that research in cognition takes place in a natural setting rather than in a simulated one they recommend that research must conform to the criterion of 'ecological validity', that is, research must be as close as possible to the natural environment in which human cognition is brought into service. On the whole, the limitations of quantitative research in psychotherapy generally are too complicated and the panacea that Grünbaum has categorically recommended for psychoanalysis must be investigated further with respect to this complexity. The force of Grünbaum's 'scotch verdict' on the questionable epistemological foundations of psychoanalysis is weak because he has not taken cognisance of the various assumptions he has made and conclusions he has uncritically inducted from the area of psychotherapeutic research, an area riddled with controversies. A clinical practitioner will correctly note that Grünbaum is too much of a philosopher, and far too preoccupied with philosophical questions to be able to treat psychotherapeutic methodology seriously and somewhat autonomously. Grünbaum's treatment of psychoanalysis disappoints a philosopher also. Grünbaum has claimed to be concerned with the 'epistemological' foundations of psychoanalysis, a cognitive issue about the nature and methods of the science. However, his analyses of pragmatic issues such as the NCT, placebo, success outcome, show that his preoccupation is rather with the therapy and not with the theory at all.

The methodological problems related to psychotherapy are only reflections of some general problems in social science research. In an enlightening paper, Danziger (1985) has noted the 'methodological circle' which inevitably marks such research. The circle refers to the theoretical, mathematical, historical and institutional imperatives which preside over and justify as 'objective', the methodological choices made in the social sciences. According to Danziger,

> if theoretical preconcepts are an unavoidable component of methodological rules, and if such rules mean that only certain kinds of observation will ever be made, then a certain predetermination of

observation by theory must follow . . . . methods based on assumptions about the nature of the subject matter only produce observations which must confirm these assumptions (1985, p. 1).

Like all other forms of human intervention, the empirical method too carries with it the burden of its historical traditions and their often tacit presuppositions. The method, according to Danziger, like any piece of human knowledge, becomes institutionalised and assumes the position of a 'methodological imperative' as the necessary and sufficient condition of all knowledge.

The analysis Danziger has provided raises questions about the epistemology of observation in the sciences which use sophisticated numerical models. In the natural sciences, Heelan (1983) and Brown (1987), among others, have shown that instrumentation brings along with its own theoretical presuppositions, often implicit and not called into question by researchers. Danziger's work has indicated that the inductive methods in social sciences are instrumental in the acquisition of knowledge and that the epistemological problems relating to instrumentation in the natural as well as social sciences are analogous. Danziger has recognised that the statistical models used in inductive research often carry tacit knowledge: theoretical assumptions which are hidden and unknown. This unknown dimension of the tool being used for research raises a number of questions; significantly, about possible discrepancies of comparison between the mathematical model used and the theory to be evaluated. For legitimate research, the theory to be tested and the mathematical model used for testing must be commensurate. On the other hand, there are no available measures of such compatibility. In all cases, there is the possibility, as seen in evaluations of psychoanalysis, for the methods in use to be 'systematically biased to favour one type of theory over another' (Danziger, 1985, p. 3).

Another factor contributing to the tacit knowledge of the supposedly 'objective' tool of the standard empirical sciences is the kind of interpretation which the researcher chooses to assume as being the 'core' theory. This is particularly a problem with theories like psychoanalysis where interpretations abound. The results of the analysis from different viewpoints of this spectrum possibly lead to different ways of looking at the results. It is worth noting that psychoanalytic critics have taken this lack of conclusivity of empirical results in psychoanalytic research as an indication of the inherent limitation of the theory as such. Thus, Grünbaum, for example, despite recognising the enormous work done in the area of psychoanalytic empirical research, has questioned the nature of this research in support of his argument that the theory rests on spurious empirical foundations (see, for example, Grünbaum, 1983c, pp. 125–28; 1986, pp. 269–70). To cite another example, Eagle has noted, after reviewing in a footnote a long list of corroboratory studies on the theory of repression, that 'not a single one of these studies provides impressive support for the Freudian concept of repression' (1986, p. 73). In another lengthy footnote, Crews (1980) has pointed out that even though a long list of corroboratory studies on repression is currently available, all these studies are 'open to challenge' and that 'their acceptance *in toto* would lend only marginal credence to general psychoanalytic theory' (p. 28).

These critics infer the spurious foundations of the theory as a science on the basis of a casual dismissal of empirical studies in the domain. This is especially ironical, given that the cure-all pill that is suggested by them, for the limitations of psychoanalysis is precisely of this sort. We will have occasion to note later that empirical research of the sort demanded by the critics is a well established tradition in psychoanalysis. Empirical work in psychoanalysis not only involves testing the cognitive claims of classical Freudian theory, but also relating the theory to the results obtained from related cognitive sciences, such as developmental, linguistic and social studies. Even though a comprehensive analysis of empirical research is unavailable, there is some evidence for the central concepts of psychoanalysis, such as the unconscious and the theory of repression. The lack of empirical warrant claimed by the critics, then, is debatable.

In any case, even if all the empirical studies unanimously show the falsity of psychoanalysis, the inference made by Grünbaum from the lack of empirical warrant to the *unscientific* nature of the theory is fallacious. Grünbaum's philosophical intuition has failed him here. In fact, the very possibility of methodological verification or falsification, which Grünbaum has acknowledged as possible for the theory makes it a science, whatever the eventual outcomes of empirical research. Contrary to the earlier inductivists and also later neo-inductivists like Adolf Grünbaum, Karl Popper's meta-science is more mature in that it only says that a theory fails to be scientific if it is not *falsifiable*. A theory *actually* found to be false, on the basis of available evidence, could be justifiably rejected but the charge of pseudo-science cannot be applied to such a theory. It would in fact be a paradigmatic science.

For Popper, the condition binding on a scientific theory is only that it should be able to specify the terms which will render it false, and not its actual falsity. For Grünbaum however, psychoanalysis is unscientific because of lack of empirical support! Very few theories would be scientific according to this criterion. Rather than incorrectly inferring the unscientific nature of psychoanalysis from the current, indeed, fertile state of cognitive research in the area, the critics can fruitfully examine the very foundations of empirical work in the social sciences in general. There are no reasons for believing that *this* work rests on impeccable foundations and any so-called epistemological consider-ation will have to focus here, rather than on the therapy as Grünbaum appears to have done.

V

It is patent that the logical-positivistic problem of demarcation, of the prospect of epistemologically separating science from pseudo-science, non-science, pre-science, speculation, belief and propaganda has in-spired both Popper's and Grünbaum's critiques of psychoanalysis. Popper clearly initiated his meta-scientific considerations by making the demarcation problem central to the philosophy of science. In Grünbaum's case, the demarcationist interests also form the almost invisible undercurrent that channels the psychoanalytic critique. Grün-baum (1983b) has tended to disown his logical-positivist and justific-ationist leanings, but his dependence on and departure from Popper's philosophy of science unwittingly enhances an interpretation of his philosophical bias as justificationist. It is not impossible to argue that Grünbaum has not only carried the demarcationist interests of logical-positivism forward by his critical appraisal of Popper, but he also has reinstated a criterion which was, since Popper, believed to be philos-ophically unjustifiable. Of course, the reference is to Grünbaum's explicit espousal of inductivist and probabilistic criteria of knowledge and demarcation. The following comments found in his texts make the interpretation that he is justificationist more than likely: '. . . in Popper's falsifiability sense of "science", psychoanalysis does qualify as science, whereas in my sense of the term it does not' (1986, p. 268); '(P)ost-Baconian inductivism has at least the capacity of challenging the scientific credentials of psychoanalytic therapeutics . . .' (1976, p. 227).

The problem of demarcation, for both Popper and Grünbaum, is raised as an epistemological issue in vivid contrast with the internal foundationalist tradition where it is an ethical issue. The central problems of a philosophy of science would be solved, for both these external foundationalists, if ways might be devised by which sciences may rest on sound epistemological grounds. Demarcating good science from other dubious ventures would provide some criteria of evaluation of available knowledge. It would permit us to know which of the available theories which claim to be knowledge really give us knowledge. This epistemological discernment between theories is inherently valuable in itself and philosophy should devise the modalities by which we may make this judgment. A philosophy of science at its best should serve epistemology for both Popper and Grünbaum.

Grünbaum has explicitly denied that he is a positivist, claiming that often it is only a swear word. While it can be granted that the term can be misused or overloaded with value based innuendoes just like any other term of categorisation, he cannot consistently deny his positivistic leanings without compromising on the empiricism that he is right in expecting psychoanalysis to adopt. Induction in empirical psychology depends on precisely the kind of philosophy that he has disclaimed is his own. Empirical psychology is based on the possibility of a theoretical reduction of the statements of a science into operationally defined and causally interpreted conditionals. Testability depends on the possibility of making a distinction between the theoretical law which stands trial and observational statements which will verify (or falsify) the statement. The distinction between theory and observation which Grünbaum has so categorically decried (1983b, p. 48), in fact stands at the epicentre of the empirical philosophy which he has advocated for psychoanalysis. The steps involved in the logical reduction of a theory to the level of testability requires this dichotomy.

There is nothing inherently problematic about the theory–observation dichotomy. Many of the so-called post-positivistic perspectives attempting to provide a rationality to science by denying this dichotomy altogether have only managed to provide 'surrogates' of truth and have ended in the sceptic's maze of relativism and solipsism (Hacking, 1983). Popper, the initiater of this critical movement to erase the dichotomy, faced some difficult semantic problems of relating the theory to the world when he tried to convert all scientific statements into their deductive structure. It is of course wrong to reduce all of a scientific theory to observation statements or protocol statements, as Popper himself pointed out. But, he effected another excess in trying to erase

the distinction altogether and bringing all observation statements into
the theoretical domain. He did not recognise the full implications of
his view that a science is *cognitive* in nature: that a science requires at
some level, though not foundationally, a psychological theory of perception, observation and scientific attention. Grünbaum's objection to
Popper's position is that Popper is mistaken in his belief that induction is
not cognitive. Even though both Popper and Grünbaum have correctly
recognised that science is cognitive they have not carried far the
implications of this recognition, caught as they are in the foundationalist battle of the primacy of criteria. Falsification and verification are
both tools or methods with which sciences work: both are cognitive in
their own ways, and entail their different emphases, procedures and
inherent logical and methodological limitations. They aim to make
generalisations in the sciences possible; their function is to specify how
scientific rules are to be applied to the world.

Common to both the philosophical critiques lies justificationism,
the claim that the scientific nature of a theory depends on the empirical
warrant that it can garner. They do differ on the philosophical criteria
which will sanction such warrant. However, both argue that a logical
circularity will be entailed by a theory, making it unscientific, unless
empirical, experimental criteria of verification are adopted. Psychoanalysis is a prime example of such a viciously circular theory for both
the thinkers. Both arrive at the decision about the probative value of a
theory on the basis of the conclusive outcome of experiments. Neither
Popper nor Grünbaum doubt the conclusivity of the experiment and
in this they are orthodox positivists. For both the thinkers, and rightly,
predicating the truth of a scientific statement is firmly linked to the
outcome of the experiment. Truth has to do with the pragmatics of a
science or with doing science. Science as an enduring activity depends
on its methodology, particularly experimentation, for the determination of truth. Anyone interested in the truth of the statement, 'The
temperature today is 36° Centigrade', would need to respond to the
question: 'What should I do to check if this is true?' Attempts to find
the truth involve providing a rationality for each method and formal
possibilities of the comparative merits of different methods, amongst a
range of actions that one might perform in order to arrive at the truth.
In the above example, some might be arguably more appropriate than
others. Thus, 'let's read the thermometer' would be considered appropriate, whereas 'flying a kite will tell us if this is true' would be
inappropriate. Philosophical issues in methodology determine the

appropriateness of certain sets of actions for arriving at the truth over certain others. They give us reasons for choosing one set of actions over others. The quest for truth in the sciences then can be systematised rationally by methodological considerations and the experiment realises the ideals set up by these considerations. This is the essence of empiricism correctly informing both Popper's and Grünbaum's critiques, and a theory's claim for truth lies in its pragmatics. However, both the critics erroneously identify the *epistemological* foundation of a theory with the *empirical* foundation of the theory. This identification is a resonance of the 'simple' view of science, a typically foundationalist view involving many problematic claims about the nature of a science, as will be seen later.

3

THE SELF, FREEDOM AND PSYCHOANALYSIS

■ ■ ■

I

The humanistic critiques of psychoanalysis focus on the science–society interphase which is a global concern today, with governmental and institutional support being made readily available for studying the impact of the various sciences on society. A 'good' science, as discussed in chapter two, is a theory that commits itself to certain epistemological normative criteria. The question of a 'human' science focuses on how a society can put such a science to humane uses. The universe of discourse within which the humanistic critiques of psychoanalysis operate is essentially valuable, raising questions in the disciplines of the politics and ethics of science. Contemporary science is institutional in its social nature, allowing us to problematise the 'organisation' of the sciences. This problem refers to its *social* organisation, of making a science respond to a society's needs. At best, a humanistic philosophy can tell us what it means for a particular science to be organised humanely by its users.

The humanistic critiques of psychoanalysis have covered two philosophical thresholds since Edmund Husserl, namely, the existentialist and the critical hermeneutic. In both, the central concepts around which the psychoanalytic critique is built are the notions of freedom, subjectivity and consciousness. The traditions are concerned with the philosophical possibility of social, political and personal autonomy of a psychologically constituted self. Freud taught that our nature is at some level gross and indomitable. The humanistic question is how we can possibly still be free. Both the humanistic traditions are concerned with formulating a philosophical denial of the so-called 'one-dimensional man' (Marcuse, 1964). This is a man who is emotionally disemboweled and is interpersonally alienated by the overpowering machinations of science and its invasive products. He has supposedly lost touch with himself, lost his integrity and forgotten how to 'be' in the world.

The critique of a science is the basic weave running through the fabric of continental thinking. With respect to epistemology, the importance of the problem of demarcation had been pointed out earlier. In ethics, too, the science–non-science distinction is significant. Classifying something as a 'science' at once brings it within a society's purview and opens it to public scrutiny. Institutions organising research can oversee the direction and possibilities of a science. The ethical commitments of a science can be checked and questioned publicly. However, this cannot be done if the possibility of making the science–non-science distinction did not exist. The demarcation question which, in Popper's view, was the fundamental philosophical problem is also ethically important. Perhaps he did not see far enough the general implications of this problem for science and its use in society.

II

Freedom of the individual as an ethical ideal, and self-consciousness as a psychological ideal, are intimately related notions in continental thought. As far as existentialism is concerned, the *nature* of human consciousness makes individual freedom possible. The existentialist notion of freedom is a psychological thesis. In hermeneutic thought, as will be seen later, freedom is at the root of the human *social agency*, and not human consciousness. Human consciousness, in the existentialist tradition, is conceived as an indubitable self-consciousness. Self-consciousness is self-reflective: it reflects upon itself and orders itself and the world. Self-consciousness re-arranges its own possibilities of being in the world with respect to purpose or teleology. Understanding of the world and others is in the light of the self's teleological possibilities. As far as existentialism is concerned, intervention in the world is with respect to individual choice and the human agency is justified in so far as consciousness is free. The tenor of the ethic proposed by existentialism is individualistic and psychologistic. It celebrates the primacy of the pre-theoretic and emotive undercurrents of human nature, the so-called irrationality of man, as the fundamental basis of human existence. Freedom in existentialism is an affective notion, referring to the instinctive response allowed by the self to situations that it finds itself in. Sartre, for example, has drawn a distinction between 'authentic' and 'inauthentic' ways of being in the world to help decide whether individualistic psychological conditions of human action are met or not. By definition, 'authenticity' of the self is its capacity to be spontaneous in action. Everything else is forced or 'inauthentic'. This does not mean that the pre-determination of a purpose by the subject is impossible. In fact, freedom embodies the possibility of such a pre-determination. However, this determination should not violate the inner affective sensibilities of the subject. The temporal coherence between affect and purpose renders an action 'free' in the existentialist tradition. The spontaneity of free action rests on this coherence.

Freedom, in the existentialist tradition, is *creative power*. It is also an aesthetic concept where the celebration of human (psychological) existence is the highest aesthetic ideal. Freedom refers to the individual capacity of human beings to speak, gesture or symbolically express themselves so that they can consciously transcend the limitations imposed on them by physical, material, social, political and historical constraints. Art is the material output of these expressions. For the existentialists, consciousness is creative because it is essentially transcendental. Its imagination is so powerful in creating possibilities over and above what actually exists, that it can nullify material constraints of any kind effortlessly. Consciousness is the psychological basis of *protest*. It is the fundamental right of an individual to say a symbolic 'No!' to oppressive forces. The existentialist recognises that the self is definitely bound by temporality, or by its own historically experienced personal time. The self has its genesis and its end in time, and a psychohistory of its evolution. However, at any point in time, it is capable of transcending these in terms of its future possibilities. The onus of making the choice rests with the self. Freedom is not an abstract possibility of the self, but a concrete possibility based on the power of transcendence of the self from the determining circumstances. The notion of freedom makes sense to the existentialist only against a recognition of facticity, those bonds—physical, material, political and historical—by which an individual is tethered to society. Facticity is the socio-historical control that is exerted on an individual in his personal time. Freedom is his imaginative capacity to envision a state where these bondages of his existence are broken down. A prisoner is free not in the literal sense of being free from his physical confinement. But he is free in the psychological sense, of being able to look at this confinement with detachment and to speculate on his future possibilities, however materially limited or emotionally distressing these may be. Freedom, for the existentialist, is *a*contextual and *a*temporal in so far as it is the conscious contemplation of the pure possibilities of a living subject. The experience of freedom is the highest aesthetic experience that the subject can have.

These reflections on the primacy of consciousness and the liberating power it has on individuals guide the epistemology that this form of humanism advocates for a social science. The 'objects' of knowledge in the sciences occupy a secondary place in epistemology, only after self-consciousness, which has been accorded the primary place. There is more than just a hint of idealism in the existentialist understanding of the 'objects' of knowledge (Ricoeur, 1981b, pp. 101–28). Objects are known by their being revealed in human consciousness. Human consciousness is capable of being a *tabula rasa*, of being in a pre-suppositionless state on which objects can be brought to stand in their original purity and essence. Consciousness has the power to transcend its own historically constituted rationality in moments of such pristine understanding. Reason and understanding are distinct in that rationality distantiates objects from their essential nature, whereas understanding approximates and essentialises them. Understanding itself is not an act of reason, but rather a pre-theoretic, 'inner eye' intuitive experience. For these humanists, a true social science 'understands' human subjects and does not rationalise.

The epistemology of existentialism is derived from Husserlian philosophy and is foundationalist. The possibility of freedom that existentialists grant to the human subject does not make its epistemology cognitive. Consciousness is a *tabula rasa* or is cognitively transparent. It does not exert its will on the object, but it absorbs the object, as such, in its essence into its presence. Even though knowledge is possible only through consciousness, this knowledge is 'objective' in the real sense, according to existentialism.

According to existentialism, even though objects are brought to stand in a state of luminescence in consciousness, consciousness is not identical to the object. It can be described autonomously in its own terms. Consciousness is always consciousness of; it is directed. It *intends* the object. Intention is an intuitive act of pure will or pure choice of the subject. Consciousness is distinctive only in its natural capacity to take on objects by acts of intentionality. The 'object' of knowledge is fixed by the preferential focus of subjective attention and at its limit, by the sheer physicality of perception, as Merleau Ponty has claimed. The theory of intentionality, at some fundamental level, aims to be a theory of attention though devoid of empirical understanding. Conscious knowledge of objects is the consequence of these experiential acts of intentionality. Knowledge is such only if it were assigned a locus with respect to the subject's intentions.

The implication of this phenomenological view of intentional and self-conscious knowledge is that no collective knowledge is possible. Empiricism, as seen earlier, aims at collective knowledge and supposes that knowledge is universal and impartial. For an empiricist, knowledge is for everybody. Knowledge, for the existential humanist, however, is the result of individual consciousness and is limited by the psychological determination of such consciousness. The leap from the experiential vision of self-consciousness to the universality of knowledge, the possibility of viewing this knowledge as binding on all human situations, is according to the tradition, a fallacious one. Knowledge is particular and subjective.

Sartre and following him the humanistic tradition of psychoanalysis have based their psychoanalytic critiques on the alleged negation of the theory to the possibility of individual freedom. The problem appears to be with the psychodynamic vocabulary defining the theory: the division of the mind into the conscious and the unconscious. The intimate relation between consciousness and freedom is threatened, for the existentialists, by the Freudian claim that not every mental act is a conscious act. Freud noted correctly that some acts need not necessarily be owned by a person, and have a dark history and evolution of their own not necessarily with the consent or control of the person. Instinctual life, according to psychoanalysis, has its own nature and mode of evolution. Consciousness is not passive, but actively participates, relates to, and changes the way objects are and also changes itself in relation to objects. Consciousness is not open to self-scrutiny, but at some point resists efforts of self-understanding. Freud taught that there are some parts of ourselves that we are happy to keep concealed from ourselves. Consciousness is not continuous, but organised into rational units at different levels.

According to existentialism, this view of consciousness can only be ascribed to the animal or the savage but not to the human subject. A human being's self-identity is derived from his self-awareness and his facticity cannot be so determined as to disallow him the possibility of freedom. In claiming that acts can also be unconscious and in some sense beyond the reach of the individual himself, psychoanalysis is denying freedom, according to the existentialist critiques. If self-knowledge is free control over oneself and one's life, then the realm of the unconscious, if it exists, is in itself threatening. Existentialism can only see a further threat in the analytic situation. For, here, the analyst lays claim to a region of the mind which is supposed to be in principle inaccessible to the analyst.[1]

III

These reflections on the nature of freedom and its centrality in existentialist thinking have important implications for the issue of the possibility of knowing the human subject or the self. They also have implications for the possibility of a social science. Within the existentialist framework, objects that are known and that which makes such knowledge possible do not enjoy the same status. The self, being the author and the arbiter of knowledge, cannot be subjected to the same conditions as the objects of the world. Philosophically, the object of knowledge and the 'self' that knows objects are qualitatively very different entities. Since the 'self', understood in terms of an intentional consciousness, is the frame of reference with which beings in the world are determined, the 'self' itself cannot be further questioned. The 'self' is the psychological, experiential *a priori* on which knowledge, including self-knowledge, is built. Paraphrasing Sartre, one may say that the presiding claim of existentialism is that the 'existence of the self precedes the essence of objects'. For the tradition, the self is a 'for-itself' (Sartre, 1956), in contrast to an object of the world which is an 'in-itself'. An in-itself is cognitively opaque and is not capable of

---

[1] Many interesting questions come to the fore in these discussions, some of them relevant to philosophical psychology, such as the issue whether unconscious acts are intentional, a debate which continues even today (see, for example, Eagle, 1988); the issue whether there are rational grounds for belief in the unconscious (Mac Intyre, 1958); and what Freud meant to achieve by the notions of psychic energy and instinctual drive (Shope, 1971).

self-reflection. Whereas a for-itself is definitively capable of formulating and projecting its own possibilities. Transcendence and teleology, using an existential or experientially close language, are characteristic of a for-itself. An object cannot know itself because it lacks consciousness; it requires the self in order to the known. The self, however, knows itself and hence does not require to be reduced to an object. Hence, for existentialism, a science that studies the self has to be constructed differently, on a normatively distinct base, than the natural sciences.

For both the existentialist and the critical hermeneutic traditions, the problem of self-consciousness, particularly its relation to freedom, is the central concern. It is in the context of this problem that the so-called hermeneutic circle of understanding became central to the existential tradition, and following this, to the critical hermeneutic tradition. The hermeneutic venture introduced the subject as a privileged participant in the reading of history. The subject is the tether around which history is woven and in which he participates. The early hermeneutic prospect of reading (primarily biblical) texts effects a problem shift in phenomenological thought to the prospect of reading the subject's individuated life context *as if* it were a text. The structure of discourse in both these cases is presumed by phenomenological thought to be the same, namely, hermeneutic. The person is the 'text' which must be 'read' within the historical context in which he is situated, by using an existential discourse of finitude and death. Reading *this* human text implies constructing a theory of understanding in terms of structures of human experience, rather than textual categories of linguistic formation.

Within the domain of the person, the hermeneutic circle aims to achieve individual freedom: of the self's escape from rational orderings constructed by the other in acts of pure choice. The question of freedom in existentialism is a problem concerning the self and its society. Between two people, which is the minimum requirement of a society, how is freedom possible? The existentialist response to this question lies in the formulation of a social theory based on the view that individuals are primary and have unlimited power and foresight in organising the social order. Commonly cherished goals of dialogue, trust, participation, care, hope, intimacy and grace preside over the theistic vision of existentialism. The theme of Sartrean philosophy is that individual freedom must be possible, *despite* society, because he sees the other as a threat to his autonomy. The atheistic existentialists are in essence more Freudian than they would like to admit in their emphases of the darker side of the human personality, in terms of aggression and narcissism. Human gaze more than speech is the basis of human contact, for it touches the unspoken but strong emotive realm of human social experience. Humanism in existentialism is any social order which permits an ideal state of individualism. Here, everyone's free choices are comfortably accommodated within society and man has unlimited scope for free expression.

IV

The hermeneutic critique of Freud (Ricoeur, 1970; Habermas, 1972) is also based on the humanistic idea that natural scientific rationality of causality cannot function in the domain of the essentially human without compromising the autonomic and ethical emancipatory possibilities of the analysed subject. The hermeneutic discourse carries the ontological and ethical concerns of existentialism forward. It retains the centrality of both the issues of the possibility of the autonomous man and of self-consciousness to philosophical thought. But it aims to correct the fundamental flaw which it believes exists in the existentialists' discourse in their responses to these central philosophical questions. Consequently, the critical hermeneutic tradition, while carrying forward the crucial existential concerns, also effects a problem shift in its understanding of human freedom and social interaction, from the aesthetic to the political domain.

The critical hermeneutic tradition aims to be a supreme theory of a free, politically active and ethically unconservative subject. A free subject is more like Dastoeievski's Raskolnikov, capable of acting in premeditated ways even if the goal is murder, rather than like Camus' Mersault who seems to ride the nihilist tide of circumstance. The existentialist inter-definition of consciousness and freedom is, for this tradition, questionable. Consciousness is not so utterly free as the existentialist imagines nor can it be so individualistic. Consciousness is limited not only psychologically, but also socially, historically and linguistically, a fact that existentialism failed to reckon with. An individualistic notion of freedom fails to be anything more than 'wild' freedom. The hermeneutic philosophers claim that the irreducible or primary universe of discourse is not the individual, as the existentialist tradition claims, but a social unit, however small.

According to Ricoeur, freedom is not spoken of in the individual context but in the social context. Human dignity and the possibility of self-assertion is in relation to social organisation and legislation. A notion of freedom which is directed inward, like the existentialist notion, is simply a nostalgic freedom, which makes social praxis impossible: the self reminisces, imagines and derives only psychological benefits about being free. Any form of social oppression can be tolerated within this psychologically defined notion of freedom. Emancipation is not a psychological, cognitive concept, but a practical concept and is understood in terms of the motivation of individuals for social action and change. Freedom, for Ricoeur, is defined vis-à-vis *institutions* and their *laws*. Broadly speaking, an 'institution' refers to all forms of social organisation in which individuals play a role and a 'law' is the legislative contract that binds individuals to these organisations. Facticity, according to existentialist thought, designates those invasive forces acting against life in a personally experienced life and time, particularly *angst* in the face of death. Facticity, for Ricoeur, is not psychological but social, relating to legislation. This shift of perspective takes the concept of freedom beyond consciousness and views it with respect to our social possibilities vis-à-vis social control. This notion of freedom makes social action possible. This is a post-modern concept of freedom, acknowledging correctly that social change might well be primarily of a legislative sort, a concept that most social movements identify with today.

Two different paradigms of freedom and emancipation are defended by the two humanistic traditions, one, in terms of the individual and the other in terms of social change. The latter arguably conforms to our contemporary social reality. Existentialism envisions a static society and not a dynamic one. A dynamic society depends on the possibility of social change and the rationality that one can provide to such change. One should be able to say that a society changes for the 'better' or the 'worse' with respect to the possibility of discrimination among human values. The existentialist view that a society accommodates everyone's values and choices leaves no scope for social change. Human nature is such that an ideal state is a goal of our society and we must strive towards it. This requires a theory of social change and social action, which the existentialist paradigm of freedom cannot allow and the hermeneutic paradigm can.

The theory of autonomy adhered to by the critical hermeneutic tradition is essentially a political theory. This, in turn, specifies how the psychology of self-consciousness is to be presented. If freedom is the goal of a primarily social and institutionalised existence, and is achieved through negotiations with legislative and political control, then self-consciousness is not intrinsically free nor fully creative as the existentialist proclaims. Social interaction is mediated through symbols or rule following, whether these are explicit or implicit. Self-consciousness mirrors this social reality rather than the reverse. The existentialist claim that psychological reality is primary, simply fails to grapple with the overwhelming normative power of human society and its insidious legislative binds. For hermeneutics, self-understanding is impossible unless the existentialist ideas of unmediated self-experience and indubitable creative consciousness are rejected. It must be substituted by a radical, linguistic discourse of human symbolic existence. The idea of 'consciousness' as a linear, uninterrupted unity of human experience is questionable, for the self is accessible to itself only through 'polysemic' mediations. The way to understand oneself is through the historical flux of ever changing personal meanings, by unceasing vacillations between processes of distanciation and recovery of the self by itself (Ricoeur, 1987b).

It is clear that there are significant differences between the existentialist and the critical traditions on the nature of freedom and consciousness and the implications of the two schools for social science are different. But they both equally affirm the metaphor of the textual nature of understanding humans in confronting the self-knowledge problem. Hermeneutics differs from existentialism in emphasising that there are *levels* of reading the human text. In doing this, it creates a new philosophical threshold, the *politics* of the self, by opening up the realm of the unconscious to hermeneutic scrutiny. The politics of the self refers to the perennial human play between psychologically compelling instinctual forces and the impact of these forces on a consciously determined public life. Psychic life is defined by schisms, discontinuity and conflict between the ego and the id. A part of one's own nature is unacceptable to one and the self invents fantastic symbols for communicating with this part. Abnormal behaviour is the result of this imaginary discourse. Ricoeur (1987a) has emphasised the inevitability of introducing the linguistic dimension into the discourse of the self, by arguing that one's own evil is addressed by the subject only through mythical detours. The hermeneutic problem is addressed only in the context of understanding evil, an issue not recognised by existentialist thought. Existentialism is content with a direct folk psychological language, with concepts such as purpose, motive, value and authenticity.

Ricoeur has stated that hermeneutics is needed only where the self also speaks an indirect language and there is the necessity to suspect speech of its apparent motives. Consciousness, a subjective realm which existentialism views as unquestionable, is deceitful and requires a hermeneutic. In some ways, this understanding of the unconscious is closer to Freudian theory than the existentialist understanding. The existentialist denial of the unconscious is, according to Ricoeur, not only a negation of the essential nature of the theory but also a negation of our own human nature. Existentialism refuted the unconscious because it argued that man is essentially free. For Ricoeur, as well as for Freud, freedom is a goal to work towards and the unconscious is an obstacle in its path towards this goal. Psychoanalysis describes how we can be free by overcoming the facticity of the unconscious.

Ricoeur has not however negated the importance of the problem of the hermeneutic circle by highlighting the linguistic dimension. Understanding a human text, in the case of existentialism, is understanding life itself. The primitive experiential force that supposedly overwhelms and overwrites rationality is forcefully represented in the stream of consciousness literature, such as Sartre's *Nausea* and Camus' *The Outsider*. For Ricoeur, the hermeneutic project of self-understanding is related to *meaning* rather than experience. The hermeneutic circle proceeds not so much 'from an intersubjective relation linking the subjectivity of the author and the subjectivity of the reader as from a connection between two discourses, the discourse of the text and the discourse of interpretation' (1987a, p. 93). Elsewhere he (1981b) has said that the 'psychology' of the author is not as important as his 'textuality'. Objecting to the literality with which the self is treated in the existentialist tradition, Ricoeur has emphasised the metaphorical relation that binds the subject to itself. Self-understanding is concerned with the relation of the subject to the literary symbols he creates about himself, the others and the world. Ricoeur's view of the self is a proto-cognitive view, and fairly consistent with the fundamental assumptions of the psychoanalytic theory of the self. However, the *empirical* implications of this view have not been followed up and have been explicity negated by Ricoeur. The residue is then a transcendental, rather than a natural, theory of the self.

Existentialist thought had, despite the introduction of the notion of *Verstehende*, caricatured it by showing it to be simply a reflection of a primordial 'givenness'. If language was experientially transparent, there would be no hermeneutic problem. For, meanings would be patent

and the need for interpretation or even the necessity of human communication would not arise at all. If we could communicate at an
experiential, non-verbal level, ambiguity in relationships, misunderstanding in communication, and other aberrations of communication
would not occur. Human negotiations have been robbed of these
realities of a society by the existentialist denial of the relative autonomy of
the linguistic dimension. Human communication is often a problem
because language is burdened with its own socio-cultural history and
grammatical or political rules of formation. Language assumes a
separate identity and introduces its own often unresearched dimensions
into human transactions. The idiolects of users, constituted by their
individuated psychohistories, confound communication further. A
theory of human communication should take into account such parameters as well and should provide a theory of misunderstanding or of
'systematically distorted communication' (Habermas, 1978) as much
as a theory of understanding. A symbol, the artefact of human communication, is a locus of gestalts of meaning, now exhibiting and now
hiding different levels of personal significances. As far as Ricoeur
(1970) is concerned, Freud was one of the 'masters of suspicion' as a
reader of human texts. He has suspected the possibility of the givenness
of consciousness and its speech acts, recommending instead the method
of 'critical' reading of these acts. Two registers, one public and the
other private, are maintained parallely and preferably incommunicado,
by the subject. According to Ricoeur, Freud sought to understand
human beings' ingenuity in hiding meanings from themselves.

Habermas' theory of abnormality is also centrally bound to a theory
of self-reflexive self-consciousness. Habermas has cautioned that hermeneutics, when used as a psychoanalytic tool, 'cannot be confined to
the procedures of philology but rather *unites linguistic analysis with
the psychological investigation of causal connections*' (1972, p. 217).
However, his further analysis of psychopathology is within the context
of personal meanings, rather than truth. He may be viewed as taking
to a logical conclusion the phenomenological idea of the subject as a
'text' and of epistemology as being confined to the construction of
personal meanings in a symbolic–mythical discourse. Habermas has
defined the state of being 'normal' in terms of a 'fit' or an equivalence
between linguistic expressions, behaviour and experience. Psychopathology is understood as a discrepancy in the narrative surreptitiously
introduced within this fit. A textual distortion, or self-misunderstand-
ing occurs in the subject, in one or all three dimensions—linguistic

expressions distortedly communicated in obsessive thoughts, actions in repetition compulsions, and experiential expression in hysterical body symptoms. Psychoanalysis is literally a 'talking cure', for both Ricoeur and Habermas. For the tradition the importance of psychoanalysis is not as a cognitive theory about the human mind, but rather as a clinical theory. It is designed to deconstruct the associations and fill in the blanks in speech. By stretching consciously rendered meanings to their psychological limits, it aims to enter into the private, misread realm of the unconscious. By picking out the distortions in 'connections of symbols', the analyst unravels the self-deceit of analysands and substitutes these with cognitively effective metaphors of living.

A number of assumptions are being made here which need to be scrutinised. The most obvious among them is the view that psychoanalysis is a clinical theory and not a cognitive theory. Another debatable assumption is that the psychohistory of the subject can be constructed from the manner and content of speech. Further, cure is assumed to ensue from the substitution of the symbolic 'metaphorical' relation that the subject has with himself. In a cognitive sense, these assumptions can perhaps be made philosophically acceptable, but such acceptance will lead to the empirical warrant that the assumptions can be given. But within the tradition, the assumptions are transcendentalist and cannot bear a natural interpretation. In asking for the empirical warrant for this proto-cognitive of psychoanalysis, we are asking for the 'truth' of these assumptions. As will be seen later, the humanistic tradition prioritises ontology over epistemology and negates the question of truth altogether for the social sciences.

For the humanists, there can be no epistemological guarantee that one set of metaphors is better than another one; just like there is no preference between two novels except one of personal taste. So long as the therapeutic goals of the personal emancipation of the subject are satisfied, the theory is 'validated'. Cure from abnormality, for the hermeneuticians, is something like editing a text. The psychoanalyst is like a grammarian, correcting the distorted text and providing rules of normal constructions. The rules are arbitrary and open ended, varying across analysands and analysts, across clinics and therapies. The limit is only the sanction by the subject who is the user of therapy. The clinic is a site where the analyst and analysand transact with different narratives of the analysand, with the aim of 'recovering' the analysand's 'self' (Ricoeur, 1970, p. 45).

The notion of freedom and human liberation are political concepts in the hermeneutic tradition, as already noted. Ricoeur and Habermas share with the critical theorists, notably Marcuse, the assumption that the psychological structure of the individual and the administrative structure of a society are the same in all matters of consequence relating to the human agency. Even the ethico-aesthetic of existentialism was based on an ethical purism. It was based on the idea that over and above all human interests, certain general human values such as liberty and equality, can be posited abstractly as universal values. According to the hermeneuticians, universalism in ethics, like determinism in metaphysics, divests human beings from choosing their own ethical goals. The notion of democracy itself, like 'freedom' and other such notions designed to uphold human dignity, is often only the guise in which ideological forces impose themselves upon human beings in order to sustain themselves. The philosophical notion of 'ideology', ideologised by the hermeneutic tradition, captures the primary need of the subject to establish his own discursive expression over all else as *both* veridical *and* judicious. In the existentialist discourse, the human agency was explained, not so much by concepts relating to decision, but rather by the unquestioned values of liberation and equality, whereas in the hermeneutic tradition, it does, because every discourse allows itself to be deconstructed in terms of its political underpinnings. Habermas has shown the limitations of discursive innocence, whether in ethics or in any other domain of human interest.

V

The humanistic critical traditions prioritise ontology over epistemology in their philosophy of social science. This shift of emphasis in philosophy, from the Kantian question of the possibility of knowledge to the possibility of being, is historically manoeuvred. Early in the history of phenomenology humanism moved from what Ricoeur (1981a) has termed 'regional' hermeneutics to 'general' hermeneutics. Regional hermeneutics initiated special methods of reading history, particularly biblical history. The paradox faced by Christian historians of the time made the concept of 'hermeneutic circle' possible. Biblical history can only be read by a contemporary language, raising the question whether the history read has not already been contaminated or 'appropriated'. The issue of the hermeneutic circle concerns the possibility of biblical understanding: if a text, comprising symbols, can be understood only by other, historically distanced symbols, then the reference of the historical text cannot be literal. And yet historical knowledge must be possible, because on this rests Christian faith. Unlike the later general hermeneutics, the regional hermeneuticians were not willing to accept the relativism implied in claiming that historical texts, like other texts, are metaphorical and referenceless.

By seeing objectionable traces of scientism in the hermeneutic project as presented by regional hermeneutics, general hermeneutics effects a set of problem shifts. These shifts are executed by the programmatic redefinition of the central hermeneutic problem as an *ontological* rather than as an *epistemological* or a methodological one. Ricoeur has noted explicitly that '[T]his movement of deregionalisation cannot be pressed to the end unless at the same time the properly *epistemological* concerns of hermeneutics—its efforts to achieve a scientific status—are subordinated to *ontological* preoccupations . . .' (Ricoeur, 1981a, p. 44). The primary philosophical question for hermeneutics no longer pertains to the logical conditions of knowledge which would lead to the possibility of affirming historical facts; rather it is about the issue of understanding individuals. Questions of reading texts can be asked in a logically equivalent way in the domain of individuals. This shift of problems from the epistemological to the ontological also transforms linguistic problems, problems about words, meanings and their historico-semantic associations, into problems of the human condition, expression and communication.

The hermeneutic problem of the subject, as seen earlier, studies the nature of human subjectivity, of how the self produces a narrative of itself in its personally experienced time. In stating the problem thus, the humanistic traditions dubiously conflate normative problems with psychological ones. The traditions raise epistemological and psychological problems as though they were both equally hermeneutic. For the traditions, problems such as interpretation, meaning, truth and understanding confront the subject and an authentic self would devise self-experientially valid responses by using the hermeneutic method. The problem about the possibility of knowledge would be solved for the traditions, if the problem of the self is resolved. The Kantian and the Socratic questions are the same for these philosophies.

The humanistic response to the solution of the self problem also sustains the conflation between epistemological issues with psychological issues. Epistemological notions such as 'meaning' and 'truth' are ambiguous within the tradition, shifting in their meaning between the normative domain and the ethics of the self. 'Meaning', for example, can be understood in its epistemological aspects as relating to the problems of understanding and interpretation, as the possibility of cognitive understanding. It can equally be understood as the *original* value upon which each and every self is built and towards which it orients itself teleologically in an authentic being. 'We choose the world, not in its contexture as in-itself but in its meaning' (Sartre, 1956, p. 465). It is important for the tradition to retain the ambiguity between its linguistic and psychological theses, because this ambiguity helps present an ontology *like* an epistemology. So long as continental thought is committed programmatically to the epistemological problem of understanding, it cannot neglect to address typically epistemological notions like meaning and truth. And yet, relating these notions to an ontology of an ineffable and theoretically irreducible self is possible only by providing these notions with personalised, psychological auras. The tradition psychologises epistemology by trying to remove its normative dimension altogether and by substituting a personal dimension.

Even as a purely psychological theory of the self, the concept of 'self-experience' is equally ambiguous. It refers both to an ineffable and pre-cognitive ground of knowledge as well as to the content which is carried in the cognitive and public inter-subjective relations. In modern psychology, the notion of self has given rise to empirical consideration of two kinds: research into the affective and non-verbal modes in which the self relates; and research into the information processing capabilities of human negotiations, an activity which is predominantly linguistic. These are two distinctive psychological paradigms. The hermeneutic tradition conflates these two paradigms rendering the discourse ambiguous.

Understanding in existentialism is defined not by the content or the logical formation of thought. It is defined by an aesthetic structure, by a subtle evocation of experiential textures, like a work of art (Gadamer, 1976, pp. 162–73). Schleirmacher has openly urged ontology to break its association with the so-called 'external', empirical epistemologies centrally concerned with the question of the determination of 'truth'. He gave up the general requirements of epistemology and oriented existentialist discourse towards pronouncing a theory of understanding with a supremely aesthetic purpose of knowing 'life moments' of 'pleasure'. Following him, philosophical focus was on the ontological question of personal 'meaning' or the 'free construction and the free expression of an individual being'. The ethico-aesthetic interest of existentialism makes epistemological considerations secondary, explicitly urging a distanciation and often a dissociation from the rational norms of knowledge.

This distanciation from epistemology and methodology is the philosophical fall-out of the 'critique of science' defended by both the humanistic traditions. Schleirmacher's distinction between 'creative' and 'objective' knowledge, Husserl's between 'phenomenological' and 'scientistic' understanding, Heidegger's distinction between 'meditative' and 'calculative' thinking, Sartre's between 'authentic' and 'inauthentic' being, is the positive response of the traditions to scientism. If science has to be human, we must accept these distinctions, according to the traditions. The vindication of science can only be based on this acceptance. These distinctions underscoring the critique of science are supposedly differences in the very nature of our cognition. The distinctions posit on the one hand, certain kinds of human cognition as being more authentic and personally emancipatory. This is a psychological thesis about the nature of cognition. On the other hand, they also make an epistemological claim that the superior cognition immediately validates the objects they intend through essential self-experience. A fundamental ontology of the subject is therefore the inevitable consequence of the tradition's appeal to epistemological credibility. The double purpose served by these distinctions advance the traditions' equivocal language by using the same concepts in both psychological and epistemological ways. The epistemological guise in which psychology is presented cannot be discarded: else the credentials of the discourse and its place in the larger organisation of human knowledge would be at stake.

Existentialist thought provided a positive psychological framework based on human experience and a literal way of viewing and presenting knowledge, inadvertently granting an objectivity that they explicitly denied. However, Ricoeur and Habermas, by defending the metaphorisation of knowledge *vis-à-vis* the politics of knowledge, make all claims to objectivity impossible. For the critical tradition, the canonical espousal in the philosophy of science, of the relation between scientific theory and reality is questionable. Realism in the sciences, specifically the human sciences, is an impossibility. 'Reality', according to these thinkers, is an ideological notion which presides over attempts to build up a scientific knowledge in human praxis. It is a powerful notion which authorises technology to enforce itself on human life and alienates humans from themselves and others. However, 'reality' is only fictitious; it is a beguiling metaphor of an imaginatively conceived and inherently political theory. The tradition espouses an anti-realistic philosophy of science, denying the realistic goals of science. The world has no independent existence apart from human constructs, and all human constructs are loaded with political interests. Science is conceived politically rather than epistemologically. The narrativisation of scientific theories advances the goal of the deconstruction of epistemology by ontology in humanistic philosophy. The tradition does not offer any frame of reference for deciding about the objectivity of knowledge, for it reduces all questions of knowledge to political questions.

As is obvious from the discussions so far, the philosophical principle which directs methodological considerations in both the existentialist and the critical hermeneutic traditions is a foundationalist one: a fundamental ontology, or a metaphysics of the self, must preside over epistemology. The metaphysics is based on the notion of an experientially indubitable or symbolically defined but a self-authored subject text. The rationale for the negation of epistemology is that the essence of that which resides ineffably beyond language must always evade the psychology which audaciously presumes to normalise it. Where it is granted that human interaction with the world cannot be effected except through such normalisations, as in the case of the critical hermeneutic tradition, psychoanalytic theory only provides the grammar or metaphor for viewing behaviour. A human scientific theory is best conceived as a more humanistic and less scientific discourse. Epistemology is simply asterisked and footnoted in the course of self-(con)textual ontological analyses. Epistemology itself remains deconstructed with reference to the ethics, aesthetics and politics of the subject's being in the world.

Traditional epistemological notions are couched in anthropocentric terms, and the 'self' is the origin and the limit within which scientific normalisations may be constructed. The status of the 'knowledge' obtained is justified not in terms of its adequate fulfilment of normative considerations but its appropriateness for being used on a particular subject. The question of the use of knowledge decides the question of the validity of knowledge. No measurements are even permissible to determine this use, for such measurements can only be abstractions from the real life situations that individuals face. Therefore, the final arbitration regarding the status of a theory as knowledge must rest with the subject himself. The self supposedly has a privileged access to its life experiential and symbolic constitution. Only this access certifies the psychoanalytic knowledge applied in the clinic as appropriate and 'true' of that self. This is a claim we refer to and critically assess for its philosophical acceptability and practical value as the 'self-access thesis'. The thesis implies that the analysand must not only freely accept that the knowledge available with the analyst be used on him; but the analysand must also attest to the *validity* of the knowledge being used in the name of making him a better and more complete individual. For the traditions, this testimony justifies the knowledge being used in the clinic.

Finally, for both the existentialist and the critical hermeneutic traditions, the condition imposed upon knowledge is such that it can address only individual contexts. Therefore, a general reservoir of knowledge is impossible and an epistemology which provides criteria for such a reservoir is misguided. Reality, especially human reality, is perspectival and no scientific epistemology can claim absolute status in its understanding of reality. Natural scientific standpoints may presume to do so but not human scientific theories. The available knowledge systems present the essentially contestable narratives or metaphors of reality between which none can be granted epistemological primacy. But ontological primacy is deemed to be possible on the basis of the proximity of the self to itself and its psychological or symbolic possibilities for autonomy. For both the traditions, epistemology itself remains deconstructed with reference to a humanistic philosophy.

VI

The humanistic concept of the self demands that the patient certify the epistemological validity of the knowledge used by the analyst in the clinic. Explicit treatment of the question of the validity of psychoanalysis in purely clinical terms has been elaborated by Ricoeur (1981c). Psychoanalysis is treated as a clinical theory and not as a cognitive theory. Errors resulting from this confusion have been discussed earlier. The clinical view of psychoanalysis disallows the possibility of its being tested outside the clinic. The theory cannot be treated as a natural theory of psychology, but only as a transcendental theory.

These are limitations of the humanistic view of psychoanalysis and robs it of its essential nature as a causal, cognitive theory of human behaviour.

'Validating' knowledge by linking it to a discourse of the subject is a questionable venture. By doing this, the humanistic traditions fallaciously assume that all statements about a person have to be *personal* statements. Truth about a person can also be stated just as any other kind of truth. It can be expressed in a qualified way, just like any other scientific statement. Human interaction is philosophically possible because we are capable of making different kinds of statements about ourselves and others. There could conceivably be first person, second person or third person statements about consciousness. These distinctions designate different levels of abstraction from introspectively known, particular kinds of self-experience to objectively known, universal, scientifically coded human experience (Chalmers, 1992; Watanabe, 1992). Thus, for example, one could justifiably say that 'I am overcome by grief', making an intimate reference to oneself and to one's emotive experiences in a particular situation. 'Are you troubled today?', inferring another's grief from overt linguistic and other expressions. 'Is grief always accompanied by tears?', asking a third person statement, about a generalised, referenceless person who experiences grief. Even when talking about one's so-called introspective and self-validating experiences, one could legitimately ask: 'Is it grief that overwhelms me today, or is it ennui? Is it just exhaustion that makes me sad? Even if I am aggrieved, do the circumstances warrant it?'. The supposedly indubitable nature of introspection has been questioned by empirical researchers like Nisbett and Ross (1980). Anyone who has read Proust's *Remembrances* cannot but doubt the infallibility of human self-consciousness and its capacity for memory, thought, emotions and even suffering. The fact that the affective realm has also to be encoded in a language in order to be scientifically comprehended or even empathically understood by the other, introduces a discursiveness taking the affective realm away from self-evidence. The state of the self is not always evident to itself. Sometimes, of course, though not as often as the existentialist imagines, emotions can be as unquestionable and irrefutable as a sound piece of deduction, as, for example, when in severe pain. Ordinary language recognises several subtle distinctions of related emotional states, such as happiness, bliss, euphoria and ecstasy, revealing the public nature of these states and their determination by linguistic and cultural subtleties.It is well known among socio-linguists, for example, that languages do not have an equal vocabulary for describing emotional and other cognitive states. Self-experience is not necessarily self-validating and brings with it all the philosophical problems of any other form of cognitive state, such as thinking, believing and inferring. The error which the internal foundationalists commit is to collapse these useful epistemological distinctions in statements about the self and pose all statements about consciousness as first person statements. Not only are these distinctions useful for scientific praxis, but also for everyday human negotiations, as Wittgenstein has indicated so clearly in his arguments against the possibility of a private language. It would become a very difficult world for ourselves and others if we insist on all statements about them to be reduced to first person statements before we relent to comprehend or sympathise. The demand for such a reduction presupposes the possibility of the conversion of all general concepts relating to the subject into person specific particulars, a task which may well be impossible, given the nature of language.

The concept of the hermeneutic circle of understanding is philosophically suspect and does not capture the essential nature of understanding. The hermeneutic circle depends on the relation between the part and the whole. Understanding is said to be a dialectical *process* of synthesis between the two relata. It is supposed to be a free flowing continuum, always momentous and always different from earlier understanding and bound to be different from future understanding, much like Heraclitus' river. Whether the hermeneutic circle is understood experientially or as a fusion of linguistic horizons, those aspects of momentariness of understanding and the discursive instability of the object of such understanding are defining of the concept. Other than all the well-known philosophical paradoxes that arise from the view of change assumed by the hermeneutic circle, continental thought describes the nature of human understanding as if it is without *any* psychological limits. Quotidian praxis tells us that if what is understood can be expressed explicitly, and more often than not this is the case, then certain understanding has been gained and further interpretation is no longer required. Our practical ability to atemporalise our understanding using ordinary language as well as the more specialised scientific language, allows us to infer that understanding is not a *process but rather a state*. A concept of understanding makes sense only where scaling is possible and logical continuity can be measured by using states of understanding as grids. Wittgenstein has rightly noted that there is an important distinction between 'understanding' and 'interpretation'. The latter signifies a process of rule making, the application of which results in completed units of knowledge or states of understanding. Contrary to the continental thinkers' claim, there is a sense of 'understanding' which is *not always* changing, novel and prone to erasure. Our day-to-day praxis depends on static features of communication. Even history writing, the exemplary hermeneutic problem, aims at adequate representation of what happened rather than at manufacturing genetic narratives divorced altogether from objectivity.

Other than the philosophical problems about the possibility of a private language and the absurdities that would result from the self-access thesis for therapy (Grünbaum, 1984, pp. 21–43), a vicious circularity is entailed by it. Any psychopathological theory, such as psychoanalysis, ascribes 'abnormality' to a subject only when the self fails to execute self or socially desired action. In the context of Anna O., for example, her self was labelled 'abnormal' because it included two contradictory components—her thirst and her compulsion to refuse water. The latter prevailed over the former, perpetrating an abnormal condition called hydrophobia. Her action, the need to refuse water, was problematised against a natural aspect of her experience, her thirst. This problem about her self could not be resolved by the psychological manoeuvres normally available to an individual in interpersonal interactions. Folk psychology, often adequate to deal with everyday personal problems, failed in her case, and she needed a 'super psychology' or a specialised discourse of understanding to resolve them.

The self-access thesis of humanistic therapy is contrary to the clinical experience of the failure of a self in coming to terms with herself. It claims that it is within the grasp of the analysed subject to understand her own illness, she has a knowledge of the psychopathological vocabulary and has the competence to use this vocabulary. Such intimate knowledge about mental illness, if it were possible and available to the self as part of everyday discourse, would render 'abnormality' normal. 'Abnormality' is a problem when a person evokes a privileged vocabulary or a 'super psychology' institutionalised by the psychotherapeutic discourse. A psychopathological theory, such as psychoanalysis, is committed to an institutionalised vocabulary. Research on human cognition is sufficiently advanced to warrant the assumption that folk psychology is not equal to a super psychology: what people may

intuitively believe is true about themselves and others may not necessarily be so. Even ostensibly 'folk psychological' presentations of
cognitive activities (Rips and Conrad, 1989) are so technical and
sophisticated as to make the designation a misnomer. Folk psychology,
like folk science, is caught in a complicated network of relations with
society and with more professional scientific organisation can no
longer be considered as sufficient unto itself nor even competitive.
The goal of therapy or 'cure' is the cognitive restructuring of the self
using these specialised discourses of human understanding. The self-
access thesis is circularly argued. 'Cure' in psychotherapy is a restitution
of the semantically incoherent self-scheme on the basis of the psychoanalyst's epistemic authority. Therefore, the process of psychotherapy
cannot presuppose the patient's self, as a coherent system which is
capable of making epistemic decisions, as the humanists have argued.
The goal of therapy cannot be the ground on which therapy is to be
based. The decision to commit a self to the psychotherapeutic contract
presumes that certain realms of self-experience are problematic and
that everyday psychology has failed. By social and institutional stipu-
lation, epistemic authority rests with the analyst. A society stipulates
that the psychotherapeutic institution takes care of its mentally ill
subjects in the best available way.

The continental traditions are naively gambling on the natural limits
on epistemology and the consequent problematisation of the nature of
truth in philosophy. There are difficulties in arriving at the truth about
abnormal behaviour, but this does not sanction the liberation of
theories about such behaviour from the quest for truth. All sciences
assume that 'truth' is one of the epistemological goals towards which its
pragmatics must converge. The psychoanalyst is called upon by a society
to intervene with a self by making use of the common pool of understanding developed by inquiring communities on the nature of self,
human cognition and mental illness. A patient's own truth cannot even
be recognised as 'truth' unless the analyst transcends the patient's individuated framework and understands the illness through the psychological theory. The competition that humanistic therapy poses between
'truths'—the 'truth' which is supposedly the patient's own truth and
the scientific truth—is no competition at all. 'Truth' is not 'personal'
but predicated only by being picked out of the common reservoir of
knowledge we possess about ourselves and the world. This knowledge
about ourselves can be coded, even if imprecisely, using available
methodological tools. This recognition of imprecision should lead to a

refinement of the methods in use, and not the denial of truth and method altogether.

Philosophically, there is no justification for the claim that granting epistemic authority to the analyst and understanding behaviour through a causal account is a negation of the autonomy of the subject. Dilman (1984) has noted that:

> Just as when we give a causal explanation of the downhill flow of the river we do not imply that its flow is not free, so too when we give an explanation of a man's action and say, for instance, that he left his wife because he was fed up with her constant nagging, we do not imply that he did not act freely (p. 141).

When we predict someone's behaviour by using the language of a psychological theory, we do not say that he cannot act otherwise. This is in the very nature of the words we use to designate psychological nature and free choice—'is' and 'can'.

When we say that 'he is obsessed' in a scientific sense, we are invoking, for example, a psychoanalytic rule that 'obsessional behaviour is the result of repressions accompanied by guilt', as a causal explanation of his behaviour. The inference that he is obsessed is derived from the causal explanatory theory which is being used in therapy. In what way does this deny freedom? The internal foundationalist could argue that in saying so the theory is claiming that the past has influenced the man into an obsessed being and, consequently, the theory is also claiming that he cannot henceforth be anything else. This argument against the possibility of a historical causal determination of a subject, a possibility dear to psychoanalysis, is untenable. To say that the past has influenced what a man is not a constraint upon the individual's freedom, because in a developmental sense, a person has created his past also. Creative expression, which is an important index of personal freedom, is very much an integral part of human development.

Freedom itself has its *psychological* limits, as Schopenhauer realised when he wrote that no man becomes this or that by simply wishing to be it. It is our psychological *nature* which enables us to conceive of teleological possibilities for ourselves. The limits to our freedom are natural, having to do with the way our minds function. For example, we naturally grant a stability to our self and feel disturbed when confronted by schizophrenic or other neurotic experiences. Not only does psychology look for some continuing thread of rationality to the self, but we ourselves do in our day-to-day practice and we are often plagued by self-questioning attitudes. Facticity not only includes our own psychological make-up but also social, political and other factors. In fact, we depend on this nature as a guide to our own and others' actions. As Wittgenstein has argued, it would be very unnerving if we surprised ourselves in our behaviour. In our everyday praxis, we fear going beyond 'our own limits' and often choose only those which are 'self-preserving', a term which reveals in ordinary language, our psychological attitude. Freud noted cynically that the conviction that one is free does not manifest itself in important decisions. We tend to cling on to and protect those aspects which we identify as our 'self' and personality changes can often be traumatic, if not impossible. Effecting these changes, in fact, is a therapeutic challenge.

VII

The issue of the nature of meaning is complex when raised in the psychoanalytic context, which is determined equally strongly by the philosophical asymmetry between norms stipulated for a logically constituted science and for a humanistically informed narrative. In the Popperian and neo-inductive external foundationalist critiques, there is no focus on the issue of the place of meaning in the sciences. This is well in keeping with the empiricistic goal of science—all epistemological conditions are satisfied by a science, if truth is decidable. This denial of the place of meaning in the sciences is clearly parallel to similar considerations in the orthodox philosophy of language culminating in Davidson. This philosophy undercuts any attempt to arrive at an autonomous theory of meaning not dependent on a theory of truth and reference. Philosophers who have directly addressed the place of meaning in the sciences have questioned this negligence of conventional thought on science and language. The epistemological status of meaning in the sciences is an important issue which has led to debates about meaning in the philosophy of science and language.

The internal foundationalist critiques of psychoanalysis have emphasised the concept of meaning for entirely different reasons. As an epistemological concept, meaning in this tradition has been associated with what Ricoeur has called the 'semantics of desire', that is, the symbolic basis around which a person constitutes his life. Meaning, according to the existentialist tradition, refers to the original purpose or value of an individual around which he defines his life. According to this tradition, meaning is a value. This value is not the result of a rational determination, but rather the inexpressible emotive ground of any rationality a self may wish to provide to life. Intention, in the existentialist tradition, is the experiential state which results in the particular constitution and agentive possibilities of a being. It is the intuitive capacity of the subject to bring to stand objects of the world in its consciousness. The hermeneutic tradition has developed the idea of intention by surrendering the experiential *a priori* for a more linguistic notion. Intention is defined in terms of a private meaning, a kind of idiolect that the subject uses. It is the (self) author's meaning that can be retrospectively read in his actions. Intention, according to the humanists, is the psychological means by which the self 'realises' itself or constitutes its own 'meaning' in either the experiential or the symbolic modes.

The notion of intention is closely associated in these traditions with meanings in the head, an association which has been under close scrutiny since Frege in the philosophy of language and mind. The views of intention as experiential and as a private language are eminently contestable. Wittgenstein has cautioned that experientially, the affective undertone paralleling an utterance cannot be compared with that accompanying a repetition of that utterance. Even if the meaning of both the utterances are the same by virtue of following the same linguistic rules, there is no way of knowing whether the emotive underpinnings are identical or different. No measurement of emotional undercurrents is possible and if 'intention' is to make sense, we must be able to codify some common rules of use of this concept in ordinary language. It cannot rest, as the humanists claim, on the bedrock of self-evidence. The language game of feelings, emotions and moods, concepts invoking inner experience, does not allow ostensive definition (Wittgenstein, 1974b, § 669).

For the existential humanists, intention is a psychological link between emotions and value. In this sense, the notion cannot shed its mystical, metaphysical status. Intention is to be understood as the psychological terminus of meaning and language use, if it is to be of any use to our understanding about ourselves. This is Wittgenstein's lesson. Language is an institution, according to him, and to understand the meaning of a sentence implies to understand the language and to commit oneself to all the rules of that institution. A language consists of symbols and rules for their use. Every sign in itself is dead and does not signify anything, attaining meaning only by its use. The possibility of attainment of meanings and the use of language is due to intentions. Signs acquire their meaning and purpose from intentions. Without assuming the human intention to use the language and to use it in particular ways, it is not possible to conceive of language at all. Wittgenstein has noted: 'If you exclude the element of intention from language, its whole function then collapses' (1975, § 63, 20). Using a Wittgensteinian analogy, a ruler held against an object does not specify its length, for there has to be someone to read it in a certain conventional, rule governed manner. A sign is alive only when it is applied according to the rules of the institution that it partakes of and the intentions with which these rules were made.

It is we who have stipulated that a scientific language is to give a picture of the world, or to refer. To provide for this referential function is the intention of having a scientific language. The relation between language and reality is intentional in nature. It relates objects of the world on the one hand and language, with its rules of formation and use, on the other. In other words, there cannot be knowledge without intention. Describing an intention implies describing what uses a sign in a thought meaningfully. That meaning itself is knowledge. Establishing a theory of knowledge as intentional depends both on the object being independent of intentions as well as the availability of a language game or an institution to represent the object by the subject. The intentional bind is one between the subject, the object, the language and the cognitive possibilities of rule following. It is in this cognitive sense that the notion of intentionality has significance for a scientific theory of the mind. This is the notion which both existentialist thinking and critical hermeneutics sought to arrive at. However, they erred in prioritising the subjective realm, disregarding the fact that consciousness is intentional, it takes on intentions because, as Wittgenstein has rightly said, there are surprises in reality. Intentions are bound both by psychological limits and the limits of reality.

The hermeneuticians rightly recognised that knowledge is intentionally constituted and meaningful, but were wrong to understand these in personal terms. The concept of intention is an integral part of any natural theory of man. It is a cognitive rather than an affective concept. It naturally relates, not to individual value, but to the social use of language. A competent use of symbols presupposes that intentionality is at work, but these symbols are not only about the self. Intentionality lies at the basis of all knowledge, including natural scientific knowledge, and not merely self-knowledge.

The fact that intentionality is an essential part of any psychology is widely recognised in philosophical psychology. Putnam (1988) has rightly observed that 'intentionality won't be reduced and won't go away' (p. 1). Johnson-Laird (1983, pp. 448–77) has also recognised and indicated directions for a psychological intentional vocabulary of consciousness and unconsciousness. There is widespread recognition that '. . . intentional content must figure essentially in psychological explanation' (Flanagan, 1984, p. 63). Intentionality refers to the directedness of the subjective consciousness to take on objects of the world through the use of language and representations. Of course, it remains to be seen what the 'self' and the 'object' mean within a psychoanalytic theory. Intention refers to that which makes 'objective' knowledge of the self and the world cognitively possible. In psychoanalytic terms, object relations, the mind's capacity to relate to objects, is possible because of intentions.

A theory of the self, a theory of the object and a meta-theory about a theory of cognition which would explain how representation of the self and the object is possible by the mind and what kinds of representations of object relations are possible, are important considerations in any theory of intention. These features of a cognitive science, more clearly explicated later, characterise psychoanalysis. Even though Freud (S.E., Vol. 14, pp. 122–23) incorrectly conceived of instincts as intentional states, he recognised the features of intention when he proposed distinctions between instinctual states and characterised them in different ways in terms of the mind's relations to objects. He stipulated conditions for formulating formal relations between mental states. In the context of instinctual states, for example, instincts were stipulated to have a force, or they 'impel' subjects to act in certain directions; they have a 'goal' or 'aim'; they take on 'objects'; they become attached to objects; and they demand 'satisfaction'.

The concept of representation in Freud's theory, refers to the capacity of the mind to order the self and objects. Representation, in the cognitive sense, identifies the intentionally structured items of the self as well as objects through symbols. A representation leads to what Johnson-Laird has called an 'intentional reference'—intended objects of understanding are structured through the pattern of symbols. A representation gives the structure of the object through symbols. The mind relates to objects through representations; representations are the 'outputs' of mental activity, including among other things, self-representations and object representations. Psychoanalysis is a theory explaining how action, normal and abnormal, ensues from these representations. These reflections raise important questions about the relation between intention and self-identity, between the mind and the self, or between intention and the unconscious, which will be discussed later.

Psychoanalysis is an intentional theory of the mind. It has a theory of the self, a theory of the object and a theory of how the self relates to itself and to objects, or a theory of representation. Its explanation of action is based on these theories.

VIII

The idiom of the metaphor in cognition in general and psychotherapy in particular is fairly widespread, deserving special attention. This idiom will be critically examined at some length because of our scepticism of the hermeneutic construal of psychoanalysis as 'narratives' or 'metaphors' of self-understanding: we must know whether the claim that the 'self' is a metaphor is a philosophical gain or loss.[2] The idiom of the metaphor in therapy is, however, not necessarily the consequence of the hermeneutic philosophical understanding of psychoanalysis, but this understanding itself is only a specific kind of response to the contemporary philosophical concern with the relation between the reality, the mind and the metaphor, particularly in the sciences.

A 'metaphor' is primarily a linguistic concept and not, for example, a concept associated with perception or logic. Even though the role of the metaphor was recognised by philosophers like Aristotle, the concept served aesthetics rather than epistemology. Only recently, the central role of metaphors in our quotidian praxis and in our more specialised scientific praxis has been recognised. An understanding of metaphors involves analyses of our linguistic communication at one level and the nature of our cognition at another level, because it is a

---

[2] The veteran Indian philosopher, Dr. Dayakrishna, often says jokingly that it is bad enough to treat the Other as an object, but it is worse to treat him like a text!

concept which lies on the border between linguistics and psychology. The interrelation between the mind and the metaphor in philosophical psychology is complex. The 'mind' has often been viewed metaphorically, as a fictional referent of psychology and metaphors have been understood as the linguistic form given to the mind's way of functioning or describing, comparing and relating objects of the world. These two concepts have been inter-defined in philosophical thought, problematising both.

The form of a metaphor is linguistic, a figure of speech like a simile, an analogy or a hyperbole. A metaphor involves two subjects, a primary subject and a secondary subject, and a relation of analogy posed between them. For example, 'Her eyes were pools of light', the primary subject is the 'eyes' and the secondary subject, 'pools'. What makes the relation between the two subjects metaphorical is the structural correspondence between them. Eyes are associated with light, reflection, watery quality and a mirroring ability, attributes that are also associated with a pool of water. The kind of relations that the secondary subject is caught in with respect to other objects are in some ways analogous to the relations of the primary subject, a correspondence which Max Black (1980) has referred to as an 'implicative complex'. For many psychoanalytic thinkers like Arlow, the metaphor 'refers to a set of linguistic processes whereby aspects of one object are carried over or transferred to another object so that the second object is spoken of as if it were the first' (for a detailed discussion, see Carveth, 1984). In Freud's own example, 'A madman is a waking dreamer', the madman is the primary subject, the waking dreamer is the secondary subject: the implicative complex here is the web of illusions that both weave around imagined objects.

The view of the mind as a metaphor within the psychotherapeutic context has been used in at least four different senses and often without always specifying the sense in which it has been used—the genetic, the epistemological, the methodological and the cognitive senses. In its genetic sense, the notion of the metaphor is used by ·philosophers of science like Hanson who view scientific theories as historically evolving theoretical systems irreducible to an essentialist and universalist meta-science of empirical justification. Within this orientation, the inquiry of what a science is will show a theory to be the result of metaphorical construction at the point of departure from historically given theories. A theory of science is viewed as a realist's metaphor for understanding phenomena inexplicable from the perspectives of available theories, through innovatively conceived theoretical grids. The genetic view of the metaphor concerns itself with the logical and sociological geneses of science through history, showing theories to be fictional or referenceless systematisations of human epistemological aims.

Freud's psychoanalysis has been subjected to genetic inquiry guided by this pattern of philosophical thinking. It has been repeatedly pointed out that the evolution of psychoanalysis as a psychodynamic theory is the result of Freud's ingenuity in metaphorically converting a neuroanatomical vocabulary into the language of the mind (Mac Intyre, 1958; Sulloway, 1979). Sociologists like Thomas Szasz and Michel Foucault have claimed that theories of mental illness only provide different innovative theoretical frameworks within which abnormal behaviour can be viewed. According to Foucault (1965), insanity is the result of the dialectical clash between reason and unreason, showing through in the geneology of thought as discontinuous epistemic constructions. Epistemological considerations are insignificant within Foucault's framework, for thought is ploughed by the sheer power of history and its cultural ramifications, making objectivity impossible. Szasz (1974) has asserted that 'mental illness is a metaphorical disease . . . (and) bodily illness stands in the same relation to mental illness as a defective television set stands to a bad television program' (pp. x–xi). The idea of illness as a metaphor has been strongly contested by Susan Sontag (1979) and Peter Sedgwick (1972). The former has decried the cultural mythicisation of illnesses and the subsequent loss of reality in dealing with the ill (for a discussion of these debates, see Carveth, 1984, pp. 508–9); the latter has discussed, from a Marxist point of view, the ideological loss ensuing from this narrativisation, a pernicious one in the context of the already scarce resources for research in mental illness. The problems that the mythicisation of an illness leads to can perhaps be intuitively understood in our own current attempts to disseminate facts to counter the myths relating to leprosy and AIDS. These inquiries of the mythicisation of mental illness have more to do with the politics, growth and evolution of the theory of psychoanalysis rather than directly with clinical therapeutic work.

In its epistemological sense, the role of the metaphor in psychotherapy is described by the internal foundationalist view that self-consciousness is elusive to espistemology. Psychopathological theories of the mind are best described as 'narratives' having no referent. Among the psychotherapists, Ricoeur, Arlow (1979), Schafer (1980) and Spence (1982) are well-known advocates of this view (see review in Wallerstein, 1986b). Freud's theory itself is caught between the 'mind as a machine' metaphor and the equally one-sided voluntaristic mythology of free will and intentionality. In its epistemological sense, the use of the metaphor in psychotherapy is fruitfully raised in the context of the issue regarding the status of any theory of the mind and its relation to reality. Philosophically, this is a question of reference, an issue which will be discussed in detail later. The question of reference is whether an ontological reduction to something akin to the gross physical realities of material sciences is possible when the domain in question is mental. Many philosophers, including Ryle, Neurath and Quine in the American analytic school of science, psychological behaviourists like Skinner and continental philosophers like Ricoeur have denied the possibility of the mind although for very different reasons. They deny thereby the very possibility of mentalistic psychology and the relevance of espistemology for such a psychology. The question confronting any epistemology of a cognitive science is to say what is the nature and status of that reality which it attempts to describe, or what is the reference, or the 'object' of a theory of the mind.

Ricoeur (1987b) has noted that a metaphor seems to defy all logic. For example, in the metaphor that 'time is a beggar', it is not possible to ask whether it is true, and if not, whether its negation is true. Calling this a 'semantic violation', Ricoeur has claimed that metaphors also result in semantic innovation, or an 'emergence of meaning' (p. 97). In keeping with his critique of scientism, he has noted that a scientific language aims to eradicate the polysemic use of language or the 'infinite' creative uses of words possible in sentences. A science, for Ricoeur, de-metaphorises language by adopting the strategies of definitions, reduction of reality to an experientially vacuous technical vocabulary and further abstraction by mathematical symbolisation, the interpretation of which is rigidly defined. The role of a metaphor in any human praxis is ' . . . to shatter and to increase our sense of reality by shattering and increasing our language. The strategy of metaphor is a heuristic fiction for the sake of redescribing reality' (Ricoeur, 1987b, p. 11). Reality, according to him, is infinitely re-describable and an authentic language is metaphorical in essence.

Responding to the question of reference, Ricoeur has noted that even though the referent cannot be an external object as in the natural sciences, the theory does have a second order referent, much as a novel has a referent. The analogy to a novel is telling, for the so-called referent of a novel does not elicit questions regarding the existence and the possibility of relations of the items described in it, whereas a theory of the mind does. We would like to know, for example, the relation of the mind to physical action, the traditional mind–body problem; whether the relation is causal, epiphenomenal or parallel; whether the mind is equivalent to physico-chemical states or whether it is superseded by other, complex but computable 'mental' states; and how the mind represents objects and itself as an object. In raising questions about the mind, we act as if it were an object, and justifiably so. We use the metaphor of the object in our treatment of the mind. The responses that a scientific community makes to these questions range, as in the other sciences, from ground level empirical research to abstract, logical and theoretical *and* meta-theoretical refinements. In other words, the response to the question of reference in psychology, just as much as in other sciences, is the entire research programme itself. Psychoanalysis, too, is a research programme in this sense, as will be evident from the following chapter. This is the possibility which Ricoeur in principle wants to deny, thereby refusing a proper treatment of the issue of reference in a science.

However we may want to philosophically wish away the object of knowledge, particularly knowledge about the human, it persists and inevitably so. The notion of uniqueness of the subject evoked by critical hermeneutics to deny the possibility of generalisation about the human is a philosophically dubious concept. Uniqueness, when not expressed, is useless, but when stated, it is only through the use of general and comparative categories. For example, to answer the question 'how many different things are there on this table?', one must be able to recognise what a 'thing' is and how one thing is 'different from' another. The uniqueness of an object, even human self-consciousness, is known through cognition and the use of a universal, rather than private, discourse.

Even I-statements have a referent. The 'generalisability constraint', or the semantic constraint binding on the use of 'here' and 'this', referring to objects (Evans, 1982), is binding on statements of self-identity also. Different predications of a particular 'I' are possible as well as different 'I's' to be predicated with the same general attribute. Statements of identity carry predicates as other statements do. We can and do, in everyday practice, attribute qualities to ourselves; and these qualities are not necessarily peculiar to us, but generalisable over other selves also. In this, I-statements have the same linguistic properties as those involving objects.

Every psychological science assumes that it is the object like the nature of the mind which makes empiricism in the science possible. Empirically, it is known that generalisability of the self of 'third person' statements of the self is possible at the cultural, cognitive, developmental, biological and genetic levels. It is clear that even in infancy, universal functions are attributable (Emde, 1988). Developmental studies have shown that the concept of self *vis-à-vis* the other is *learned*. Affective modes of being and self-experience may well be learnt as a result of infant–caregiver relationships or the phenomena of 'social referencing'. Even in adult life, the range of emotions are not infinite but limited, and often describable. It is true that at this point of our scientific evolution, one does not have the visionary zeal to say that all cure in psychotherapy is effected genetically. It is, however, wrong to deny the strong biological nature of our being, a nature which is determined not so much by the metaphoric transfer of mental contents through narratives, but by the indeterminate mutability of our genes! Social scientists cannot but naturally assume that their common research concerns deal with something that exists in the world that can be humanly understood. It appears that the humanists are refuting such an obvious fact as that human beings can be humanly known.

The epistemology of a science requires not only that the mind makes objects to be in the world but also that the world makes a contribution to the types and nature of objects that the mind makes. The mind 'makes mind', i.e., the mind constructs scientific metaphors about itself, just as it constitutes a physical object. But the mind has its own natural limits, and in this sense is not metaphorical. A theory of psychology understands the mind in its non-metaphorical aspects. A theory of the mind refers to the natural mind, even though that theory itself is cognitively constrained. In narrativising psychoanalysis, critical hermeneutics ignores the question of reference altogether, an important one for any theory claiming the status of knowledge.

The general problem in Ricoeur's philosophy is his view of language. Language is not, as Ricoeur has claimed, essentially metaphorical. No form of language, whether natural, scientific or poetic can essentially be so. The use of metaphor depends upon *departures* from literalness, from established or commonly consented meanings of words, and not upon a total negation of literalness. In the metaphoric association between 'eyes' and 'pools' in the earlier example, what eyes are is understood indirectly by knowing what pools are in their literal sense. The 'semantic innovation' that Ricoeur has mentioned is not about creating new meanings for words, but rather a re-configuration of the existing relations between objects and their qualities. Semantic innovation involves a novel use of language. Contrary to Ricoeur's claim, not only scientific language but also ordinary language by and large is unmetaphorical and is constrained by the conscious adoption of various strategies, such as simplicity, clarity and coherence, to achieve its intended goals. If language were basically metaphorical, the natural distinction between literalness and metaphoricity, a distinction on which even poetic discourse seems to depend, would disappear.

The third sense in which the mind is used as a metaphor in the context of psychotherapy is the methodological sense. In this sense, metaphors are used to describe the nature of the transference/counter-transference relationship between the analyst and the analysand (Carveth, 1984). The classical psychoanalytic theory refers to the analyst as a 'mirror', a 'surgeon', a 'father', a 'midwife', etc. For the object relations tradition, typified in Winnicott, Spitz and others, analysis is 'mothering'. There are different metaphors of the analytic exchange such as 'catharsis', 'interpersonal', 'semiotic analysis', 'hermeneutics', 'pure interpretation' and 'corrective emotional experience'. The methodological sense of metaphor in psychotherapy is useful for the development of thumbrules for praxis.

Finally, and most importantly, the concept of metaphor is also used in the cognitive or psychological sense. The mind is viewed, metaphorically speaking, as a metaphor creating psychological assembly, expressing the idea that we relate to the world through the metaphors we create. The relationship between the metaphor and human agency has been pointed out in literature. A metaphor is not only a literary or a linguistic device but serves an important psychological role or a cognitive function in relating to the world and people. When we say, for example, 'He *attacked every weak point* in my argument', we are implicitly using the 'argument is war' metaphor; or, 'We've been working on this problem all day and now we're *running out of steam*', we are implicitly using the 'mind as machine' metaphor. According to Lakoff and Johnson, '. . . metaphor is pervasive in everyday life, not just in language but in thought and action. Our ordinary conceptual system in terms of which we both think and act is fundamentally metaphorical in nature . . .' (1980, p. 3). There is no epistemological

relativism in this view, because it does not deny the normative possibility of knowing how the mind makes metaphors. In fact, this
cognitive view of metaphors is a prototype for a scientific theory of the
mind. With such a theory, it is possible to specify the philosophical
and psychological limits working on the mind.

Metaphors can be 'dead' or 'live' as Carveth has pointed out, or
even 'frozen' or 'fresh' as Nelson Goodman has indicated, depending
on whether their metaphorical force is retained by a judicious use or
whether they lose it through overuse. Metaphors are not static but
dynamic, varying from literalness to metaphoricity, depending on the
use. Thus, for example, even though the expression 'the legs of the
chair' is nominally a metaphor, we overlook its metaphorical nature
and view the chair as possessing legs. Here we have a dead metaphor:
the similarity between the primary and the secondary subjects (between
human or animal legs and the chair's) is treated as an identity. The use
of metaphors involves a cognitive play between identity and differentiation of objects and attributes. These relations could be cognitively
effected in terms of either the whole object or part thereof. The
differentiation between 'dead' and 'live' metaphors, between the mental
capacity to identify or differentiate the internal relations of an object,
is significant in psychotherapy.

Abnormality can be viewed as the cognitive incapacity to differentiate
between the metaphorical and literal or between imagined object
associations and the real associations. Freud proposed that normally
the mind is able to make a semantic difference between psychic reality
and external reality. Normally, a judicious use of metaphors involves a
skilful control over them by manipulating identities and differences
and requires rules of language acquisition and its use, such as competence and performance. It also requires sustaining the distinction
between literalness and metaphoricity. The primary process is very
fertile in metaphorical thinking, and works through processes of free
association. For example, the processes involved in dreaming such as
displacement, condensation, substitution and projection involve the
transfer of relations from one psychological object to another. The Rat
Man's case study documented by Freud, for example, is rich with such
associations effected under neuroses. These processes of metaphorisation
are performed, as it were, in an automated or mechanical way. The
ego, a conscious, secondary cognitive state oriented towards reality
testing, has no part to play and no control over the construction of
these metaphors. In disorders such as paranoia, schizophrenia and

obsessive fears and anxieties, metaphors are 'dead', for the subject has no conscious control over them. Carveth has noted that '. . . the neurotic's problem is *not* that his thinking is metaphorical but rather that he is *possessed* by his metaphor . . . rather than being in *possession* of it; . . .' (1984, p. 512). It is as if the person who refers to the 'legs of a chair' also cleans them, carves them, cooks and tries to eat them. One of the aims of therapy is to reorganise the analysand's cognitive functioning in such a way that he is able to restore the metaphorical relations of objects contained in his primary process metaphors as conscious and controlled relations. Cognitive change in therapy essentially involves the attainment of the user's recognition that the objects of his primary processes have changed from their metaphorical status to a literal status, obtained by the unconscious transfer of qualities, relations and emotions associated with past objects to present objects. In its cognitive sense, the concept of metaphor is useful to psychoanalysis.

IX

What remains for our critical inquiry is the problem of prioritising ontology over epistemology, the humanist appeal that a human science must dissociate itself from normative epistemological considerations in favour of an ontological theory of the self. Psychoanalytic research implies the range of activities that a scientific community performs in order to arrive at a normatively adequate representation of psychopathological reality. This, as argued earlier, is the science's response to the question of reference. The likelihood of achieving this depends on conforming to some philosophical standard of knowledge, involving notional considerations of what scientific activity is and what a psychological theory should be like.

Psychoanalytic knowledge refers to cognitive knowledge about our conscious and unconscious behaviour. Psychoanalytic therapy, on the other hand, involves the *application* of knowledge thus attained by clinicians, using practical indices of treatment, success and cure. Our discussions on Grünbaum have pointedly shown that the therapeutic and cognitive norms do not necessarily overlap. There is of course, as already noted, an interdependence between therapy and research. A therapy not based upon extra-clinical research on abnormal cognition would not be able to relate or contribute to any common reservoir of psychopathological knowledge. A scientific psychopathological theory should definitely contribute to the understanding of human (abnormal) behaviour by responding to common cognitive questions faced by research communities in the area. The possibility of this common addressal presupposes the transcendence of the different applications or interpretations of theories in the clinic using criteria of comparability, so that their relative merits for cognitive problems can be assessed. This commitment of a science to being a socio-cognitive discourse, involving agreement and often measurements of relative theoretical acceptability, is binding on psychoanalysis as well. The justification of using psychoanalysis in contemporary psychotherapeutic practice rests on its capacity to assess and define its own status *vis-à-vis* other psychotherapeutic systems, its empirical and theoretical explanatory merits *and* therapeutic successes; in other words, in terms of both its theoretic competence and therapeutic performance. All these issues are epistemological in nature, and contemporary research in the field has focused on these issues. The continuing insularity of psychoanalysis from the mainstream psychiatry, the fragmentation of psychoanalysis into new theoretically uninformed but clinically effective applications, and the administrative problems these pose for the institutionalisation and organisation of psychoanalysis are real questions facing the community today. One way to mitigate these problems of psychoanalytic therapy would be to promote empirical research, and establish a comprehensive and inter-disciplinary data pool of the sort envisioned by Grünbaum. The continental construals of psychoanalysis neglect the reality of these epistemological problems and the urgency the community faces in solving them, advocating instead the further narrativisation of the *theory* by different *applications*.

Granting epistemic authority to the patient using a humanistic argument is clearly a conflation of issues: between the attempt to understand the cognitive underpinnings of abnormal behaviour and the morality of the *use* of this knowledge by the psychoanalyst in his relations with the patient. The ethical problem facing psychotherapy relates to subjecting a person in psychological distress to the social, administrative, economic and moral imperatives of the psychotherapeutic institution, and to the judicious use of the science by its practitioners. It is not *per se* about the development of a theoretical, cognitive data base about abnormal behaviour. Of course, it can be granted that such a data base can never be built up outside of extra-epistemological imperatives. It can even be granted that it is to a large extent determined and promoted by these imperatives, leading to the necessity for a politics of psychiatry. But from this possibility, it cannot be inferred that all research is simply the endorsement of these imperatives. Often, critical questioning of these imperatives has been done by social scientists, even in the history of discourses on mental illness. This is possible because knowledge has grown despite these imperatives generating its own research possibilities.

The humanists assert that knowledge is power, but countering power does not imply that one must deny knowledge. One cannot possibly question the very relevance of epistemology on the grounds that all knowledge is dehumanising and that it is underpinned ideologically. Our capacity to make judgments even about the relative merits and demerits of different sciences and their relative impacts on human society assumes that transcendence of ideologies is possible using norms and standards. Even if such considerations cannot be 'interestingly atemporal', as Cushing has warned, epistemological anarchy is not warranted. To know that a theory is being promoted from a certain ideological basis will have no important consequences for the human agency unless methods are devised which reaffirm the ideals of knowledge. Knowledge *per se* is not ideological, rather knowledge can be *used* ideologically. The ethico-political deconstruction of epistemology is certainly important to combat the injudicious use of knowledge against the marginalised communities. This deconstruction will be useless unless it is further specified what knowledge *is* to substitute that which has been rejected and how research communities must go about acquiring such knowledge and implementing it.

The ethical question of humanism arises in clinics, it concerns the individual analysts who *use* the knowledge available to them for treating mental illness. It is understandable to demand that a psychoanalyst be morally responsible to uphold human dignity with respect to his patients. But sense seems to fail us when a demand for human dignity is made on a theory. The facticity of limits to contemporary social science research—in terms of methodology and theoretical sophistication and in terms of the poorly examined political priorities which guide mental health research—makes us question the judiciousness of demanding that the institutionally engineered professionals uphold exaggerated ideals of humanism. The moral imperatives of the therapeutic institution extend well beyond the space of the clinic, as much as the science does. Just as extra-clinical considerations determine the knowledge base on which therapy rests, so also, extra-clinical socio-political considerations determine the range of ethical actions available to individual psychoanalysts. Policies of practice, the judiciousness or otherwise of particular practices such as electro shock therapy, forced interventions and drug use, are not determined simply by individual practitioners but by the institutionalised contracts drafted by administrative, political and practising communities. The humanists are wrong in their assumption that the humanistic ideal should rest with the practitioner alone. The ethics of therapy is not only a clinical issue, as the humanists imagine. The inference to be drawn from these considerations is not that individual practitioners need not treat their patients humanely but only that the exhortation of humanism from practitioners may often be exaggerated and well beyond what practitioners are capable of. This may be because they are committed to the ethical goals of the larger psychiatric, political and social institutions of which they are a part. That these goals can be questioned by the practitioners, social scientists and other concerned intellectuals is of course a redeeming thought.

The ethical question in the contemporary, politically motivated world is not primarily about the freedom of an individual but about a social and legislative commitment to allow individual freedom. Granting individual freedom is a social contract that a society enters into, a state's polity, legislature and the judiciary are expected to play important roles in ensuring this. A society commits itself, by consensus, to relieve individuals from bondage. Any ideal society would allow for the kind of psychological freedom that existentialism envisions. But freedom is a 'top-down' process, beginning with social consciousness and consensus and trickling down to individuals, as the critical hermeneuticians have rightly pointed out. The perverted cannibal who silently melts into the crowd as the curtain falls in *The Silence of the Lambs* is truly free, in the existentialist sense. Yet as a social being, partaking of the same social reality into which he has vanished, it is hard to feel elated by his release. Again, the frenetic mob which recently brought down the Masjid in Ayodhya was free to do so. As was evident, no force could stop this in a state which practices a passive secularism. Yet, as social and ethical beings who find life so blatantly, violently and expertly devalued by another's freedom, we are often forced to prescribe social limits to individual freedom, a claim that any existentialist would deny. The notion of freedom makes sense in the context of institutions and society. Freedom is possible where a society conscientiously reviews its legislation because the existing norms marginalise and victimise certain sections of it. Humanism in psychotherapy refers to the ability of a society to effectively assimilate and use the knowledge available to it, for ameliorating the suffering of the mentally ill and restoring their human dignity.

Ethical considerations and the commitment to the inherent value of human life can in fact motivate new research possibilities. Such considerations will still have to answer the epistemological question of how to go about this research. Humanism cannot be an argument with which to proscribe our pragmatic and rationally guided search for patterns of human (abnormal) behaviour, presumed to cut across individual clinics, cases and professionals. There are of course problems of devising standards and methodologies which would take into account the varieties of psychological contexts, and the intricate networking of individuals within societies, but these problems relate to epistemology and not ethics.

4

PSYCHOANALYSIS: A SCIENCE OF COGNITION

■ ■ ■

I

Foundationalism, we have seen, sought to exclude psychoanalysis from the realm of knowledge on philosophically problematic grounds. Even though the rudiments of a fresh foundation for psychoanalysis have been broadly hinted at, a positive characterisation of psychoanalysis as a cognitive science is yet to be developed. This has been attempted here and in the following chapter. Before doing this, it is important to understand why the foundational issue has acquired the status of a fundamental issue in the philosophy of science. There are, indeed, important historical and sociological reasons for this. The determination of the foundational question, its genesis in the history of philosophy and its devastating impact on psychoanalysis has a historiological rationale. The ostracism of psychoanalysis from the realm of knowledge is the logical culmination of a historically constituted movement of philosophical thought.

The patent conflict between the epistemological and the ethical realms of knowledge was productive to thought, after and largely in response to the Enlightenment in nineteenth century Europe. This was the historical context within which the question about the foundations of sciences was raised as an important issue. It was then problematised as a philosophical imperative—as a question which each and every science has to address itself to.[1] Raising this question was philosophically required because of the growing recognition that 'science doing' and 'science making' were two different tasks in the development of a

[1] The historical material for developing these ideas have been gathered from Jahnke and Otte (1981); Izenberg (1976); Weckowicz and Liebel-Weckowicz (1990).

science. This recognition spelt out for the first time the difference between 'science' and 'meta-science'. The need to raise the question of the 'foundations' of science separately from the question of 'verification' became a philosophical possibility. Bolzano, a representative of the scientific community of his times,

> distinguishes between 'making certain' (*Gewissmachung*) and 'foundation' (*Begruendung*) when discussing the mathematical sciences. While 'making certain' means a mere formal demonstration or subjective illustration, 'foundation' aims at establishing the objective connection between the various truths .... Since consideration which lead to both of these belong to the class of proofs, one could call such proofs objective proofs or 'foundations' to distinguish them from others which lead only to one and not at the same time to the other . . . (Jahnke, 1981, p. 86).

The difference that Bolzano drew for the mathematical sciences was echoed by scientists of other disciplines. The difference that they sought to establish was really between science as having an overall socio-cognitive rationality and science as simply a method of demonstration or verification. The former came to be known as the 'foundational' issue.

The nineteenth century science of science had two aspects: first, a preoccupation with the 'adversity of empirical reality' to be obtained through a thorough going empiricism; and second, a focus on the 'social-communicative function of science' (p. 79). This is a consolidated view of science as being both a human, value related activity as well as an empirically bound, truth related activity. At the bottom of this view, predictably, were interests of demarcation. The meta-science aimed to fulfil the principle 'that science must be guided by empirical reality, and not by preconceived notions' (p. 78). Scientists had already expressed concern about what it means to do 'science'. Popper's central question is an old one in a new form. From this point of view, science reoriented itself from substance concepts to concepts of function or relation, from essences to accidents, or from ontology to epistemology in the natural sciences. It was no longer possible to believe that what is 'seen' is what is 'real', that is, what 'appeared' is 'real'. The difference between phenomena and noumena, between appearance and reality assumed a new significance in the philosophy of science. Epistemology concerned itself, not with the study of essences, but with the connections between accidents. Predictability and control referred to how well we can manage phenomena procedurally, whether these procedures are formal and mathematical or experimental.

Science, according to the nineteenth century philosophy, was an evolving human language, with the aim to do certain things. It did not automatically show a gross reality, but showed reality as a diversity. However, a scientific theory would be fit for human use only in so far as it also completed him as a human being. The right view of science, according to this ostensibly primitive, but actually cohesive philosophy of science, would include not only the epistemological but also the human. The paradox between the two, even though well recognised, was not perceived as being counter-productive, but was a natural viewpoint to hold. This tension between science as human and empirical is also evident in Freud's texts. Freud worked within these historically given perceptions of science as empirical-positivistic (in the Comtean sense) as well as humanistic and voluntaristic (*à la* Schopenhauer). The essential tension, productive in the meta-science of the nineteenth century, seems to have degenerated into separate and combative philosophical positions each reducing science to a one-dimensionality. English empiricism and logical-positivism have carried forward the justificationary dimension of knowledge construction, whereas the idealistic and phenomenological schools of philosophical thinking took the socio-historical view of scientific knowledge to its logical culmination.

The issue of the foundations of the human sciences problematised[2] by the thinkers of the late nineteenth century assumed an independent course of development. These debates were based on the alleged peculiarity of the human social subject and pursued the hermeneutic programme of evolving a new humanistic language for the human social sciences. Such a language would radically argue for the independent methodological construction of the human sciences, denying the normative canons of the so-called Baconian sciences. Underlining this programme of the construction of a new language for the human sciences was an implicit critical characterisation of the nineteenth century science as mechanistic. This is a primitive view of science

────────────

[2] Weckowicz and Liebel-Weckowicz (1990, pp. 315–60) have traced the development of the 'controversy about the method of social science' to the last part of the nineteenth century, when 'German universities became a forum for a debate called the methods controversy' (p. 320).

maintained to date by the critical hermeneutics. It was probably easy and even justified at a certain historical point to make this character-isation because of the growing perspectives of the empiricistic and pragmatic views of science based simply on the systematising principles of usability, predictability and control. Modern science, however, is more introspective and sees the socio-cognitive nature of its praxis.

The issue of the foundations of the human sciences came through with greater force in philosophical history because the histories of these sciences are very meagre in comparison to the prodigious history of some of the representative natural sciences. Psychoanalysis, for instance, was not an individuated science until a little over 100 years ago. The word 'psychiatry' was not used until the year 1846, and was included in the Oxford English Dictionary only in the year 1937 (Weckowicz and Liebel-Weckowicz, 1990, p. 109). Even this short history of the human sciences, particularly the psychiatric sciences, has been constantly overshadowed by unrealistic anxieties about the possibility of matching up with the Baconian sciences. All this indi-cates how a science like psychoanalysis is inadvertently implicated in the larger historical movement of a philosophy of science. The seces-sionist responses to the productive tension which existed in the nine-teenth century meta-science have unwittingly made their impact in shaping the philosophical context, criteria and the vocabulary within which the debate about the status of psychoanalytic theory can take place.

The conflict of foundationalist philosophies, their prioritised epistemological norms and separate philosophical interests has led to the well known 'crisis' in psychoanalysis; normatively, as seen in the previous chapters, it is neither allowed to be a science nor is it allowed *not* to be a science! Popper, at the point of philosophical departure from logical-positivists, has rightly recognised that science is *cognitive* and initiated a methodological reconsideration of science. But he foundationalised falsifiability, a claim which Grünbaum and other neo-inductivists have questioned, for whom induction is *equally* cogni-tive and *equally* foundational. The external foundationalists correctly emphasise that science is cognitive, but erroneously equate epistemology with the question of empirical justification. This is a reduction of the socio-cognitive rationality of science to its methodology. A psychology of perception and observation foundationalising the philosophy of empiricism is only a partial acknowledgement of the full-blown socio-cognitive venture that scientific activity is. The internal foundationalists' insertion into these debates is important, for it highlights the neglected aspects of the justificationist philosophy of science: first, in the epistemological context, in arguing for the indispensability of the semantic notions of meaning and intentionality for both a philosophy of science and of the mind, and second, in terms of directing our philosophical consciousness towards moral issues in the use of psychoanalytic knowledge. It is, however, true that these germinal intuitions of continental thought have not been formulated in a philosophically satisfying way. They are caught in mystical and onto-logically foundationalist notions of a self-perceiving self.

The philosophy of science is at present concerned about the intimate relation between psychology and epistemology. It no longer seems possible to deny the mental basis of knowledge. Philosophy is sceptical about non-cognitive theories of scientific knowledge such as those propounded by foundationalism. As Kant and Wittgenstein both showed, knowledge and representation of knowledge have psycho-logical limits. Many thinkers now seek ways of 'naturalising' knowledge by eliminating its normative base and enhancing its empirical base by formulating neuro-philosophies or empirical psychology. The claim to the mental basis of knowledge is not however an attempt to naturalise knowledge by explaining it psychologically. Epistemology, or the normative determination of knowledge, is not entirely redundant nor entirely reducible to psychology. Psychological limits to knowledge can be understood and represented as knowledge on the basis of normative considerations. To attempt this is to confuse the philo-sophical difference between *what* is knowledge and *how* we acquire knowledge, or between the contents of knowledge and the process of obtaining that knowledge. This is an unforgettable lesson that Popper taught philosophy. Even the attempt to understand our psychological nature would be rendered impossible unless we have the criteria of independently establishing what has been acquired as knowledge. The inter-disciplinary nature of epistemology and cognitive psychology rests on the interrelation between and even inter-definition of language and mind, between epistemic norms and cognition: epistemology even though limited by natural psychological conditions is still at some level normative.

The norms that one accords to psychoanalysis will have to suit its essential nature as a cognitive psychological theory. Leaving the ethical question of humanism aside for the moment, the epistemological foundation to be given should normatively encompass the themes individually emphasised by the philosophical foundationalists. Only a thorough-going empiricism can answer the realist's question of reference, but psychoanalysis cannot equate reference with behaviour. The empiricism that psychoanalysis espouses should allow for the possibility of the conception of a distinctively mental realm in terms of concepts of meaning, intentionality, consciousness and unconsciousness. Psychoanalysis is an intentional psychology. A cognitive epistemology must be provided to the theory, rather than empiricist/behaviouristic or hermeneutic/personal view of knowledge.

II

Even psychoanalysts hold the view that psychoanalysis is by nature a clinical theory. This has been discussed earlier, in the introduction, where certain important methodological questions which this leads to were elaborated upon. This informs us about the problems of the clinical view and lead us on, later, to formulate a cognitive view of the theory. Foundationalism, as said earlier, has its adherents among practitioners too. They hold the view that abnormal behaviour can be understood in purely clinical terms, on the basis of a foundationalist epistemology of an immediately given object or subject. The spectrum of clinical positions in their presumptions, are of both external and internal foundationalist kinds and claim: (*a*) that the clinical theory fits clinical facts, a claim based on the primacy and purity of clinical observation, (*b*) that the clinical theory is 'experience-near' and should be based on an interpersonal self-psychology of reasons and motives. This attempt 'to save the clinical phenomena' by programmatically eliminating the meta-psychology or reducing it to its clinical form has aroused the concern of many psychoanalytic thinkers such as Robert Holt and Heinz Kohut.

Not all thinkers, however, uncritically assume this prevailing stance, such as Hartmann (1958), Rangell (1985), and more recently, Edelson (1989) and Opatow (1989). Eagle, a critic of the clinical approaches to therapy, does not claim that therapy can or should be based on the possibilities of pristine observation in the clinic. Emphasising in his works (1984) and elsewhere (1988) that all forms of behaviour have a cognitive basis, Eagle has noted,

> whatever the inadequacies of Freud's . . . metapsychology, he
> was . . . correct in searching for a deeper level of explanation in the

substrate and processes underlying the behaviour we carry out and the goals we pursue .... It is this search for a deeper level of explanation rather than the specific content that I take to be the significance of Freud's metapsychology. To limit psychoanalysis to the so-called clinical theory and reject *any* form of deeper theoretical account is to ... accept an inadequate and truncated form of explanation as well as to isolate psychoanalysis from an enriching body of facts and perspectives (1984, p. 149).

Holt himself, despite his lasting critique (1976, 1981b, 1985) of metapsychology, later conceded that the philosophical necessity of a metapsychology would have to be accepted in the end.

Freud's meta-psychological model of the mind is not merely a web of metaphysical speculations as some of these practitioners have assumed, but rather what Eagle has called the 'deeper level', causal-explanatory cognitive theory of the mind. As such it is the indispensable and defining core of the psychoanalytic theory. It is what captures the essential nature of psychoanalysis as a cognitive theory. Meta-psychology makes many assumptions about human cognition, like any other cognitive science. It includes definitively psychoanalytic concepts of consciousness, preconsciousness and unconsciousness; their structural differentiation into the concepts of ego, id and superego; the intentional mental states, such as wishing, believing, imagining and fantasising attributable to these systems; their affective and cognitive representations; their internal relations and mutations; the concept of the self, its internal structure and its external agentive functions; a theory of object and intrapsychic conflict; and the countless number of mental processes by which the ego 'resolves' its intrapsychic and interpersonal conflicts, such as the well studied defense mechanisms. Psychoanalysis describes by using the vocabulary of consciousness and unconsciousness, primary and secondary processes, or the ego and the id, what it means for a subject to be a self and what it means for a subject to relate to objects. Psychoanalysis gives a theory of the self and a theory of the object in order to explain behaviour. The self and the object are inter-defined in the theory.

The science also assumes that the self and the object are natural items in the world because the mind perceives them as such. The self is not metaphysically prior, within the theory, but rather the mind. A conception of the self and the object is possible for a person, only because of the way the mind organises items of the world. The mind can take on many functions, among them, representing the self that it embodies, other selves and natural objects. Psychoanalytic science provides the mind with a cognitive/realistic status, rather than an empiricistic/behaviouristic or hermeneutic/intuitive status.

The foundationalistic theories granted the mind only a phenomenalistic status. Both empiricism and hermeneutics are sceptical responses to the reality of the mind that knowledge and language try to capture. Both equate scientific realism with granting the possibility of physical entities. This is an equation which is questionable even in sophisticated physical theories, and for psychology it leads to the impossibility of mind talk. The foundationalist's position is as if he has supposed that all things in the world are 'chairs': only this person will need an account of the ontological status of something which is not a chair, but say, a table. A table will not be a real object in his scheme of things. The alternatives before the person are to either reduce the phenomenal presentations of a table to a chair, or to deny real status to the table. In a similar way, only the assumption that everything which is real is palpable can lead to the foundationalist's stance that either it must be so reduced or it must be denied the status of reality altogether. The foundationalist theories subscribe to an anti-realism with respect to the mind.

Perspectivisation of the theory as a cognitive theory defends the concept of the mind against the sceptical excesses that both the foundationalist traditions were open to. A cognitive view of the mind such as psychoanalysis attempts to provide through its meta-psychology overcomes this scepticism, by making realism about the mind scientifically possible again. The theoretical and methodological sophistication of the discipline can give us well formed psychoanalytic theories of the self and the object. The philosophical problem, however, is what kind of realism is possible in a theory of the mind and whether we can meaningfully explain what the mind is. A cognitive view of knowledge fundamentally recognises that the mental realm has an independent status of its own which can be given a philosophically adequate form of representation and methodological individuation. In psychoanalysis, it is meta-psychology which makes realism possible. It is true, as Holt (1981a) has shown, that the notion of meta-psychology underwent several changes and was put to different intellectual *and* non-intellectual uses in the metamorphoses of Freud's conceptual thinking. Among other things, meta-psychology meant a purely physicalist theory of the mind, by reduction of the mind to neuro-physiology; a psycho-biological identity theory of the mind in terms of an evolutionary biology (also see Sulloway, 1979); and importantly, a functionalist depth psychology, by reference to a theory of the unconscious. It is no longer necessary to argue for the relative credibility of the different theories of the mind involved. Whether any of these are philosophically vindicated or not in psychology, we must acknowledge the importance of different facets of the mind and the need for an integrated theory of the mind. That human cognition is not a matter of the mind alone and requires, at some level, the acceptance of a connection with the material aspects of being, is a claim as indispensable for a theory of the mind as that the mind is not matter alone. Psychoanalytic meta-psychology *is* the theory of the mind that Freud proposed, and contains a set of interrelated cognitive concepts and claims about psychologically normal and deviant behaviour. This meta-psychology theorises about what a normal and an abnormal mind looks like, how they are structured and how they result in behaviour. Freud held that meta-psychology was 'the most complete description of (mental processes) of which we can at present conceive' (S.E., Vol. 20, p. 109). Meta-psychology *is* the cognitive theory in psychoanalysis. As such, it is precisely the kind of theory that is amenable to extra-clinical testing. It describes the kind of entity the mind is and answers the question of reference. Empiricism in psychoanalysis, or the possibility of verifying psychoanalytic laws, follows from meta-psychology and not from the clinical theory. In other words, meta-psychology is meant to be an extra-clinical theory of abnormal behaviour.

III

The assertion that an extra-clinically given meta-psychology is philosophically required is the first step towards building the foundations of psychoanalysis as a cognitive theory. It will be seen later that extra-clinical research of the cognitive claims of psychoanalysis can and do adequately stand warrant for the probative value of some of the central concepts of the theory. However, Grünbaum's recognition of therapy as the application of extra-clinical is still myopic in its lack of understanding of the full import of the notion of 'extra-clinical'. The extra-clinical determination of the psychoanalytic, cognitive theory of the mind is not *only* the empirical justification of its laws, but also the socio-cognitive rationale within which psychoanalysis is evolving. The science itself goes beyond therapy and is extra-clinical in a very general way.

'Extra-clinicality' designates the general rules presupposed by any therapy. The extra-clinical determination of therapy refers to the rational, normative determination of therapy. Therapy is the point of intersection for the skilful use of different kinds of normative considerations, among which empirical consideration is only one. For example, Freud's clinical studies are the result of his participation in the extra-clinical research programme that he was actively involved in for understanding abnormal behaviour. The determination of the nature of hysteria and the clinical possibilities of treatment depended upon Freud's prior participation in canonical polemics and philosophical discussions about mental illness. The theory of man and mind emerging from these debates had a very large role to play in the kind of therapeutic choices that Freud made. Therapeutic strategies adopted by clinicians are guided by extra-clinically given *theoretical* differentiation.

Grünbaum's rather narrow view of extra-clinicality is indeed consistent with his explicit restriction of attention to the truth value of psychoanalysis. His singular interest in verification limited his conception of extra-clinicality to the justification of the cognitive claims of psychoanalysis. But this restriction itself is questionable because of its narrow implications for the more general issue of the epistemological or scientific foundations of the theory.

Our broad view of the 'extra-clinical' socio-cognitive determination of the theory is in some ways similar to and derived from Lakatos' view of science as a 'research programme'. This view argued that scientific praxis is not to be understood in terms of purely experimental manoeuvres in the laboratory, but in terms of the science's overall participation in a community's efforts to understand particular domains. Scientific praxis is seen within the fold of a larger, philosophically, socially and historically defined rationality, rather than in terms of purely methodological norms. Lakatos' meta-science stands Popper's on its head: Popper had placed methodology at the head of scientific priorities as the oracle which exposes false theories. The notion of a 'research programme' is meant to capture the breadth of the community enterprise that a science is, in the holistic spirit of the nineteenth century meta-science. The notion of a research programme encompasses the historical, socio-cognitive nature of scientific activity.

It takes a science beyond empiricism and methodology and situates it in the context of the historicity of scientific tradition and interest relativity of communities. The problem of verification is only a small part of the research programme.

However, Lakatos' attempt to understand the growth of scientific knowledge has often been at the *expense* of methodological interests leading to a widespread recognition of scientific relativism (for critical discussions, see Hacking, 1983; Hesse and Arbib, 1986, pp. 6–10). This is an implication which is as objectionable philosophically as the universalism of a purely methodological view of science. A purely historical understanding of a science is questionable as an attempt to justify the epistemological foundations of a science. One cannot justify a science by providing a logic of discovery. The fact that a theory has a logical history is true not only of science, but of all kinds of theories. Theories of philosophy, art, religion, among others, equally exhibit a historical rationale. The principle of historical rationality will not work as a demarcation principle. The validation of the epistemological foundations has to do with normative and not historical considerations. Scientific praxis equally requires an epistemological vocabulary that axiomatically assumes a historical transcendence and determines the criteria of validation for a science.

But as both science and meta-science change and evolve in time, normative evaluations of a science must be contemporary. The evaluation of scientificity of particular decisions at critical junctures of science requires not only a continuity with the traditions' logical history but also normative evaluations using epistemic norms. It is useful to situate a theory within the context of discovery to show the logical evolution of scientific knowledge. However, the justification for its *continued* use in contemporary scientific praxis remains an open question which cannot be answered by a community except by taking fresh stock of the theory *vis-à-vis* some philosophically acceptable set of epistemological commitments and its conformity to these commitments.

Thus, our socio-cognitive view of science is close to the research programme view in so far as the latter permits normative considerations. The notion of a research programme may be understood in two ways: first, as a practical notion, referring to the range of activities that a scientific community performs, guided by certain epistemological norms; and second, as a historical notion, referring to the logic of discovery of a science. The first sense can be meaningfully used for our perspective of a science. Lakatos' meta-science does not make this distinction and hence is led to relativistic implications.

Any therapy depends upon a vast background information drawn from the larger research programme. Extra-clinicality is only partially an empirical notion and includes other epistemological and non-epistemological norms and choices. A therapy is a praxis, the nature, aims and goals of which are normatively constrained, whether these norms are social, institutional or philosophical. In terms of information about cognition, a therapy cannot be its own source of knowledge and draws on extra-clinical knowledge and belief. A therapy is one of the particularised sites or service outlets for the use of knowledge about human beings obtained through cognitive research. Derivation of this knowledge is not only from within the discipline but also from other related fields of cognitive inquiry. A therapy explicitly or otherwise inducts philosophical viewpoints, cultural or social biases, ethical choices and prejudices of the practitioners. Not only is a therapy determined normatively but is also determined by a separately justified rationality of therapeutic practices and customs. This has occasioned wide debates recently on a 'theory of therapy' which evaluate philosophical controls on therapeutic practices. Ideally, the psychoanalytic theory should be supported by a theory about psychoanalytic practice or therapy, about what kinds of practices contribute to ideal analyst–analysand negotiations. Ethically, too, choices are pre-given in a therapy through sociological and political considerations extending far beyond the possibilities of the clinic. Policies about mental health, for example, and priorities of mental health research determine therapy as fundamentally as the cognitive realm. It is in this very general sense that any therapy, including psychoanalytic therapy, is determined 'extra-clinically'.

These different philosophical, epistemological, historical, cultural, social and ethical aspects of a research programme guide the development of psychoanalytic therapy (Sulloway, 1979; Jones, 1961; Ellenberger, 1970; Roazen, 1975). Freud, for example, faced two research problems relating to hysteria and hypnosis. These were specific debates in psychiatry, deriving from the general controversy in which all of nineteenth century science was embroiled: the vitalist versus mechanist debates about the very nature of reality. In the medical context, this controversy took the form of debates between physicalists, or those who argued for a somatic psychopathology and the 'psychiker', or those who argued in favour of a psychological basis of mental illness (Weckowicz and Liebel-Weckowicz, 1990, pp. 109–52).

Until Charcot, some of the hysteric's somatic manifestations, for instance, paralysis, had been conflated with the organic form of paralysis. Organic paralysis is caused by lesions of certain parts of the brain. Paralysis of the arm, a common symptom in hysteria, was thus believed to be caused by lesions in the arm centre of the brain, near the fissure of Rolando. However, the analysis revealed no such lesions. Also, as Freud witnessed in 1885, when working under Charcot, traumatic paralysis could be artificially induced in hypnotic trances. This meant that this paralysis was to be seen as etiologically different from organic paralysis, for it could not be localised in the brain. Recognising that Charcot's studies restored human dignity to hysterics, Freud launched clinical case studies, just as Charcot had done on traumatic paralyses, showing that hyterical paralyses 'are largely independent of the regular anatomical distributions governing known instances of *organic* paralysis' (S.E., Vol. 3, p. 27). Freud worked out the etiological differences between hysterical and anatomical paralyses. For example, organic cerebral paralysis affected the hand and not the shoulders, but in hysteria, the opposite was seen. Hysterical paralysis could be alleviated or induced by hypnosis, whereas anatomical paralysis could not. Freud concluded that hysteria 'behaves as though anatomy did not exist or as though it had no knowledge of it' (S.E., Vol. 1, p. 169). Freud speculated that hysteria appeared to be caused by 'functional' lesions rather than organic lesions, a germinal cognitive idea. It appeared to be guided by the *mental* concept that the patient had of the 'arm' rather than of the anatomy. The connection between symptom and cause seemed to be 'symbolic' rather than physiological. Freud evolved a psychopathological metaphor analogously based upon the physical but different from the physical.

Anna O., the first psychoanalytic patient, exhibited a variety of hysteric symptoms (S.E., Vol. 2, pp. 21–47)—paralysis of extremities on the right side of her body, and sometimes paralysis of the left side, ocular and hearing problems, difficulties with the posture of her head, a nervous cough, resistance to drinking liquids, suicidal impulses, and forgetting her native tongue, German. She exhibited delirious states of 'absences', a term describing states when her personality changed to what she called her 'bad self', followed by a 'cloudy' state of autohypnosis. When she woke up from this trance, she could not recall her hallucinatory phases.

In the treatment of this patient, Breuer noted several phenomeno-logical traits—the patient had an immense capacity for recall; by merely showing her an orange, which she had substituted for water, she could go into her 'bad self'; in the hypnotic state, if Breuer related to her the words that she had uttered during her absences, she could recall the forgotten details of her hallucinations; this recall was accompanied by strong emotions and relieved her symptoms and restored a sense of calmness; the patient could, aided by her extra-ordinary power of recall, trace the occurrence of her symptoms right back to the first time, at which point the symptoms disappeared.

These phenomena in themselves were very productive in terms of theoretical possibilities. On the face of it, there were the somatic symptoms which did not figure within the domain of a pure physiology. This implied, of course, that the practitioner had a thorough know-ledge of the organic or neuro-physiological bases of abnormal func-tioning. The rejection of a physiological model was further confirmed by the fact that the symptoms could be induced simply by showing her the substituted orange. The extraordinary memory and the emotions accompanying recall astonishingly alleviated the symptoms. Breuer used the cognitive notions of 'abreaction' and 'catharsis', respectively, to describe the processes of recall charged with emotion and subse-quent symptom relief.

In using these notions, Breuer made many assumptions about the process of memory—certain past experiences, more often unpleasant or distasteful, had the tendency of lingering on in that cognitive capacity called 'memory' in some way or the other; this process of lingering was directly related to the emotions that a person attached to it; further, an extremely negative value could result in the 'memory' being 'repressed'; it was possible to bring out and know these repressed thoughts by manipulating cognition in certain ways; the overcoming of repression could be an intense emotional experience; only an intense experience was curative; etc. An entire *cognitive theory* about affect, memory and a proto-theory of the internal representation of the self and object relation is involved in this understanding of Anna O. Breuer, in other words, was using a proto-explanatory theory about human abnormal cognition, in order to understand the observations made in the clinic.

The therapeutic choices in the clinic were also guided by a theory of therapy. This theory argued for the benefits and limitations of particular kinds of practices, their essential features, and also defined specifically therapeutic notions such as transference and countertransference. During Freud's time, debate was rife on the technique of hypnosis. Theodor Meynert, in whose anatomical laboratory Freud worked, strongly opposed hypnosis on the ethical grounds that it reduced a human being 'to a creature without will or reason, and his mental degeneration is only hastened by it' (quoted in Sulloway, 1979, p. 42). His objection was based on the fact that hypnosis released sexual impulses in the subcortical region of the brain. He also pointed out the possible danger of making healthy people morbid. However, both Charcot and Meynert agreed that hypnosis had a physiological basis, contrary to Bernheim, who believed that hypnosis was a psychological process. Bernheim disagreed with Charcot on the claim that only neuropaths were hypnotisable. He argued that suggestibility was common to everyone, and that hypnosis was ideogenic. Charcot endorsed the somatic view that hypnosis occurred naturally as an organic reaction to sensory stimulation during hypnotism.

Freud faced an ethical and philosophical problem with Bernheim's position on the technique. The idea that hypnotisability is psychological would imply that the physiological symptoms are not genuine. As far as Freud was concerned, this implied a regression to pre-Charcot days, when hysteria was dismissed as 'lawless' and irrational. While ethically this was unpalatable, Freud clearly believed in the 'rationality' of human behaviour, and could not eschew the position that it was not possible to explain hysterical behaviour as 'caused' through understandable and specifiable, causal cognitive processes. Freud also believed that nature was bi-polar and human behaviour could not be understood except as an interaction between the somatic and the psychic. According to him, Bernheim's views were 'one-sided' (Freud, 1954, p. 58), though the only defense he could put up for Charcot's was *ethical*, and at the expense of his epistemological problems with Charcot. Freud's own conclusion to this debate was that hypnosis was equally a physiological phenomenon as it was a psychical one. He compared hypnosis to sleep, where a psychical component such as an intention to close one's eyes automatically led to the physiological effect of sleep. A confirmed dualist, he maintained that 'there are both psychical and physiological phenomena in hypnotism and hypnotism itself can be brought about in the one manner or the other' (S.E., Vol. 1, p. 81).

Freud faced some practical problems in using the method of hypnosis. Among them were that not all patients were completely hypnotisable, the discovery that even Bernheim was unable to bring about a complete hypnosis, and the subsequent admission by Bernheim that his private practice was somehow less conducive to hypnosis than his hospital. Bernheim's suggestion that patients who were hypnotised to the stage of somnolence with amnesia were also capable, *when awake*, of recalling early events which they could not before, compelled Freud to look for alternative theoretical and technical possibilities. If what Bernheim said was true, the hypnotic method was not significant to understanding the way the hysteric mind worked, and he could still induce the patient to recall without hypnosis.

The process of 'hypnosis' did not add anything significant to his conceptual geography of understanding mental illness but on the contrary, seemed to subtract from it. Hypnosis had worked, but apparently blindly. Though it could relieve some symptoms, it could not effect an enduring cure. Some of the symptoms were seen to be substituted by other symptoms. The clinicians were unable to explain *how* hypnotism worked. Freud gave up hypnosis altogether, alternatively developing pressure and concentration techniques, and finally the free association method. However, he retained the original concepts he had arrived at with the help of hypnosis, the ideas of catharsis and abreaction based on a process of recall. Freud realised, in this process, that under hypnosis patients could recall early unpleasant events as if automatically. When they were not hypnotised, they seemed to have a lot of difficulty in effecting this recall, even though eventually they could. Their initial protestations, alleged inability to recall, etc., along with the fact that Freud had to use significant force and persuasion, seemed to indicate that there was some kind of force at work in the patient, 'which was opposed to the pathogenic ideas being conscious (being remembered)' (S.E., Vol. 2, p. 268). Hypnosis seemed to have hidden this 'interplay of forces'. 'The use of hypnosis is bound to hide . . . resistance' (S.E., Vol. 14, p. 16). Freud said, 'From all this there arose, as it were automatically, the thought of *defense*' (S.E., Vol. 2, p. 269).

Thus, Freud was led to formulate his psychoanalytic theory not only on the basis of his observations of clinical behaviour, but also his participation in debates among the general medical community, his theoretical preoccupations, his objections to alternative theories, his technical limitations and preferences, his view of human nature and values. He postulated that the mind was somehow structured as many interacting sub-systems, each definable in its own terms and essential features. Freud's psychological theory of the mind was the logical outcome of an entire research programme. Other than epistemological considerations, such as the nature of a science and the availability of knowledge at any particular time, therapy is also determined by philosophical, social mindsets and sheer cultural differentiations. Current therapy is equally dependent upon a vast realm of extra-clinical considerations, such as, available research on cognition, general philosophical, political and ethical considerations and purely theoretical problems in the domain of psychopathology.

IV

Our reorientation of the philosophical foundations of psychoanalysis from an empiricistic/hermeneutic clinical approach to a cognitive extra-clinical approach is made within the current preoccupation of philosophy with the nature of a cognitive science. If psychoanalysis is a cognitive theory, then some of the epistemological norms binding on any such theory should be binding on psychoanalysis too. Thus, when we describe psychoanalysis as a cognitive theory, we are also committed to address many of the philosophical questions facing the cognitive sciences.

Any cognitive science subscribes to the view that knowledge is a symbolic representation. It asserts that knowledge is the result of the linguistic possibilities available to us and our cognitive capacities to construct representations using these. For a cognitive science, knowledge aims to understand reality. Language and mind work together in order that we may know reality. Any cognitive science grants the realism of the Kantian claim that '. . . our view of the world is causally dependent both on the way the world is and on the way we are' (Johnson-Laird, 1983, p. 402). Freud's psychodynamic theory of the mind appears to have conceded by the use of a historically different and arguably deficit vocabulary, the modern functionalist idea that cognition is possible because the mind is a system which makes and manipulates symbols. Understanding action, speech and the entire repertoire of what is called 'typically' human behaviour is possible because of the subject's conscious or unconscious relation with these symbols. Interaction with the world, with others, and with oneself is possible through a mental manipulation of the linguistic possibilities of symbols and what they signify.

Human action, according to any cognitive theory, is the result of the representational capacities of human cognition. Philosophically, any theory of action also requires a theory of representation (Papineau, 1990). *Prima facie*, action may be explained to have ensued from a belief irrespective of whether the belief is true or false, making a theory of representation redundant for a theory of action. For example, a woman who obsessionally holds up her finger thinking that the world rests on it, is acting upon a belief which is scientifically false. But this is precisely the kind of action that begs explanation at a deeper level, and attributions of belief simply fail to explain at this level. Human action can be explained if one knows the intention or purpose from which action has ensued. That which has to be invoked, such as mental contents of objects, in order to give the intention is the representation.

Freud's theory is a formal cognitive theory of the abnormal mind. Freud nurtured the idea that the abnormal mind could be understood as analogous to a machine, as a psychic organisation of 'systems'. Behaviour is the functional output of this system. These ideas have been dealt with elaborately in his *Interpretation of Dreams* and *Project for a Scientific Psychology*, among other works, where he has compared the abnormal mind to a compound microscope and referred to it as the 'psychic apparatus'. Freud pictured 'the instrument which carried out our mental functions as resembling a compound microscope' (S.E., Vol. 5, p. 574). Being aware that this is an analogy, he used it only to make the 'complications of mental functioning intelligible by dissecting the function and assigning its different constituents to different component parts of the apparatus' (S.E., Vol. 5, p. 575). This definition of the mind was what Freud called a systemic definition, signifying 'inclusion in a system and possessing certain characteristics'. According to Freud, psychoanalysis listed the mental structures and processes by which abnormal behaviour could be explained as having been caused. This is a typically functionalist aim: 'what determines which kind a mental particular belongs to is its causal role in the mental life of the organism' (Fodor, 1981, p. 11). Freud's endeavour too, 'tries to delineate the structure of a process, whilst leaving it largely unspecified just how this structure is (or is to be) realized' (Lockwood, 1989, p. 26). The interesting consequence of the computational analogy for a theory of the mind has been the possibility of defining the structure of cognition in abstract terms, independent of the question of its physical realisation. Fodor (1981) has referred to the 'level of abstraction at which the generalizations of psychology are most naturally pitched and, as things appear to be turning out, that level of abstraction collapses across the differences between physically quite different kinds of systems' (p. 8).

Freud's need for a vocabulary which could be used to talk about a peculiarly cognitive realm which is capable of being understood in its own terms, which may be construed as causally efficient on behaviour and which explained clinical phenomena, was fulfilled by his meta-psychology. This meta-psychology allowed Freud the epistemic distance required to understand clinical behaviour through the mediation of the uniquely psychological vocabulary that he evolved. Freud did not aim to be 'describing clinical facts' in using this meta-psychology. Rather, he was interested in knowing those psychological principles of human cognition which could explain human behaviour and then make clinical practice possible. Understanding human behaviour was the primary question for Freud, rather than explaining clinical phenomena. He believed that once the former was accomplished, the latter would naturally follow.

Freud was wrong, of course, to have believed that the clinic could empirically justify this theory and in this he was methodologically naive. But his philosophical rationale for postulating a meta-psychology is impeccable, that is, to make an extra-clinical cognitive theory possible. The Freudian meta-psychology is the extra-clinical cognitive theory. The fact that he based this theory largely in the clinic casts a doubt only on the method he sought to validate this cognitive theory, as Grünbaum has rightly pointed out, but it does not render Freud's psychology 'clinical'. By his meta-psychology, Freud fulfilled a much felt need for a causal model of the mind abstracted from the clinic. If this were not the case, Freud need not have postulated the difference between the 'clinical' and the 'meta-psychological' theory.

In formulating general principles for a theory of the mind, it is patent that Freud's primary interest in the development of psycho-analysis was epistemological rather than ontological. Two questions can possibly be raised in research programmes focusing on the abnormal mind—whether the abnormal mind exists, and how it can be understood. The latter is the Kantian epistemological question relating to the possibility of synthetic knowledge about the abnormal mind, whereas the former is directly ontological. No doubt, the onto-logical question is unavoidable, but such a question is perhaps most usefully subsumed, as seen earlier, under epistemology. Freud's problem was, given the clinical representations of abnormality in affect, speech and behaviour or the symptomatology, what kind of causal processes could be hypothesised as functional explanations of such behaviour using a mentalistic vocabulary.

Justifying his need for a meta-psychology epistemologically, Freud noted:

> It (the concept of the 'Unconscious') is necessary because the data of consciousness have a very large number of gaps in them; both in healthy and in sick persons psychic acts often occur which can be explained only by presupposing other acts, of which, nevertheless, consciousness affords no evidence . . . . All these conscious acts remain disconnected and unintelligible if we insist upon claiming that every mental act that occurs in us must also necessarily be experienced by us through consciousness; on the other hand, they fall into a demonstrable connection if we interpolate between them the unconscious acts which we have inferred (S.E., Vol. 19, p. 235).

The passage is heavy in its philosophical import. Freud's argument for the unconscious is that what could count as clinical observation—'the data of consciousness'—is incomplete. Taking clinical observation for granted did not give Freud the understanding required for helping resolve problems about certain kinds of human behaviour and such understanding was necessary for therapy to be possible. If these forms of behaviour must be 'explained', then this could be done only by 'presupposing' mental acts other than those which are conscious. 'Evidence' for these acts is problematic because what we always have is conscious or overt behaviour. Yet, parapraxes, dreams and neurotic behaviour cannot be explained, if one is determined 'to hold fast to the claim' that only conscious experience—what is strictly observable in the clinic—is legitimate. If these behaviours must 'fall into demonstrable connection', we must 'interpolate' unconscious acts, which are 'inferred'.

The differentiation of meta-psychology from clinical theory is philosophically needed because on this depends the possibility of separating clinical claims from cognitive claims. By implication, the possibility of empirical justification depends on this differentiation. The distinction between the cognitive theory and the clinical dimension of this theory has been maintained, clarified and advanced conceptually in different forms by many psychoanalytic researchers and practitioners, such as Wallerstein, Sandler and Joffe, Ketty and Gill. The differences between the 'non-experiential' and 'experiential' realms, 'constructs' and 'phenomena', 'mechanism' and 'outcome', 'process' and 'content', etc. embody the conceptual difference between the organisation of the mind as specified by the cognitive theory and its clinical behavioural manifestations. Sustaining the essential and well acknowledged difference between the science and therapy in psychoanalysis is possible because of the conceptual difference that Freud proposed between meta-psychology and its clinical features. Freudian psychoanalysis provides a scientific theory for understanding human abnormal behaviour. The nature and formal organisation of the theory is determined by responses to different kinds of research problems in psychoanalysis. Meta-psychology is a theory of psychology, making cognitive claims about the psychodynamic, intentional and conflictual nature of the mind. As such, verifying the truth of psycho-analytic laws depends on the possibility of meta-psychological general-isations. Meta-psychology states the lawful domain of psychoanalysis and the essential features of its referent; it is an object-laden ontology and its function is to 'refer to the underlying existential structure and conceptualize entities that actually exist' (Opatow, 1989, p. 648) using the laws of psychology. The referent of psychoanalytic theory is the structure of the mind that the theory specifies. The theory specifies the mental structures and processes that the theory attributes to abnormal behaviour, using essentially psychodynamic and intentional concepts.

An epistemology for psychoanalysis is mainly concerned with providing philosophical rules for developing a meta-psychology of this nature. That is, the epistemology would provide answers to issues relating to the construction, nature, scope and validation of knowledge of a psychoanalytic cognitive science. Such an epistemology would be a philosophical theory of definition, delimitation, truth, meaning and explanation with respect to the cognitive theory. The epistemology would state the rationality of each with respect to the larger realistic goals of the scientific research programme.

The problem of demarcation plays an important role in the epis-temology. Ideally, demarcatory discussions should also contribute to specific questions relating to the nature and scope of the theory. In the context of psychoanalysis, interest in demarcation should not be restricted to whether the theory is a science or not. This question should be answered only by an examination of the nature of the theory being evaluated and by addressing its specific theoretical problems, such as the delimitation of an intentional, psychoanalytic theory of the mind, strengthening the linguistic basis of the theory, its definitive concepts and their interrelations, and the inductive, empirical basis for its referent. The issue of demarcation not only concerns whether psychoanalysis is a science or not, but also knowledge about the linguistic rules of the theory and the empirical possibilities of these rules. The question of demarcation is decided by examining the specific nature of a science. It implies defining the sense of the theory and identifying its reference, and how these can be adequately represented epistemologically and validated empirically. The foundational issue of psychoanalysis must be defined with respect to an understanding of the nature of psychoanalysis as a cognitive science.

To say this is not to claim that *henceforth*, psychoanalysis will function in this way—as a cognitive science. But rather that foundationalism ignored the essential nature of the theory as a cognitive science. The philosophical critiques of psychoanalysis misunderstood the nature of the theory and hence made incorrect evaluations. Our philosophical view of science and psychoanalysis attempts to present, in a way that the foundationalists did not, the psychoanalytic research programme as it exists. We are not breaking new grounds for psychology, but re-orienting philosophical thinking about psychology so that it can be seen from within the unifying epistemological principles of a different perspective. By providing a cognitivist foundation for psychoanalysis, we are not setting the theory or its methodology on an entirely new groove. Rather, we are only stating what seems to have been obvious all along about the nature of the theory from within the research programme itself; critical philosophy, using its external norms, has lost sight of this nature. We aim from a cognitivist epistemological basis, to restore philosophical vision.

V

A psychoanalytic functional explanation of human behaviour must fulfil certain philosophical commitments in order to be a philosophically acceptable theory of cognition. These commitments are binding on any kind of psychological explanation that is offered as 'functional'. Importantly, such an explanation must draw from a psychological vocabulary which will outline the features of the cognitive system in terms of mental structures and processes. A functional explanation derives from a uniquely mentalistic vocabulary, which Freud himself recognised as indispensable. Flanagan (1984) has referred to 'the thesis of the Autonomy of Psychological Explanation' which Freud appeared to have held: 'the thesis that the science of the mind should proceed to frame its principles in terms of its own specialized vocabulary without trying to force translations into the vocabulary of any already existing natural science' (p. 60). Freud's psychology made it theoretically possible to talk about two distinct but formally relatable sets of mental states and processes. Freud postulated a divided mind comprising consciousness and unconsciousness, or the later differentiated concepts of the superego, ego and id. These fundamental concepts of the mind went through epistemic vicissitudes, getting repeatedly clarified through the topographical, structural and energic models of the mind. Freud's theory of the mind is not really a comprehensive theory of the mind, but comprises at least three models, each embodying its own suppositions, implications and limitations. If treated as a comprehensive theory, they lead to paradoxes, contradictions and conflicts.

The topographical notion of the mind uses a spatial metaphor: any mental element 'which is now *present* to my consciousness may become *absent* the next moment, and may become *present again*, after an interval, unchanged . . .' (S.E., Vol. 12, p. 260). Consciousness and unconsciousness are defined in terms of their presence or absence to *awareness*. In this model of the mind, there is no explicit connection drawn between memory and consciousness; the historicity of memory, the intentional and conflictual nature of cognition or the socio-ecological determination of human personality and behaviour is largely neglected. This simple view of consciousness is close to the existentialist view requiring no causal etiological explanations but restricts itself to phenomenological descriptions of the contents of consciousness.

Further differentiation of this topographical conception by Freud led to the second definition, the 'dynamic' view of the mind, where he used an archaeological metaphor. Some unconscious memories could, according to this view, be recovered through a simple process of recollection; these contents were designated as the 'preconscious'. Freud reserved the term 'unconscious' for those which could not be so recovered. This view attains structural differentiation of the mind to some degree and recognises intra-psychic conflict, though it is not yet a full-blown cognitive theory and still lacks a comprehensive explanatory theory of memory, intentionality and behaviour.

Interestingly, Freud made a distinction between cognitively non-problematic mental phenomena and those that were problematic, dispelling the usual doubt that Freudian theory viewed all behaviour as pathological. By itself, an act of forgetting, for example, does not beg to be explained. However, repeated memory lapses accompanied by strong affective responses did. What required to be clinically explained is something that Freud knew he had to decide upon and scrupulously judge. In the problematic cases, recovery seemed to involve a lot of psychotherapeutic effort: suggestions and counter-suggestions, untold transferences, affective outpourings, aggressions and sullen silences, and so on.

The third energic view of the mind aims to correct the problems of the other two views and is based on a physical metaphor. A theory of human action requires to explain how change and mobility are philosophically possible and, to satisfy this requirement, Freud postulated the notion of 'psychic energy'. The model assumes that the mind is disposed to make certain mental manoeuvres to reach psychic stability, like the movements of a pendulum, set in motion, eventually attaining equilibrial states. The principle of homeostasis or nirvana is the principle defining the goals of mental processes. Subjects are psychologically disposed to attain a semantic state of stability by stabilising the intentional relation between the mental state and the object. The fundamental hypothesis that Freud proposed is that the mind wishes to relate stably to itself, others and objects of the world. The structural differentiation of the superego, the ego and the id was made by Freud to establish a theory which would show that the mind satisfied this aim. Abnormality was viewed in relation to the fulfilment of this aim. The energic view of the mind is a complex theory, specifying several mental states and processes, the interrelations and transformations between the mental states, and the causal transformations from state to representation to action.

In all these three conceptions of the mind Freud held on to a few guiding cognitive principles: (*a*) the mind is 'organized at different levels' of functioning—the conscious and the unconscious; (*b*) it is necessary and possible to 'compute' the cognitive nature and the relations between these systems in terms of both subject organising principles and object-ladenness; and (*c*) the aim of psychoanalytic meta-psychology is to provide syntactic, semantic and pragmatic rationales for computing these mental states and the processes by which they are internally as well as externally related. Arguably, it is the energic model which is the most sophisticated epistemologically and comes closest to satisfying the psychoanalytic definition of a conflictual and intentional mind. Though the other two models carry the germinal ideas of a structurally and functionally differentiated mind, they fail to grapple with issues of the differentiation of processes, object attachments and subject organising principles of mental life. This failure as a theory of psychology also signifies an epistemological failure of these models to be presented more formally, the possibility of which depends upon these differentiations.

That the suggested model of the mind be 'computable' is a necessary requirement of any cognitive science: the theory must show how the structures attributed to the system cause overt behaviour, using what may be called 'effective' procedures of a formal semantic theory. An effective procedure comprises the set of logical, and often mathematical, steps or the algorithms that would be required in detailing the processing and transfer of information from the unconscious, automated states to the conscious, agentive states. Pioneering attempts have been made in mathematical representations of psychoanalysis and the usefulness of such attempts have been lauded by analysts like Edelson. However, mathematisation of the theory is not the only way of its formalisation, other methods of knowledge representation can be and have been applied as well.

Formalisation, which Ricoeur has derided as the denudation of metaphorical quality from language, is indispensable. It serves the purpose of presenting a hypothesis in the epistemological form of a scientific law. Even the so-called 'coherence' of the 'narrative', the epistemological goal of the hermeneutic theory of psychoanalysis, would not be obvious unless formalisation of some nature is rigorously pursued. The possibilities of formulating effective procedures for psychoanalysis, for example, the algorithms computable for the defense mechanisms, complete psychoanalysis as a theory of understanding abnormal behaviour. The formalisation of psychodynamic processes such as conversion, sublimation, condensation, projection, repression, defense and resistance, serve the function of causally relating the mental system with overt behaviour. The energic model, whatever its metaphysical excesses and the limitations of its means of representation, formally gives the possibilities of causal agency of the system. Thereby it specifies the range of normal and abnormal actions possible for different mental states. Freud proposed a theory of how human action was caused by unconscious and conscious mental states by specifying these processes. Freud's meta-psychological distinction between the superego, the ego and the id provided the basic conceptual battery for formulating and integrating principles of information processing of the mind, on the basis of which the subject's behaviour could be explained. The theory not only explained actions which occurred in the clinic, but also possible actions not always seen in the clinic. Freud wanted his theory to explain the causal rules by which unconscious contents could be read by relating speech or actions with their unconscious pathogens. The theory specifies how mental states are transformed into action. Some analysts have argued that a causal transformational semantics, or a depth grammar, is required for psychoanalysis (Edelson, 1977, 1986b, 1989). Freud's 'energic' metaphor of the mind seeks to provide such a logic.

Systems of consciousness and unconsciousness are cognitive structures dissociated from each other, and related in their contents only through what Ricoeur has rightly called 'mythical' detours. However, they are *psycho*-mythical detours or 'imaginary' in a psychologically specific sense. Through its rigorous systematisation, psychology can identify the kinds of mythical detours that individuals engage in. The ego refers to the intentional, conscious and reality directed aspects of the mind: it is the organising principle of the mind, the central processing unit as it were. The id is not intentional but pleasure seeking and unconscious.

Both the conscious and the unconscious process information in different ways. The mind is more than the ego in including the unconscious realm also. The attribution of intentionality cannot be made to the unconscious which works, as it were, automatically and uncontrollably. The 'existence', or in other words, the causal efficacy of the unconscious is well documented in literature on cognition. Brewin (1989) has noted, while explicating the mental schema that can be assigned to the conscious and unconscious systems of the mind:

> Converging lines of evidence point . . . to the existence of two forms of information processing, one under the control of and one not under the control of the individual. Automatic processes are rapid, relatively inflexible, and difficult to modify; require minimal attention to occur; and may be activated without intention or awareness (p. 381).

Research in the primary process is also included in the psychoanalytic research programme. Holt (1976) has been sceptical of a *rigid* dichotomisation of the primary and the secondary processes and also of Freud's inclusion of all para-conscious phenomena under the rubric of the primary process. However, he has granted that underlying many such phenomena there *is* a conceptual unity which we may 'as well continue to call', as Freud did, the primary process. Referring to extensive extra-clinical research using Rorschach responses, Holt has noted: 'the statistical explorations of the various categories and scores derived from them support the proposition that Freud's descriptions of the empirical varieties of primary-process products ... describe something unitary' (p. 89). Evidence from these researches reveals that not only is the unconscious an empirical reality of cognition and not merely a meta-psychological fiction; it also shows that Freud was essentially correct in his understanding of the primary process as that which seeks immediate gratification and the secondary process as that which seeks realistic gratification. Despite the current status of this research and its theoretical and methodological problems, Holt has succeeded in showing the epistemological possibility of the measurement of the primary process and its differentiation on the basis of its relation to behaviour. This is a possibility which philosophical sceptics like Mac Intyre have questioned.

The question of the self in psychoanalysis is related to the ownership of mental contents. The mind processes and stores information at both the conscious and unconscious levels, but the contents may or may not be 'owned' by the ego (Eagle, 1988): 'What is distinctively psycho-analytic was Freud's claim that mental contents remained unintegrated within the personality, not because of constitutional weakness or because they were experienced in hypnoid states, but because they were purposively disowned and extruded from consciousness and from one's dominant ego organization' (p. 92). Alienation, or the relegation of certain mental contents to the realm of the unowned, is not a moral issue as it was made out to be by Sartre. Rather, it is a cognitive issue relating to the processes which control us in a way that certain cognitive or experiential aspects of our being are not perceived to be within the purview of our consciousness or action, and even ascribed to another, absent or 'bad' self, as happened in the case of Anna O. There is ample empirical evidence to show that conscious thought does not necessarily determine behaviour.

Eagle has pointed to evidence from studies on memory such as Tulving's to show that there is a difference between 'semantic' and 'episodic' memory. The latter stores information in an autobiographical, socio-temporal way. The former does not store information in a personalised way, and hence information codified in this memory is not 'owned': it is information that can be processed, as if abstractly, even when the *basis* for that information is oneself. Thus information about oneself need not always be ascribed by a person to himself. There is a cognitive sense in which a mental content can be 'mine' or 'not mine', a sense which is determined with respect to the literal ascription of mental contents to subjects. Of all mental contents attributed to the self, not every one of them needs to be owned. Some of them are disowned, and these are rendered unconscious. The disowned, unconscious mental contents are not themselves intentional, even though it is true that they are purposively disowned. This purposiveness indicates the intentional nature of the ego which disowns them, and not of the unconscious. Ricoeur and Habermas were intuitively and metaphorically correct in attributing 'self-deceit' to patients. Ego organisation cognitively transfers certain thoughts from the episodic to semantic memory, symbolically disowning it. Freud's aim was to show that the unconscious mental contents were purposively disowned by the ego and that these contents were however integrated into the overall organisation of the subject by pathological conflict resolution.

Though empirically the unconscious is a warranted cognitive realm, the philosophical dilemma for psychoanalysis has been whether the theoretical inference from conscious behaviour to the unconscious is legitimate. The sceptre hovering over a psychodynamic theory of the mind is that since the unconscious is unobservable and elusive, we cannot know it except indirectly, raising fundamental epistemological puzzles and intellectual paradoxes. Even as a psychological theory, the unconscious and the conscious require to relate and influence each other, because experience, both clinical and ordinary, shows that the two systems work in collusion. Even if some acts are unconscious and disowned by the ego, they are not altogether chaotic. They can be brought into some demonstrable connection with the rest of the psychological constitution of the subject. To make this connection demonstrable was Freud's therapeutic and theoretic concern. Sulloway (1979) has highlighted Freud's preoccupation with the issue of 'choice of neuroses' throughout his intellectual development. This issue focuses on how definite aspects of the subject's psychological constitution are necessarily related to specific forms of neurotic behaviour;

and how certain constellations of ego organisation choose specific routes of neurotic conflict resolution. A greater organising principle, other than the ego, is also to be assumed to be present in the mind. In literature (Weiss, 1988), there are two acknowledged notions of the unconscious, first, the 'dynamic unconscious' hypothesis, where the subject has no control over the unconscious; and second, the 'unconscious control' hypothesis, where the subject has some control over the unconscious, showing the unconscious to be the result of an agent's purposiveness. There is empirical evidence for the latter. This could indicate either that the ego assumes a higher order function of integration or that there is the need for the assumption of some hierarchical internal organisation and differentiation of subjective principles, such as, subsumption of the ego under the concept of the self.

Classical psychoanalysts such as Hartmann and Rapaport have argued in favour of the former, claiming a conceptual equivalence of the self and the ego. Kohut's self-psychology, Horney's socio-cultural psychology, Sullivan's interpersonal psychology and Adler's ego psychology have de-emphasised the ego and have argued for the self. This difference is not merely a linguistic difference, but a conceptual or cognitive one. The concept of the ego is distinctively and inseparably related to the concept of intra-psychic conflict, articulated specifically in terms of a theory of object relations. These are concepts which are dispensable to self-psychologists (for elaborate discussions see Wallerstein, 1983), but indispensable to ego psychologists. This philosophical difference between the self and the object has percolated into these theoretic differentiations in psychoanalysis also. Thinkers like Wallerstein and Rangell have attempted to evolve a more integrated vocabulary including the essential components of both a theory of the self and a theory of the object. The self may be referred to as the 'complex' cognitive or endopsychic representation of its own physical and psychological organisation, effected by the ego. The self is the result of a cognitive processing of information about its internal wholistic/particular organisation. The self can, in essence, be the object of the subject's intention, or what is referred to in the self-psychological tradition as a 'self object'.

An objection has been pertinently raised (Rangell, 1985) that while the psychoanalytic community at large sees the need for differentiation of subject organising principles of the mind, such differentiation is not recognised by the theory for the object of cognition. 'While the

individual as the subject of psychoanalytic study has gradually under-
gone increasing differentiation, as forces and structures interacting
within come to be further understood, the internal organization of the
object has been largely overlooked' (p. 303). According to Rangell,
what has been overlooked is that the intentional, object relation of the
mind need not necessarily be a relation to the whole object, but rather
to different parts, attributes or qualities of the object. The complex
theory of the subject is, for Rangell, to be supported by a complex
theory of the object. The mind relates both to itself and the object in a
complex way.

An object is the representational content that the subject's mental
states take on. All objects have a cognitive status. However, a differentiation of kinds of objects is necessary and Freud himself drew a
distinction between 'external' and 'internal' objects. The mind assigns
items either to an external reality or to an internal reality: 'Indications
of discharge through speech are also in a sense indications of reality—
but of thought reality not of external reality'. The need for a distinction became obvious to Freud when he had to painfully abandon his
'seduction' theory of hysteria, where he understood more clearly the
role played by fantasised objects. With respect to neurotics, Freud
said, 'What characterizes neurotics is that they prefer psychical to
factual reality and react just as seriously to thoughts as normal people
do to realities'. Freud noted elsewhere that 'frustration in regard to the
object brings on the outbreak of neurosis and that the neurosis involves
the renunciation of the real object'.

This Freudian notion of the cognitive capacity of the mind to order
things into two realms, the external and the internal, the real and the
imaginary, has been assimilated into contemporary psychoanalysis.
Jacques Lacan, for whom psychoanalysis is semiotic analysis, has made
a commensurate difference between the register of the 'symbolic' and
the register of the 'imaginary'. Edelson (1989), carrying this analogy
with language further, has used Chomsky's model of a transformational
generative grammar, and has viewed psychoanalysis as consisting of a
surface structure grammar of the 'conscious' and a deep structure
grammar of the 'unconscious'. Each of these grammars, Edelson has
shown, poses its own linguistic possibilities of formulation, formalisation, interpretation, translation and use, to a psychoanalyst. Piaget
noted a similar difference between the processes of assimilation to
internal reality, and accommodation to external reality. Edelson has
found it fruitful to use Susan Langer's distinction between 'discursive

symbols' and 'presentational symbols' as equivalent to Freud's distinction between psychic reality and external reality. The relations of the mind to these two kinds of object representations are different in nature, regulated in their motivations by two different principles of mental functioning, the reality principle and the pleasure principle. The relations with external object representations are relatively rigid, with attributions being defined by the philosophical principles of rationality of logic and language. The relations with internal objects are highly mutable and volatile, transgressing these principles through free associations. The secondary process functions metaphorically, transferring names, parts, qualities and attributes of one object to another imaginarily.

Exhaustive developmental, experimental cognitive studies by psychoanalytic researchers between the fifties to the eighties, such as those by Mahler and her colleagues, Blancks, Kramer, Settlage and others (Rangell, 1985; Posener, 1989) provide support for the empirical validity of psychoanalytic perspectives of self and object relations. These researches grew out of an internal criticism that even though Freud dealt extensively with developmental phenomena, such as oedipal life, and the processes of maturation from oral through anal to genital stages, he neglected research on children and depended, for his developmental views, on 'adultomorphic' premises. Following Anna Freud's attempt to set the stage for developmental psychoanalysis, and Piaget's work, psychoanalytic research has enfolded within itself the insights derived from these integrated researches on development. Particularly, the developmental and evolutionary nature of cognitive concept formation about both the self and object, the semantic separation of self and object and its differentiation through various stages of life have been extensively studied in the case of infants at different developmental stages, in adolescents, in parenthood and in adulthood.

VI

An epistemology for psychoanalysis acknowledges the extra-clinical normative determination of therapy through a meta-psychological theory and the nature of that theory as cognitive. The referent of the psychoanalytic cognitive theory is the ontological structure of the mind that it describes, defines and empirically verifies through its research programme. The intention of the scientific research programme is to arrive at a 'working model' of this structure. This intention moves all psychoanalytic research traditions, such as the self-psychological model and the object relations model of psychoanalysis, and the developmental model which is a kind of an attempt to integrate the two. The formulation of a 'core' psychoanalytic theory however, is, confounded because of the pluri-theoretical perspectives guiding these different empirical research traditions (Wallerstein, 1988, 1990). The referent of the theory, or the assumption that underlying all these plural perspectives is a common object, is also complicated. The extension of the theory is in fact overdetermined because the meaning or the intention of the theory is not precisely delimited.

The 'meaning' of psychoanalysis is problematised because of various contributing factors, including the fragmentation of Freud's theory into theoretically redefined models. This plurality need not be viewed as a threat for it is an invariable feature of all sciences, established or growing. However, a sense of urgency *is* instilled in one when confronted by philosophies, such as the existential and hermeneutic, which programmatically eschew the normative and epistemological advantages of science and herald the possibility of a purely speculative eclecticism untempered by empirical work. The use of Freud's theory in different disciplines and varied contexts, such as anthropology, literary criticism, social and political theory, and culture studies is not inherently pernicious. But it does obscure the meta-scientific commitments of a predominantly and self-definitively psychopathological theory. The 'causal' metaphor and the 'textual' metaphor of psychoanalysis, even though they generate stimulating philosophical issues and demarcate the philosophical limits of psychoanalysis, needlessly complicate pragmatics when they assume the further task of 'interpreting' Freud with *aclinical* interests.

The philosophical considerations of psychoanalysis have not contributed to the integration of plural perspectives into one semantic theory of understanding. On the contrary, by providing conflicting metaphors of the theory and its method they have pulled the science away from a much required theoretical integration. These two metaphors may be called two kinds of 'rhetoric' because of the singularly obdurate way in which these two discourses have been historically opposed and given as mutually exclusive methodological options to the psychoanalytic community in particular, and the social scientific community in general. It is patent that reading Freud's texts will not provide us with any cogent philosophical rationale for justifying one rhetoric over the other. A decision of the 'right' interpretation based on the text is really of no help: for the texts present a kaleidoscopic gestalt, showing us one or the other type of interpretation, the causal and the humanistic, depending upon our view.

Problems of translation from German to English have contributed to these philosophical forgings of diverse interpretations. It is peculiar that most of the European impressions of Freud have been singularly humanistic while the Anglo-American impressions have been more or less positivistic. The translator's preferences shape and guide the direction of the Freudian exegetic. Thus, for instance, Bettelheim (1983) has argued that the positivistic view of Freud as a mechanist is a distortion of his essential humanism. According to Bettelheim, this distortion is a consequence of James Strachey's biased efforts in his translations to present a respectable account of Sigmund Freud as a scientist. Socio-linguists may say that this interpretative schism in Freudian interpretation has arisen out of differences in the cultural outlooks in the reading of Freud.

Donald Carveth (1982) has rightly said in response to Bettelheim's claim about Strachey's scientistic preferences that it 'is appealing, but won't wash. Like the cultural milieu in which he worked, Freud suffered from the problem of "two souls in one breast": the romantic-humanist lived in continual tension with the positivist-reductionist' (p. 61). Hesse and Arbib (1986) have similarly noted:

> In Freud, then, we see the merging of at least two horizons as he comes to address the 'facts' of his self-analysis and the analysis of his patients the neurological perspective, which became implicit after 1895, yet surely shaped the essential terms of his metapsychology; and the humanistic perspective, especially the resonance of the Greek myths (p. 107).[3]

Edelson's observation must also be borne in mind, that the insecurity about the foundational status of psychoanalysis has led to an indiscriminate borrowing from psychologies which are presumed to be epistemically stronger. This borrowing has led to a number of mixed discourses often advocating the fruitfulness of being so 'mixed'. In an eclecticism which sooner or later leads to a diffusion and erasure of

---

[3] For detailed discussions, see Izenberg (1976).

theoretical boundaries, the requirement of what Edelson has called the 'core' theory is lost. There are, of course, practical and therapeutic advantages of being open to all theoretical possibilities. However, cognitive claims cannot be theoretically loose but must be epistemically rigorous and controlled. Such control is lost when there is no measure of comparability of theoretical competence and therapeutic performance between these different interpretations. The scientific challenge facing a practitioner would be to synthetically bring these possibilities together into some systematic, rational order and be able to choose truth tested and epistemologically strong explanatory claims from these for use in the clinic.

Freud himself contributed to the theoretic fragmentation, his profuse psychoanalytic writing, spread over the last 40 years of his life, is not at all conducive for providing such a 'unified discourse' of his theory. Many of his notions went through epistemic vicissitudes, and he clarified, revised, specified, rejected and altered his views. Wallerstein (1988) has noted the multi-perspectival psychoanalytic approaches to therapy, and has said that we have, existing side by side,

the American ego psychological (and by now post-ego psychological) school, the Kleinian, the Bionian, the (British) object-relational sometimes narrowed down to the Winnicottian, the Lacanian (largely outside but to a considerable extent in Europe and in Latin America inside our official ranks), and even in the United States, so long the stronghold of the unquestioning monolithic hegemony of the ego psychological metapsychology paradigm of Hartmann and Rapaport, where we have, however, recently witnessed the rise of Kohut's self psychology as a major alternative psychoanalytical theoretical perspective and, to a lesser extent as new schools, Mahler's developmental approach and Schafer's new voice or new idiom for psychoanalysis (p. 7).

Wallerstein has taken the problematic position as the central argument of both this (1988) paper as well as of a more recent paper (1990), that the 'common ground' of psychoanalysis lies in its *clinical* work. The comparability of diagnostic and prognostic possibilities of treatment and the allegedly comparable clinical successes of different theoretical models of psychoanalysis is used as an argument for the unity of the research programme.

However, it has been seen that dependence on the clinic for the

resolution of problems of theoretical delimitation, validation and verification, or providing a philosophical rationale for psychoanalysis as a
theory of cognition on the basis of its clinical efficacy, is eminently
questionable. It is correct to believe that both the therapy and the
science do require a common criteria of truth, that link success to
truth. Both a psychoanalytic clinician as well as a scientist need the
truth of the theory. Therapy and research are both built upon an
expectation that only a true claim 'p' leads to condition 's' through
actions $u \rightarrow z$ (where 'p' is a proposition, 's' is success and 'u to z'
are a set of actions that a therapist or a scientist has to perform). The
truth of 'p' is not concluded or inferred from success, but the satisfaction of the criteria of success is premised upon the truth of 'p'. For
example, glass can be cut with a diamond because diamond has the
physical properties required for cutting glass.

Similarly, a clinician erroneously infers the 'truth' of the law from
the success of his therapy, but he is justified in using a law provided he
knows it to be true. What is true extra-clinically is the truth to be used
in the clinic. What is 'true' is the same for both theory and therapy by
virtue of the empirical conditioning of the theory's meta-psychology and
it is this that justifies the use of the theory for therapy too. However,
'success' is defined in both therapy and research using different criteria
and different sets of goals. Thus, it would be problematic to equate the
logic of therapeutic inferences with the logic of research despite there
being a common truth for both research and therapy.

The rationale for clinical practice can only be extra-clinical, particularly relating to the responses of the community to the issues of
deciding the meaning and truth, or philosophical problems of the sense
and reference of psychoanalysis. The question of the possibility of theoretical unification of psychoanalysis or the determination of the meaning
of psychoanalysis cannot be brushed aside as clinically irrelevant.
There are well-known sociological problems of therapeutic fragmentation. The fact that there are over 250 unintegrated forms of psychotherapies has to be directly confronted. This clinical fragmentation
leads to several problems (Gill and Hoffman, 1982) such as the lack of
epistemological and methodological control in the clinic, allowing a
licentiousness with respect to therapeutic practices, philosophical
assumptions made about therapeutic notions such as transference,
counter-transference and cure, and about what constitutes a sound
approach to the patient, making an extra-clinical theory of therapy an
essential requirement.

Even though Wallerstein has erroneously argued for a clinical basis for the unity of psychoanalytic perspectives, he has perspicuously noted that the post-Freudian evolutes cannot be viewed as 'paradigms' in the Kuhnian sense, but rather as different models of the general psychoanalytic theory, implicitly granting the possibility of *theoretical* unity which he has openly denied. A paradigm connotes a division or discontinuity in the growth of knowledge and the theoretical incommensurability between two theories. Integration and the cumulative growth of knowledge is impossible. This view of scientific knowledge questions the possibility of stability of objective reference of theories, a possibility which is indispensable to a science with realistic goals. Freudian, Jungian and Adlerian psychoanalysis may perhaps be considered as paradigms. There would, of course, be certain unresolved questions whether this view is normative, based on the *a priori* theoretical differentiation between these theories, or whether it is political, based on the fact that institutionalisation of these theories has been historically different. The integration of psychoanalysis must be theoretic rather than clinically defined. The epistemology for such an integration allows the plural interpretative perspectives, or clinical models to discursively participate in an overall meta-psychology.

It is here that cognitive science contributes significantly by revealing the usefulness of the distinction between a theory and a model. The meaning of a theory is the precise delimitation of the different models of the theory with respect to the general theory. Philosophically, meaning is not derived from a theory of truth nor from a theory of translation. There is an important difference between knowing a proposition and knowing the truth of that proposition (Dummett, 1975). The former is based on the linguistic possibilities of statements and the latter on the procedural possibilities. A translation theory of meaning is circular, for effecting translations is premised upon knowing meanings. The meaning of a model has been given when every concept of the model has been defined and the rules for its use have been specified, and when it has been formally cast in the form of a theory of understanding. Specifying the meaning of psychoanalysis is individuating the different models of psychoanalysis.

Cognitive science is sympathetic to the delimitation requirement of models of the mind like psychoanalytic theory and provides the criteria required and procedures to be adopted for such delimitation. Understanding abnormal behaviour using these models would imply being committed to the condition of satisfying 'the principle of finitism'

(Johnson-Laird, 1983), i.e., the principle that the psychoanalytic theoretic 'cannot represent an infinite domain' (p. 398). The individuation of psychoanalysis in terms of its models is the delimitation of the theory with respect to its domain. Every model is to be meaningfully rendered by specifying its definition, scope and aims. Whatever Freud may have said about all the various aspects of cognition, the justification for the use of the general theory of psychopathology would be based upon evaluations and normative decisions regarding which of the clinical models are in a position to adequately stand up to modern conceptual, empirical and technical developments in psychotherapy. This is consistent with what Freud said: '(P)sychoanalysis has never claimed to provide a complete theory of human mentality in general, but only expected that what it offered should be applied to supplement and correct the knowledge acquired by other means' (S.E., Vol. 14, p. 50). Freud understood the need for delimitation of the theory and emphasised at several places that psychoanalysts should be concerned with '. . . what psychoanalysis is, how it differs from other ways of investigating the life of the mind, and precisely what should be called psychoanalysis and what would better be described by some other name' (S.E., Vol. 20, p. 7).

The delimitation of psychoanalysis occurs at two levels—first, at the general level of showing how psychoanalytic theory is different from, or the same as, other psychological and psychopathological models, such as behaviour therapy, cognitive science, developmental models; and second, at the level of delimiting clinical models from the general theory and specifying the interrelations between the model and the theory. The science of psychoanalysis is thus internally organised, in terms of the organisation between the general theory and its clinical models and the rationality that can be assigned to the relation between the two; and also externally organised, in terms of its relative differentiation from other related cognitive theories of abnormal behaviour. A theory of meaning for psychoanalysis would have to provide an adequate rationality for representation of knowledge at both these levels.

This view of psychoanalysis, its differentiation into the general meta-psychological theory and clinical interpretative models, is a cognitive view of science. Cognition naturally acts through the processes of naming, categorisation and hierarchical ordering. Scientific activity being essentially cognitive has these features too. The two foundationalist positions advocated two conflicting paradigms of scientific knowledge. External foundationalism, in attempting to bestow scientific theories with a unifying rationality, chose to reject the essential difference between the general theory and the clinical models by focusing exclusively on Freud's texts. Internal foundationalism characterised scientific theories as being perspectival and lacking a unifying rationality and viewed psychoanalysis as purely clinical; this, again, is a neglect of the essential difference. The cognitive view of science and psychoanalysis maintains the philosophical and practical difference between the clinical models and meta-psychology. The cognitive view of science is philosophically close to Wittgenstein's family resemblance theory: the clinical models form a family, drawing from and departing from meta-psychology. However, it is still possible to logically and empirically systematise the relations between any two models and between any model and the general theory. The cognitive view provides a comprehensive view of the structure of psychoanalysis as a science.

5

PSYCHOANALYSIS, SCIENTIFIC KNOWLEDGE AND HUMANISM

∎ ∎ ∎

I

Scientific knowledge is cognitive, intentional and empirical; psycho-analysis, as a human science, aims to be knowledge in this sense. The claim that scientific knowledge is cognitive implies that knowledge is a representation of the world effected by the mind's capacity to mani-pulate and organise symbols according to its perceptions of the world. Epistemology for a science needs ways of saying both that knowledge is intentional and also not subjective; is represented and also not narrativised. An acceptance of the notion of intention is not neces-sarily the rejection of empiricism, for intentions are not private, unspeakable entities uniquely experienced by the self. Rather, they can be brought within the purview of philosophical and psychological principles. There must be a possibility of providing a rationality to knowledge despite the fact that knowledge has its origins in the self. A science has realistic goals and expects to organise the world according to certain methods. These methods are limited, of course, due to creative and material constraints. These limitations notwithstanding, empiricism embodies the realistic goals of a science. These ideas form the basis of our characterisation of science as socio-cognitive.

This characterisation of science emphasises the social nature of knowledge. To say that knowledge is social does not imply that it is *relative* to a society, but that knowledge is in the *public* domain. The socio-cognitive characterisation of science does not mean that know-ledge is definitely based on *social* perceptions. It means that ideally, knowledge is for everyone. There are well-known problems about relativising knowledge to a society, even knowledge about the human, just as there are problems about relativising it to the self. The claim that science is socio-cognitive is not intended as a claim about its cultural determination, but about its psychological determination. It claims that knowledge is both generalisable *across* social differences and that human cognition makes this generalisability possible. Human nature is assumed to have a commonness which is embodied in a society. Knowledge, it is also assumed, is the product of this commonness rather than of the differences between individuals or between societies. We would say that this commonness is the very basis of our life experience: the possibility of a society depends on this assumption.

The psychological notion of intention is central to the socio-cognitive view of scientific knowledge. Intention implies that which brings a self in relation to itself, society and objects of the world, through the use of a language. Intention connects knowledge with the world. Intentionality is not an empty, experiential directedness. It has a cognitive dimension and comprises the range of psychological functions that the mind performs in relation to the world. The mind not only experiences objects through intentionality; it also assigns patterns and meanings to symbols through which it represents objects. The mind categorises its experience in terms of objects, it defines these categories and makes demarcations and differentiations among them. Knowledge of the self and the world is possible because of these intentional functions of the mind.

The psychologically constituted nature of knowledge is, however, not only relative to the human mind but also to reality. It should be possible to state both the nature of the mind and cognition that makes knowledge possible as well as the nature of the object. That knowledge is cognitive and intentional rules out neither the psychological nor the objective constraints of knowledge. The naturalness of knowledge refers to both the mind and its intended object.

The hermeneutic position that a science of psychology cannot be and should not be objective immediately denies the psychological intentional basis of knowledge. Any notion of intention is philosophically incomplete unless it specifies both its objective and subjective referents. A theory of intentionality includes both a theory of the self and a theory of the object. It describes how the mind organises both the self and the object. A theory of the object is required for intentionality to be possible. The empiricistic denial of intention, on the other hand, is a denial of objectivity, because objects would be like the

Kantian noumena, unsaid and unknown unless intended. A philo-sophical sceptic who denies either the intentional or the objective constitution of knowledge is effectively, a double sceptic, denying both.

There are both subjective and objective constraints on knowledge and these constraints are equally specifiable. Epistemology provides the criteria for the possibility of describing how something exists outside the mind. This is binding on a theory of the mind as well. It does seem rather absurd to say that 'the mind exists outside the mind' and methodological reductions of the mind to its phenomenological status constitute the philosophical responses to this absurdity. How-ever, this seeming absurdity is only equal to the linguistic absurdities and other logical paradoxes that such reductionism issues forth, for instance, 'the mind is a fiction' raises the question of *what* created it. Any response to this question will have to necessarily be in terms of a theory of the mind, where the mind is treated as a natural object. Equally absurd is the claim that 'the mind is the brain'; it raises the question of how this claim is even philosophically possible, without assigning some autonomous epistemic status to the nature of 'claims'. To do this, a theory of intentionality is required. The apparent absurdity of saying that the mind exists outside the mind will disappear, once its linguistic formulation is changed to saying that third person scientific statements about the mind can be constructed in logical independence of the mind which thinks about it.

Knowledge not only has a cognitive nature, but also a normative nature. Knowing the self and the world is a first order function of the mind. However, there are second order, philosophical functions which specify how the first order functions are to be accomplished. These second order functions also need systematisation and representation; they require the mind's attention. Intentionality should not be under-stood only in terms of the construction of a first order semantic vocabulary such as objects, but also the second order meta-vocabulary. The latter would specify the criteria for the ordering of items and the goals of such ordering. The discipline which results from the first order function is called science, and that which results from the second order function is known as epistemology. Both science and epistemology are equally intentional and equally socio-cognitive.

It is important to retain the normative dimension of knowledge. There is a philosophical difference between the logically *a priori* and the psychologically *a priori*. It is this difference which distinguishes the normative from the cognitive: what is psychologically necessary may not be logically necessary. The psychological constitution of knowledge in terms of the universalisability of human psychological nature and knowledge as the output of this nature, is not equal to its logical determination. Knowledge as intentional and perceptual are psychological notions and specify *how* knowledge is obtained. Yet the norms binding on them are to be given logically independent of these notions by indicating in a philosophically adequate way *what* knowledge, intention and perception are. The psychological basis specifies the empirical conditions of knowledge, and the normative basis provides the rational conditions of knowledge. Knowledge has both natural and normative limits. This view of science as being cognitively determined is itself a normative view of science and not a natural view of science. It states that science is such, because the claims that it makes are philosophically viable and not because empirically all sciences have these features.

Even though all knowledge is symbolically represented, there are cognitive distinctions between different organisations of knowledge and also criteria for such distinctions. Symbols are individuated, differentiated, arranged, systematised and named; they are given meanings, purposes and goals; rules are specified for their use. The structural organisation and use of symbols is made on the basis of the intentions of a community speaking a particular language. It is arranged into different languages and discourses. The philosophical problem of demarcation, posed by both the foundationalist traditions, relates to differentiating organisations of symbols into discourses. It is a response to the need for making discursive distinctions among human, intentional orderings of symbols. Epistemology provides the criteria for making these distinctions legitimately. Science, too, is a human discourse. It is a language game, systematically ordered into disciplines and sub-disciplines, each with its own specific aims. As a language, science is rule bound with realistic goals. An epistemology of science specifies how the realistic goals of a science are fulfilled, by proposing a theory of truth, meaning and explanation.

II

Truth in a science is a semantic, epistemological notion serving the pragmatics of attaining scientific knowledge and not a syntactic, ontological one. Popper's and Grünbaum's views of science assume that truth *is* ontological. This is the early Wittgensteinian view of knowledge which states that an artificial logical language is the syntax which directly gives the picture of the world. Truth, according to this primitive view of science, is syntactical. This equivalence between language and ontology, between syntax and truth, is questionable. Truth and objectivity are linked not directly, but indirectly with ontology, through experiment. The relation between truth and the world is a semantic one, and not a syntactic one. A logical syntax does not directly lead to truth, but we intend the connection between the syntax and the world by means of scientific procedure. The notions of meaning and intentionality are presupposed in a science's quest for truth, for they refer to our capacity to make a scientific language intend the world. Truth is what we make the scientific language do by assigning it a particular status with respect to the language game.

Truth is epistemological and not ontological. The goals of truth and objectivity of a science are attained by manipulating the methodological and pragmatic possibilities of the notion of truth. Philosophical theories of truth lead to what Tarski (1949) has called a meta-language, that is, making an object language possible. The language of truth is a language which we use in specific ways in a science. In so far as it is a language, it is presided over by intentions. The intention of assigning a place to truth in science is to bring knowledge within the scope of human cognition. Truth, like other epistemological notions, serves a cognitive function making objectivity possible and is equally determined by the limitations of language, particularly the formal language in which it is usually cast, and limitations of perceptual and non-perceptual cognition. There can be (and is) agreement and disagreement about truth, for truth is not a self-evident ontology. The epistemological discursiveness of 'truth' is patent in the canonical disagreements between coherence, correspondence, consensual and pragmatic notions of truth.

The place of truth in a philosophy of science is to provide ways of making an extra-theoretic reference to an object. Philosophically, truth is a notion by which we can say that the intentional connection with the representation of an object refers to something outside that representational connection itself. Truth is intimately linked with the possibility of picking out items which naturally fall within the extension of a concept. Truth has to do with extension. The truth of a law in a scientific theory helps researchers to pick out natural objects in the world named by that law.

Truth gives us the philosophical sanction or justification to intervene with objects of reality included in the conceptual inventory of a theory. Truth is at the basis of action and practice. We are able to act in the world when we believe that the assumptions we make about the world are actually true. Certain procedures independently validate these assumptions as being in fact true. For example, if we know that sugar is sweet, we might want to add sugar to coffee if we like sweetened coffee.

This is the case whether the reality in question is given by a theory of the external world or by a theory of human psychology. The manipulation of not only objects, but also ourselves and society is possible because of this. Freedom to act, our faith that our choices are rational, is based on another belief that what we believe about the world and ourselves is also true. In cognitive sciences like psychoanalysis too, it is truth which makes therapy possible. The aim of knowing truth, in psychoanalysis, is to provide what Mc Culloch (1986) has called an 'intervention strategy', that is, to provide a framework 'essentially to act upon a system or produce or prevent change in it' (p. 72). The notion of truth lies at the basis of action: it gives us some prior conception about what *is* in the world so that we can manipulate that which is.

This semantic view of truth is not a specification of a 'theory' of truth in the classical sense, but uses the Wittgensteinian notion of a criterion. Wittgenstein differentiated between a 'criterion' and a 'symptom': 'X' is a criterion by virtue of a definition, convention or a rule of language. If 'a' satisfied criterion 'x' of 'b', 'a' is necessarily equal to 'b'. 'X' is only a symptom if such a rule cannot be provided and no necessity is entailed in the identity relation between 'a' and 'b'. For example, an animal being a mammal is necessary if it is viviparous but not if it is biped, for viviparity defines a mammal, but not being biped. Pragmatically, sciences use the *criteria* of truth rather than a theory of truth, where the criteria specify the methodological rules. Truth is a language game and there are many ways of playing this game. What is possible in the sciences are only the criteria of truth. As a language game, truth has an aim, namely, empirical justification. The aim to arrive at truths through the adoption of the procedures of science is rule bound. Wittgenstein (1974b) has noted that 'justifying the evidence, comes to an end;—but the end is not certain propositions striking us immediately as true, i.e., it is not a kind of seeing on our part; it is our acting, which lies at the bottom of our language-game' (§ 204).

Science needs a notion of truth, because truth is useful for its pragmatic ends. But scientists can develop different criteria to use at different times. Psychoanalysis also has to use different criteria of truth. For example, when Freud inquired into hysterical behaviour, his methodological interest was directed at giving him an accurate picture of the psychic structure of a hysterical mind (Rubinstein, 1983). The criterion for determining truth here was correspondence, or the view that a logical picture would lead to a picture of the world. When Freud gave up the seduction theory as an aetiological explanation of hysteria and proposed an alternative theory of infantile sexuality, he used the criterion that different truths must cohere together: the number of fathers who were child abusers was not compatible with the number predicted by his theory. The intended function of a criterion of truth in a science is empiricism. That is, to allow scientists to say that the items intended by the theory have to be empirically justified as existing, in whatever form, physical or psychic, independent of the theory as an object of the world.

To claim that scientific knowledge is 'objective' is to propose a theory of the object and the methods by which this object may be 'real'ised by the methodological criteria of truth. Truth gives us 'objective' knowledge in this sense. This is true of both the human sciences as well as the natural sciences: the philosophical characterisation of an 'object' of knowledge is the same, whether the object to be known is human or natural. Epistemology provides *formal* criteria for assigning an 'object' status to an item. Epistemology also specifies the conditions that must be necessarily fulfilled for labelling something an 'object'. Philosophically, an object is describable on the basis of these criteria. For example, it is assigned features and patterns, primary and secondary qualities; it is introduced into different sets and classes of objects; its relations with respect to space and time are specified; it is assigned quantities such as numbers, identities and plurality; it is compared and indexed taxonomically, etc.

The difference between human and natural objects of knowledge is not due to any formal or radical difference in what constitutes an object. The difference is rather in the *contents* of characterisation of these objects. Humans cannot be precluded from the realm of objects on formal, philosophical grounds. As objects of scientific knowledge, humans share the philosophical features of natural objects. Epistemologically, humans and natural things must be put on a par, if knowledge is to be formally possible.

Both physical and human objects of knowledge share several common formal features. Physical objects are also unique; there is an indeterminacy about their nature due to an essential indeterminateness and variability; natural objects are historically constituted and temporal. On the other hand, humans share with natural objects possibilities of generalisability and stability of nature and action. The epistemological limits to both human and natural objects are the same: at some point, physical objects vanish beyond our language into ineffability where we are burdened with a scepticism; and contrariwise, human objects do emerge out of indeterminateness into the eminently effable luminescence of language and knowledge. Issues of knowledge and scepticism, of our being able to say in philosophically adequate ways, when we 'know' and when we do not, are common to both the human and the natural sciences.

However, concession can be made to the natural, empirical difference that sets humans apart from other objects. Human sciences differ from the natural sciences on account of the difference in their intrinsic *nature* between humans and other objects. Intentionality, consciousness and freedom, notions which appear to set humans apart from physical objects, are natural and not formal features of being human.

To 'find' truth is to be able to say that the structure that language has captured exists in the world. Decisions, mainly procedural, are involved in our being able to say this. The task of finding truth involves specifying ways of action and scientific communities attempt to find truth by specifying the rules of experiment. Here, there is the assumption of a pragmatic criterion of truth, that empirical success is related to truth. The instrumentality of truth is, nevertheless, tied to some conceivable correspondence with reality. In doing science we *expect* to learn more about the world we live in. Any attribution of a semantic nature to truth must accept this intention built into all sciences that our cognition provides an item of a language to refer to natural kinds of objects. A reality commitment is inherent in all scientific ventures. As seen earlier, a science must respond to the issue of object reference: of what language refers to and how this reference is stable across temporal or cultural changes in language. The possibility of objective knowledge depends on this. A scientific methodology specifies when objective knowledge in this sense has been obtained. The reality commitment of a theory is the *a priori* on which scientific research programmes are based. This commitment is primarily a cognitive commitment, a tacit expectation, or an intention on the part of scientific communities to carry on with the task of knowledge construction by assuming that truth orders objects of the world, that objects exist outside our cognitive or subjective pictures of them. Scientific research presupposes this intention. Finding truth through method is the satisfaction of this intention.

Realism in science, whether 'scientific' or 'prospective' (Brown, 1990), is an epistemic attitude, referring to this intentional commitment of scientific communities. Realism 'among the growing number of philosophical theories which like many scientific theories are partly metaphysical and partly empirical; it has implications beyond experience but is testable by experience' (Leplin, 1984, p. 7). Realism, as a philosophical view of science, requires a theory of the object referred to by the domain of that science; the possibility of referential stability across interpretative differences; a theory of experiment specifying *how* objective knowledge is obtained; and a theory of evidence specifying *when* such knowledge has in fact been obtained. It was seen in the previous chapter how psychoanalysis embodies these intentions by being committed to resolving the problems of delimitation of the general theory and its different models; the unification of these models theoretically; as well as in relation to empirical, extra-clinical research.

The objectivity of a science is linked to truth, and truth is tied to procedure and experiment. Experiment, the central agenda of any scientist, is an autonomous activity having its own rationality. It has a formal determination, and its goals and function are fixed with reference to the larger scientific programme (Hacking, 1983, 1988; Brown, 1987; Heelan, 1988). Experiment is premised upon the philosophical *a priori* that a hypothesis is capable of being tested for truth independently, that is, the outcome of the experiment can conclusively state the truth or the falsity of the hypothesis. The ideal condition that all notions of experiment strive to obtain is for ways of devising experiments so that it could be legitimately said that the data obtained through observation has been treated independently of the hypotheses being tested. Current debates (Achinstein, 1983) on epistemic control, relevant evidence, confirmation, particularly in induction and probability theories, seek to philosophically satisfy this ideal. The theory–observation distinction denied by post-positivistic thinking is in fact the rationale on which all experiments are based. It should be possible to say *a priori* regarding any individuated experiment, the hypothesis that is being tested, and the phenomenal presentations which will or will not bear out the hypothesis. This should be possible despite the background laws and other assumptions being made. The epistemological and methodological conditions that Popper and Grünbaum have correctly imposed upon the sciences, such as falsifiability and the 'declared consequence restriction', are attempts to obviate the possibility that data may be theoretically contaminated.

A scientific methodology provides norms for evolving procedures which overcome this problem of contamination. If it is unconditionally granted that all evidence is epistemically contaminated by the theory, the fundamental question as to why scientists accumulate evidence remains unexplained. Scientific activity will itself be depleted of any rationality whatsoever. An explanation of the evidence collecting activity of scientists is possible only in terms of the realist assumptions that scientific theories do intend to make reality commitments; and also that there are legitimate ways of making cognitive distinctions between 'theory' and 'observation' in our scientific procedures. Establishing this legitimacy in experiment allows us to say that a theory has a referent independent of it. Explaining the empirical success of science, which is obvious to everyone, is possible only if we assume that nature is law-like and that we are in a position to know these laws. Freud made these assumptions in his science. The empiricistic ideal (of defining philosophical standards that will render experimental evidence conclusive) satisfies the cognitive principle that science makes reality commitments.

Of course, there are inherent limitations to justification and methods, which defy the assimilation of the world into neat sets of lawfulness. Empirical justification, too, like other epistemological ventures has to do with rule following and linguistic decision-making, as Wittgenstein has pointed out. The statement, 'this is red' is justified because 'redness' is a concept which is linguistically determined, involving our capacity for the acquisition and use of language. Wittgenstein asked in his *Philosophical Investigations*, 'How do I recognize that this is red?—I see that it is *this*: and then I know that that is what this is called' (1974a, § 380). The language of observation is a language; it is neither pre-linguistic nor pre-theoretic. Observation cannot be any more private or ostensive than feelings and emotions. The 'thisness' of observation would have no practical implications for a science unless systematically codified in a scientific language.

That this codification of observation is in relation to the theory, or the overall goals of the science is of course to be granted in a qualified way. Observation becomes relevant to a researcher only when a cognitive structure has been attached to it. It is possible for a researcher to say what is an observation only against the non-problematically assumed background theory and its universe of facts. However, to affirm the cognitive basis of all methods of observation is not to claim that all observation language is theory language. Experiment requires the pragmatic distinction between the non-problematically assumed background theory and the evidential premises which will render a problematic law, after experiment, non-problematic or 'proved'. The possibility of testability, truth and objectivity lies in this distinction. A science requires ways of saying both that observation is based on the theoretical and procedural selectivity of the researcher, and that despite this, research proceeds because of the possibility of making empirically relevant observations (Glymour, 1983). It is one thing to say that all observation makes sense only against the use of a cognitive map and another thing to conclude from this that in scientific practice it is not possible to say what will count as an 'observation'. For example, to see a hammer as a 'hammer' is indeed to use a cognitive structure about tools, but the hammer would not thereby be rendered a non-observation or an illusion to someone looking at the hammer who is not used to the language game of hammers.

Given the complex science of today, its sophisticated instrumentation and tools of analyses, it is indeed a misnomer to call, say, the photoelectronic flash in a nuclear chamber or the electronic printer output which gives us the measurable details of the frequency of neutrino interactions as observations, without invoking a theory. Epistemic components are certainly involved in scientific observation. We do not 'see' neutrinos any more than we see the mind, though we do 'see' something (flashes or patterns of behaviour) which allows us to talk coherently about truth, confirmability and evidence and even about the existence of neutrinos and mind. The theoretical links or laws between objects can be worked out, but empirically testing for these will clinch the case in favour of some and not the others. For this, it must be granted that perceptual seeing is also required: that over and above theory and method, their separate rationalities and limitations, there is a way of speaking about observation which will allow researchers to make useful cognitive distinctions between truth and falsity, evidence, confirmation, etc.

The response to the problem of theory-ladenness of all observation is not to deny the distinction between theory and observation altogether. Rather, a separate philosophical rationality to observation must be provided as contemporary philosophers have realised, a rationality which will sustain the cognitive enterprise that science is. Philosophical denials of the distinction rarely took into account the fundamentally cognitive nature of observation, simply examining the notion either historically or in the abstract terms of the science itself and its linguistic or theoretic formation. To understand the place of observation in experiment, a cognitive theory of perception is also required.

Using studies on cognition, Brewer and Lambert (1992) have shown how observation is indeed theoretical as Hanson and Kuhn, among others, have claimed. These studies, however, stress that where the incoming sensory stimulus is unambiguous and strong, theoretical dependence is low, and such dependence becomes higher where the stimulus is weak. Other than showing that theory dependence of observation is measurable, this study points to the gross perceptual nature of observation, limited by our biological nature and enhanced by instrumentation, which cannot be disregarded.[1]

Pierre Duhem's classic paper on the inconclusivity of experiment and of the open-endedness to providing 'evidence' to laws is widely used to argue for the inconclusivity of verification and truth. Thus, Waismann (1968) has noted: 'An experiential statement is, as a rule, not conclusively verifiable for two different reasons: (1) because of the existence of an unlimited number of tests; (2) because of the open texture of the terms involved' (p. 41). The assuredly open-textured nature of the experiment indicates only that science progresses by collating and assimilating different, even conflicting, truths obtained through the experiment. But it cannot be inferred from this that the experiment is inconclusive. Only when one holds on to the idea that science leads to ultimate and final truths and science is composed of only such truths, one questions the conclusivity of the experiment. Experiments, and the truths borne out by such experiments, are conclusive, notwithstanding that future experiments may undermine these truths and favour others. Working towards conclusivity provides the desired epistemological framework to systematise knowledge. Conclusivity is defined with respect to our cognition and methodology

[1] Also see Brown (1987) for extensive discussions on the nature of observation particularly with respect to instrumentation, and for discussions regarding the Hanson–Kordig controversy about what Galileo actually 'saw'.

specifies the cognitive criteria of conclusivity such as induction o falsification.

Reality itself has an important role to play in experiment. Experiment is important in science because it allows reality to assume a role in its outcome. In any experiment, there is, over and above the interests of the research communities, their epistemological choices, experimental design, criteria of testing and observability, etc., the unknown input of reality which decides the outcome of the experiment. Objectivity in scientific research is a cognitive ideal of measuring this uncontrolled and uncontrollable input. The need for experiment is to allow for the surprises that reality might have in store for us, which can potentially question our theoretical models and their methodological derivatives and impel us to reconsider them. Of the range of activities that scientists perform, it is through the experiment that reality can show itself to us.

An instrumental view of scientific method is held by some philosophers, such as Larry Laudan. They have argued that observation, truth and scientific method are instrumental in fulfilling a science's larger aims. This view that the method fulfils the aims of a science is partially correct as was discussed at some length in the introduction. However, an essentially instrumental view of scientific method overlooks the normative dimension of method. Larry Laudan's view, for example, cannot be justified because he has emphasised the instrumental dimension over the normative (for critical discussions of this view of science, see Siegel, 1990). The instrumental view of science falters because it cannot grant epistemological restraint on subjective or social beliefs and relativises the goals of the science with respect to the subject and society. Siegel has argued against this position with the help of an example: the double-bind method of empirically testing for drug efficacy is arguably better than the single-bind method not because the merits of the former are instrumentally better than the latter; but because of the capacity of the former to respond adequately to normative issues in methodology. Methodologically, the double-bind can overcome many of the problems of the single-bind method. The choice of a method in a science, a choice which its methodology aims to prescribe, is to allow for talk about rationality in a non-instrumental sense.

We clearly endorse the external foundationalists' emphasis on the normativity of knowledge and the conclusivity of the experiment in the determination of truth, though the reduction of methodology and truth to a single criterion and single method is questionable. The idea that unless extra-clinical *inductive* evidence is provided for psycho-analysis, the foundational problems of the science remain unresolved may be a novel idea to philosophers of science, coming as it does in the wake of Popperian philosophy. But it is not new to the psychoanalytic community. Even Freud, though sceptical of extra-clinical testing, demanded inductive generalisability over cases for holding on to his causal claims, which motivated him to document his case studies with philosophical sensitivity and rigour. Since Freud's times, however, there have been several related trends of interdisciplinary researches in psychoanalysis, some of which have been referred to in earlier discus-sions of the self and object theory. Amply representative of the empiricistic tradition, Wallerstein (1986b) has rightly noted in a review essay:

> I have simply tried to indicate that I feel there is sufficient warrant for such empirical testing in ways that are alert to the subtlety and complexity of subjective clinical phenomena, while simultaneously loyal to the canons of objective scientific method, and that this *has* been pursued as an activity, within psychoanalysis before and since the rise of the various challenges to the propriety of such activity from the various quarters I have addressed in my consideration of the place of our discipline as a science, the hermeneutic-pheno-menological challenge in its various expressions, and more cursorily, the claims of the logical-positivists, of Karl Popper, and most currently, of Adolf Grünbaum (p. 25).

Some of the trends that Wallerstein has perceived as important and contributing to modern psychoanalytic research include (*a*) studies in infant and child development, beginning with Margaret Fries and Sibylle Escalona in the forties, extending through Mahler, and continuing in the works of John Bowlby, Sylvia Brody, Rene Spitz and Peter Wolff. These works have led to methods of psychobiological monitoring by Robert Emde, Annelise Korner, Lou Sander, Daniel Stern, among others. (*b*) Studies in psycho-semantics, which began in the thirties, by Flanders Dunbar, Franz Alexander and Thomas French, Felix Deutsch and Sydney Margolin, leading to modern behavioural medicine. (*c*) Development of psychophysiology, with contributions from Charles Fisher, understanding psychoanalytic theory through research in behavioural and neuroscientific ventures. (*d*) Experimental cognitive studies within a psychoanalytic theory of dreams, imagery and suggestion, initiated in the twenties by Otto Poetzl, Allers and Teler, amplified in the fifties by Fisher, and extended by George Klein. Wallerstein himself, along with others like Thoma and Kachele in Germany, Hartvig Dahl, Merton Gill, Mardi Horowitz, Otto Kernberg, Luborsky and Strupp, has been long involved in defining, organising and collating an empirical pool that will stand warrant for psychoanalytic laws. Wallerstein (1986b) has recognised, as do Holt, Edelson, Marmor (1986) and others, that the contributions to this empirical pool come from 'several other lines of psychoanalytic research activity either intrinsic to and contained within the corpus of psychoanalytic theory, or representing interfaces with cognate realms of intelligence of human behaviour' (p. 20). It is possible to view psychoanalysis, contra Grünbaum, as a discipline with many ramifications of research bound by empirical criteria.

'Truth' for not only psychoanalysis comes from several different sources. We may note that a tradition of direct extra-clinical quantitative testing exists in the research programme, such as those undertaken by Kline (1972, 1986), Fisher and Greenberg (1977), Eysenck and Wilson (1973); extra-clinical case studies using epistemologically refined models of documenting and analysing cases, such as pursued by Luborsky (1986), Marshall Edelson, Rubinstein, Silberschatz, Gill and Hoffman; social interaction studies in families by Hauser, Powers, Nom, Jacobson and Follansbee; and other indirect empirical work such as in the cognitive sciences, neurosciences, animal studies, child psychiatry and psycho-linguistics. This methodological complexity does compound the question of arriving at truth, begging further methodological reconsiderations. It is not immediately clear whether these different sciences share the same theoretical premises and how their methodologies are comparable. But it does not necessitate the rejection of the concept of truth altogether, as the humanists have argued, nor its relativity or inconclusivity. Rather, as Hesse (1974) has noted of the sciences in general

Sometimes comprehensive theories of maximum empirical content are appropriate, sometimes instrumentalist predictions, sometimes inductive inferences. It is a naive reading of the history of science to suppose that different methodologies are necessarily in conflict, given their different aims. The logic of science should provide a comparative study of such methodologies, rather than a partisan polemic on behalf of some against others (p. 7).

Not every problem faced by a researcher in a science is related to truth and evidence and scientists do not regularly find themselves in a quandary about the truth of a law. Epistemology for a science requires not only a theory of truth and evidence but also a theory of meaning and explanation. The former falls within the methodological realm involving the autonomous scrutiny of experimental possibilities, while the latter is associated with the linguistic nature of a scientific theory, necessitating the resolution of problems of definition and the delimitation of the central concepts of the theory.

An epistemology for science needs to make a distinction between truth and evidence on the one hand, and meaning and explanation on the other. Hempel believed that statistical relevance *is* causal relevance and that truth *explains* causally. Hempelian viewpoints have often philosophically argued that '(A) necessary condition for a sentence's stating a deterministic law of nature is that it be a true, universally quantified generalization' (Ruben, 1990, p. 100). However, this unqualified equivalence between explanation, statistical relevance and causal relevance is questionable (Sober, 1987). The explanatory possibilities of a phenomenon are many, given the multi-model nature of the sciences. For example, the Freudian theory is sustainably interpreted as many psychotherapeutic models such as the systems model, the ego psychological model and the object relations model, all of which are independently testable. For the general theory, different sets of truth claims can be derived for testing because of the possibility of different interpretations of the theory. Truth testing involves selective inferences from the general theory. There will always be sets of empirically untreated theory and unwarranted assumptions, which however may be required to hold the conceptual vocabulary together for providing explanations. Making sense of the empirically treated part may be impossible if we root out the untreated parts. Empirical verification is always an incomplete, on-going activity. This is why a scientific epistemology needs an explanation. An explanation makes use of the relations existing between the central concepts of a theory. Sometimes an explanation also contains a true hypothesis or a law.

The earlier, simple view of science believed that a scientific explanation is merely specifying true hypotheses of a theory. Today, many philosophers acknowledge that a scientific explanation goes beyond the truth of a theory's laws. An explanation gives a causal story and statistical analysis gives *evidence* for this story. Laws or truths of a science have the feature of being *embedded* in an explanatory causal model, evidence for which comes from statistical analysis. The explanatory theory is broader than the true theory. It may be the case that the explanatory theory is not fully supported by empirical facts. However, without the explanatory theory, the empirically warranted truths may be meaningless. Contrary to the traditional view that truths are epistemologically final and head the priorities of knowledge, it is now recognised that truth is 'incompleteable within the terms of its own vocabulary' (Ruben, 1990, p. 116). Kinoshita has referred to this explanatory background commitment on which truth rests as a 'realm of discourse' (Kinoshita, 1990, p. 305). A truth would not be recognisable as a truth unless it is viewed in the context of an explanatory theory.

The various Freudian interpretations may be viewed as explanatory models of psychoanalysis. Explanatory models have a clinical nature, compared to the general theory, which has a cognitive nature. The theory and observable consequences of a science are essentially cognitive: they are universal and idealised descriptions of phenomena statistically generalised over many instances. Epistemologically, what makes this scientific generality applicable to particular instances is a notion of explanation. A scientific theory being abstract, cannot directly be applied to particular phenomena. Truth and evidence, being probabilistic, cannot be particular. An explanation underlies an understanding of particulars. Knowing the uniqueness of an object is possible by providing an explanation. An explanation, such as a clinical explanation of abnormal behaviour, draws from the theory and available empirical research, and integrates them into a causal story of particular presentations of abnormal behaviour in the clinic. A clinical psychoanalytic model is an explanatory model because it aims to be an integrated model, drawing from both the general theory and existing empirical work. A scientific explanation of a particular clinical phenomenon is neither strictly theoretical, nor strictly observational: it brings together different logical and empirical relations into a meaningful causal narrative. A general theory such as general meta-psychology is not explanatory, only the clinical models are explanatory. We have already elaborated the role of the clinical models and how they explain by providing us '. . . with an inventory of what sorts of entities, mechanisms, processes, etc. (observable and unobservable) exist, and tell us something about the relations between them' (Gasper, 1990, p. 292). Philosophically, scientific explanations 'explain by telling us of an entity what it is' (Kinoshita, 1990, p. 304).

Yet, we know the epistemological problems in the clinic and must acknowledge the need for sufficient controls for differentiating good explanations from bad ones. This is recognised in the psychoanalytic research programme and many researchers are involved with refining the procedural aspects of the case study method. The objection of lack of controls and consequent epistemic contamination is believed to be minimised to a large extent by introducing both external and internal controls in the case study method. External forms of 'control' in the clinic have been mainly in the form of recording instruments, such as a tape recorder or video. There are ethical problems involved here, but clearly the epistemic advantage of using these external controls are evident and documented. Another form of external control is to make documentation open to public scrutiny and accessible to interested researchers, an attempt which is recent and growing in response to vocal objections to the secrecy traditionally maintained by psychoanalytic clinicians. Edelson, for instance, has noted: 'Psychoanalysis is a body of knowledge that is important to a wider intellectual and scientific community than that comprised by psychoanalytic practitioners. In its documentation, it should follow the scholarly practices, and accept the standards, of that community' (1986b, p. 97). Sherwood has also observed that 'in perhaps no other field was so great a body of theory been built upon such a small public record of raw data' (1969, p. 70). Wallerstein (1986a) and Holt (1985) have lamented the reluctance of psychoanalysis to divulge data for research purposes. As a palliative, Holt has referred to Dahl's meticulous collection of a library of case study material. Other than these, attempts have been made to include controls within the case study method itself. The presentation of a case as a 'causal story' can be written with lucidity and rigour provided a few discursive tools are used. Edelson, for example, has worked out in some detail the conditions that must be met for preparing a case study.

Given this complexity of the theory and method in psychoanalysis, philosophers can address a number of questions other than the orthodox foundationalist one of the scientific nature of psychoanalysis. They can, for example, attempt to make the prevailing psychoanalytic methodology stronger by considering the following problems that extra-clinical studies face: despite the empirical data available from within the discipline and from without, through the adoption of different types of experimental methods, a comprehensive collation and analysis of this data and the integration of this analysis with respect to meta-psychology is yet to be accomplished. This is a problem which is faced by most other social sciences as well, where there is excessive but unintegrated data. Since evidence relevant to psychoanalysis cannot be clinical evidence in the classical sense, philosophy can specify how extra-clinical evidence could be integrated into the clinical explanatory models, raising questions about the logical and empirical relations between therapy and research, and between the pragmatics of the clinic and those of knowledge. Ironically, it is interesting to note that often there is a large but tacit import of 'extra-clinical' standards into the clinic. For example, the psychoanalytic community being part of the larger Western psychiatric discourse, depends upon the comprehensive indices of mental illness stipulated by this institution, such as the DSM Manual of psychiatry. However, measures of comparability between these therapeutic indices and the theory being used in therapy are intuitive and unsystematised. The area of psychotherapeutic research in general and psychoanalysis in particular throws up many interesting theoretical and methodological problems. Philosophers can contribute positively to these debates.

The epistemological rationale provided to science in terms of computability of meaning and verification by experiment is conventionally referred to as a semantic view of science. A semantic view is based upon the idea that scientific theories are formal systems comprising a set of representations, schemas, models or computations. They represent reality by using formal, usually mathematical, possibilities of their language and they are usually subsumable under unifying logical rationalities. Verification is methodologically complex and involves the evolution of an autonomous philosophy of confirmation. The status of psychoanalysis as knowledge can be sustained on the basis of the possibilities of capitalising on a recognition of these two features of scientific theories, its formal and theoretical complexity and possibilities of theoretic coherence; and its empirical and methodological complexity and possibilities of empirical convergence. Psychoanalysis recognises both that theoretical multiplicity is to be tempered by a search for a common ground and that the research programme must confront the issue of being able to process, consistently and repeatedly, the phenomenal presentations that fall within its domain by the methodological determination of truth.

Our view of science as being 'socio-cognitive' in nature is philosophically close to this semantic view of science. Even at the cost of repetition it may be said that this view of science recognises a cognitive as well as a normative dimension of science. Science is viewed as a class of *events* occurring in a society, intentionally pursued by agents interested in knowing certain kinds of reality and determined by different philosophical criteria or norms. Psychoanalysis pursues the task of resolving problems relating to the delimitation and integration of the general theory and its clinical models, normatively presented through a theory of meaning and explanation. Equally important is the empirical realm of science, raising pertinent questions about devising appropriate methodologies, possibilities of comparability between them, and the collection and synthesis of data based upon normative criteria of truth and experiment. A philosophy of science recognises and allocates the right place to all these with respect to the self-defined goals of the research programme, thereby specifying the philosophical 'foundations' of the theory. We have come full circle: outlining the philosophical foundations of a scientific theory is to provide the overall socio-cognitive rationality for that science. It is to describe the rationality of that science in terms of its entire range of activities. Surely, the foundational problem is a normative one at a philosophical level. However, an apt response to it takes into account the theoretical and methodological complexity of the scientific research programme.

III

A consideration of psychoanalytic criticism has indicated that foundationalism, as a view of science, is philosophically unacceptable. Its epistemology is questionable and hence, its evaluation of the science itself is wrong. The alternative is not an argument for an anti-foundationalism. Many philosophers, mainly from the continent, support this position. For them, knowledge has no foundations and to attempt to provide one will be futile. However, in its philosophical excesses, this position equals the foundationalist positions. We have explicitly recognised the relevance of foundational questions and have argued that psychoanalysis can be given a scientific rationality which is not foundationalist. Understanding the philosophical nature of psychoanalysis as being an essentially cognitive theory, we have sought to provide an overall epistemic rationale for the research programme.

We must still attend to the humanistic query: whether the search for a scientific rationality, particularly in terms of causal laws, is a threat to autonomy in domains where the object of study is human. The relation between science and violence has aroused the concern of many social scientists today. If all scientific rationality is to be viewed sceptically, then so will this rationality which we have tried to provide for psychoanalysis. The sciences, particularly the human sciences, have carved out their own invincible niche in society and their presence can no longer be negated. There are very few convincing arguments against the promotion of science as a social activity. All that we claim to know about the world and ourselves seems to hinge upon one or the other science. There must be a philosophical way of saying both that the search for scientific laws is a legitimate and necessary epistemological exercise and also that the freedom of man is not thereby squandered by this venture; that a science can no more shirk its humanistic commitments than it can its epistemological determination.

Knowledge is by definition a collective or what is called a socio-cognitive exercise. The socio-cognitive view of science not only points to the universality and generalisability of knowledge but also to the *situatedness* of a science in a society. Science is public because language games are public. Relativisation of knowledge with respect to individual consciousness or social perspectives together with a disregard for epistemology is a denial of the social cognitive nature of knowledge. Any philosophical viewpoint which denies the normatively determined embeddedness of knowledge in a society will confront these three questions: for whom is it constructed, what for and how. These are the three philosophical disgraces of solipsism, relativism and agnosticism Solipsism is an intellectual disgrace because an individual does not require to know anything at all if he actually believes that the world comprises only himself. In a relativistic world where anything goes, rationality for choice is lost. An agnostic who denies the need for knowledge would fail to reach beyond the phenomenal and differentiate between the real and the illusory. The organisation of objects and the self into knowledge requires the competent use of normatively given criteria.

The notion of causality is one such criterion used for understanding the spatio-temporal patterning and necessary relations between objects in the world. 'It enables us to see order in and make sense of phenomena which otherwise would seem haphazard and arbitrary . . .' (Dilman, 1984, p. 153). The reason why the empirical proposal for viewing human behaviour as describable by causal laws is loathed by humanistic philosophy is because traditional philosophy viewed causality as an ontological, and not as an epistemological problem. In its traditional, ontological sense, causes were opposed to free will. Any argument for causality first had to respond to the charge of fatalism. However, contemporary philosophy of science does not necessarily oppose causality of free will. Causality is, as Wittgenstein has said, the 'form of a law'. The 'law' of causality raises epistemological problems, such as those relating to the nature of causal explanations, distinctions between causal, accidental or coincidental associations, common causes, and the relation between statistical and causal relevance. Modern considerations of causality, particularly in the context of its use in the methodology of the social sciences, is increasingly epistemological.

The shift from an ontological to an epistemological understanding of causality renders the notion cognitive: science seeks natural ways of ordering objects in relations. There is indeed the expectation in all causal perspectives that the laws and explanations defined in the theory occur extra-theoretically, that the necessary relation holds in reality. Causality does *ontologise* knowledge. However, the expectation that the world conforms to causal laws reflects our ways of ordering things in the world. We are compelled, by our philosophical requirements, to explain phenomena in a law-like manner. A causal law specifies, in terms permissible by the theory, what is the necessary empirical connection between objects in a domain and the methodology verifies this connection. A causal law is empirical because its truth value is decided by the experiment, and it is necessary because it is law-like. A causal law has the form of a synthetic *a priori* statement. The necessity is a logical and not an ontological one, by virtue of its being cast in the form of a biconditional.

The view of causality as the ontological basis of determinism erroneously describes a science as the logical study of essences. Sciences study accidents, and necessary relations may be said to hold between accidents by virtue of our perception of them. Objectivity, or the objectness of objects, opens the way for the causal necessity. The 'thisness' of red is compelling, though the necessity is not an ontological one but a psychological one. Realism implies that objects are given in some pre-determined way to our enterprise of knowing. The naturalness of objects makes scientific knowledge possible. If this is true, we may speak of the object and causal relations between objects as naturally necessary where 'natural' is defined cognitively. The synthetic *a priori* nature of causal laws involves making epistemic decisions with respect to the nature of objects delimited by a specific domain, the possibilities of logical formalisation of the necessary relations between these objects and verification of these relations. There are objective and pragmatic limits to causal explanations set by the research communities.

Causality is inevitably linked to generalisability and predictability over cases. Predictability is an important part of science and it makes science credible as knowledge. It gives an economy and neatness to thought and to the construction of knowledge. If we are condemned to see pictures of the world anyway, we may as well have harsh and clear pictures rather than softly focused, amorphous ones. Formal predictability and statistical measurements of rational belief in a theoretical system indicate that the picture of the world described by a theory is complete to a measurable degree. Quantification of objects, assigning numbers to things of the world and the possibilities of measurement are not merely scientific abstractions. Rather, they are based on our cognition of identities and differences between objects. Mathematisation of objects is natural and not artificial, related to the way we perceive and order the world. Assigning numbers to things is not possible unless we can recognise both that one object is the same as the other, and also that one object is unique. Knowing one chair as another chair, for example, is not possible unless we can perceive both that this chair is identical to the first chair in specifiable ways and also that this chair is distinct from the other. Recognition of repetition, a function involving both perception and thought, lies at the basis of mathematisation. Quantification lies at the very basis of our pictures of the world, whether these pictures are rendered in an ordinary language or in a scientific language. Community agreement and instrumentality of science are the consequences of cognitively completed pictures. Phenomena make sense and can be used commonly and repeatedly once the picture is specified using a particular language game.

The hermeneutic fear of scientific abstraction is rooted in the belief that if one can predict another's behaviour one can also *control* it in some ways. This is a rather naive view of social behaviour and change. Our social experience of violence and aggression in society, deviant behaviour, delinquency, criminality, addictions and other forms of maladaptive behaviour shows an intransigency despite the availability of scientific knowledge and its possibilities of predictability. The fact that we know in a general way why these behaviours are caused and how they can be corrected has not mitigated the occurrence nor has it effected a complete cure. The social fact is that in spite of our knowledge of these forms of behaviour, our control over them seems negligible.

That control of human behaviour is difficult despite predictability is a cause for therapeutic concern and challenge. Human nature has a grossness which may be impossible to overcome, despite our knowledge.

Given the ideal ethical conditions in the clinic, such as the patient's consent and motivation to therapy and the psychoanalyst's intentions, self-control is the goal of therapy. The consent sanctions the fact that, given a therapist's competence, cognitive change can be effected in a way such that patterns of behaviour can be modified in foreseeable ways. If this is control, then it is accepted and *required* for therapeutic change. Forced interventions such as the enforcement of therapy on unwilling subjects, hospitalisation for achieving political goals, drugging a patient forcibly, do raise the problem of appropriation of the subject leading to several ethical dilemmas for the therapist and society at large. This indicates that there are two forms of control, one ethically legitimate and the other unethical, depending on whether control furthers the goals of therapy and the interest of the patient or not.

It is important to note, however, that the causal laws and the possibilities of predictability are the same in both cases of control. The truth and falsity of the knowledge used in therapy does not vary with the ethical and unethical uses of this knowledge. The ethical problem of control throws up the question of using knowledge for goals external to therapy and not about the formation or the contents of knowledge. When illegitimate forms of control are used, what is questioned is not the validity of the knowledge, but rather the way it has been used.

'Laws' are of two kinds—natural and socio-cultural—and they differ in their philosophical nature. A natural causal law such as in psycho-analysis states how the present has fully grown out of the past and gives epistemic guarantees for saying how, if we know the prevailing conditions, we can know future states. Causal laws are deterministic as opposed to cultural laws, which are mechanistic. A mechanistic law is like a computer programme, indetermined and man-made. It is rooted in social constructions and consensus. Freedom is opposed to mechanism and not to causal determinism. We are free because we can effect legislative changes in our socio-cultural determination. We can change our cultural laws because we have made them. The humanistic thinkers conflate the philosophical distinction between natural and cultural laws, i.e., between determinism and mechanism.

The questions of causality and freedom are qualitatively different, and do not belong to the same domain. The former is an epistemological and cognitive question relating to the possibility of knowledge given our natural and linguistic limitations, while the latter is concerned with our social organisation. Freedom is not a cognitive concept. It may perhaps be said that it is cognitive to the extent that all therapy ideally aims at making the patient 'free' of his illness or disorder. Used in this way, it is not an exalted concept at all in the hermeneutic sense and is simply analogous to saying that a person is 'free' of his migraines. In this sense, freedom refers simply to a general sense of psychological well-being given by cognitive self-experiential and objective parameters.

As used by the continental thinkers freedom is a *value*. In this sense, it is a concept idealised by all ethical perspectives whether they are explicitly humanistic or not. Just as one of the intended goals of science is objectivity, one of the intended goals of ethics is freedom. Philosophically, freedom, like any other philosophical notion, is given by both normative and pragmatic criteria. It is not necessarily self-evident or axiomatic as the continental thinkers claim. Normatively, philosophers have tried to understand freedom in terms of rational choice. For the existentialist, freedom is manifested in dialogue and inter-subjective communication. The critical hermeneutics state that it is action which must be free. Pragmatically, ethics also specifies how freedom may be attained, for example, through protest or through negotiations. Philosophical and methodological criteria can be outlined for the ethical notion of freedom. Pre-theoretic notions of freedom are not philosophically possible.

The continental thinkers proposed two distinct paradigms of freedom: one advocating an individual, psychological freedom, and the other pertaining to social and legislative. The issue of freedom may be raised both with respect to the individual and institutions. One can meaningfully ask if an individual is free under particular circumstances and contexts and whether an institution allows the freedom of individuals through its legislation. These constitute two different kinds of ethical considerations.

In the therapeutic context, the question of freedom has been raised by the critical humanists only with respect to the individual, particularly the analysand. They raise the question of humanism as if it were only a clinical issue and related only to the patient. This is rather curious because the psychoanalyst is also vulnerable to oppression though the structures of oppression of the patient and the analyst in the two cases may not be the same. It is well recognised in psychoanalytic theory that everyday interaction with abnormality is often a threat to the analyst's sense of self and that identification of the analysand with the analyst may work the other way too. Counter-transference is a serious problem for many therapists. Psychotherapists could also be oppressed by institutional and other political pressures. The ethical question of the analysand's freedom may be legitimately raised at both the individual as well as the institutional levels. At the individual level, a professional ethic would provide an ethical rationality for clinical practices while at the social level, political negotiations and policy change are targeted. Humanism is not merely a clinical issue; it is a far more complex issue than the humanists have conceived of.

Psychoanalysis, like any other theory of man, may be seen as an affirmation of the free will of man rather than as a theory of suppression of speech and domination. Freud saw the analysand in the clinic as an active and free participant in the dialogue. Indeed, the therapeutic efficacy of the theory is at stake by a denial of the patient's participation in his cure. The psychotherapeutic contract itself would be rendered in principle impossible except upon the premise of free will. Ideally, the therapy begins at the point when the patient submits to the recognition that he is indeed what he is nominated as: a 'patient' in need of psychotherapeutic help and desiring cure. Freud said, 'The primary motive force in the therapy is the patients' suffering and the wish to be cured that arises from it' (S.E., Vol. 12, p. 143). Freud maintained that if the analytic process must endure this motive force 'must be maintained till the end of the treatment'. The voice of the patient is an indispensable part of the psychoanalytic dialogue and the force which moves the dialogue is the patient's self-interest in effecting his own cure. In so far as the psychoanalyst is interested in the patient, the onus is upon the analyst to ensure through a theory of therapy, that the patient does present himself as a continuing participant in the psychotherapeutic exchange. A theory of therapy would provide an ethical rationality for particular clinical practices, such as possibilities of communication, interpersonal interaction, the uses and abuses of dialogue and silences, and scope for interpretation in the face of the patient's distress. It is a theory of therapy that can answer ethical questions relating to the individual, using a therapy.

Just as epistemic controls are needed for making correct scientific explanations in the clinic, it is important that a theory of communication be formulated for adequate ethical controls within the process of communication. There must be ways of stating when communication is 'free' and when it is not, requiring an examination of clinical notions of empathy, listening, therapist's attention, verbal and non-verbal responses, etc. One of Freud's own recommendations for a theory of communication was the cultivation of an 'evenly suspended attention'. He said:

> As soon as anyone deliberately concentrates his attention to a certain degree, he begins to select from the material before him; one point will be fixed in his mind with particular clearness and some other will be correspondingly disregarded, and in making this selection he will be following his expectations and inclinations. This, however, is precisely what must not be done (S.E., Vol. 12, p. 112).

In order to grant the patient maximum attention possible, Freud suggested that a manner of listening and communication, 'like a telephone receiver', be adopted. This recommendation is substantiated by detailed analyses of a number of specific things that a practitioner must and must not do—not take notes during the analysis, vividly remember the names and the problems of the patients, cultivate an 'emotional coldness' or 'opacity', 'avoiding speculation or brooding over cases while they are in analysis' (S.E., Vol. 12, p. 114), etc. Even though at the beginning of this document, Freud cautioned that the psychoanalytic method suited his constitution and may not suit others, it is a fair claim that he would have desired *any* form of psychoanalytic therapy to be well equipped with a model of communication and inter-subjective interaction.

The progress of analysis also depends on the capacity of the patient to recount, as he desires, the development of his life and illness; the scope of the analysis being limited by the extent to which he is able to perform such a recount. Referring to the goal of analysis, Freud warned that it may prove counter-productive for the analysand if the analyst expected more of the patient than the patient was capable of giving. Realistic goals must be set, to which the patient can meaningfully attach himself. If the aim of the analysis is to make room for the re-functioning of the patient's 'reality principle', which in Freud's view was equal to rational choice, then, the patient's recognition of what is possible for him must be constrained by his structure of being and not by the analyst's prescriptions. Freud suggested,

> Not every neurotic has a high talent for sublimation; one can assume of many of them that they would not have fallen ill at all if

they had possessed the art of sublimating their instincts. If we press them unduly towards sublimation and cut them off from the most accessible and convenient instinctual satisfactions, we shall usually make life even harder for them than they feel it in any case (S.E., Vol. 12, p. 119).

Freud was of the view that the inauguration, the progress and the culmination of therapy was premised on the free will of the subject.

Psychoanalysis does not aim to lay the basis for oppression and domination. On the other hand, it is premised on the recognition of the free will of the subject. The problem of freedom in the context of the clinic is one of the patient's consent to analysis and his satisfaction with the analysis. These require an examination of the ethical dimensions of clinical practice and the political or administrative norms which determine such practice. These are clinical issues and not cognitive issues and the possibility of freedom in the clinic rests upon these considerations.

The continental thinkers rightly pointed out the naivete of believing that knowledge is impartial. Knowledge, ideally and definitively, is for everyone, but politics does not allow it to be so. To be able to use knowledge is a privilege, as seen in the preferential use that psychotherapy in particular, and medical practice in general, is put to. The availability of this knowledge is often determined by the individual's socio-economic status. Our social and political organisation is such that not everyone is allowed free access to the available knowledge. This is the social reality and social change must aim to counter this.

However, the alternative is not to argue that the ideal conditions of freedom should decide the *validity* of knowledge. This is clearly false, for we do not define what knowledge is on the basis of ethical criteria. A science is determined by epistemological considerations. Epistemology provides the criteria for the commitment with which a scientific community self-reflectively scrutinises and reviews its own method of operation. But every science does make an impact on human life, on its quality and its aesthetic. Ethics studies this impact. Epistemology makes a theory a well formed science and ethics makes it a human science.

This is true of both the physical and the human sciences. Even in the physical sciences the capacity of scientific theories to order phenomena according to laws is not a sanction for the oppression of nature. No scientific theory, whether natural or social, aims to provide a philosophical foundation for oppression. For instance, the stars and planets are studied and an astronomical theory formulated in order to construct navigational maps, predict seasons, etc., but there is no claim here that the objects under study are to submit to the laws. When one explains how the moon rises or sets, one does not thereby aim to control the movement of the moon.

The continental argument that only the human sciences are accountable for the question of humanism is myopic at best. The implications of this view are in fact a clear sanction for technological domination which is primarily natural scientific. Natural sciences as much as the human sciences are indeed accountable for the broader question of freedom. The idea that only humans are free and attempts to study human beings should confront the question of freedom before it builds its epistemological foundations is anthropocentric. This idea denies what every environmentalist intuitively knows, that nature too, in a sense, is free and that the sciences must address the question of the freedom of nature from man and consequently, the question of man's freedom in the context of the serious damage he has done to nature.

Any science can be put to bad use, as can be clearly seen from the threat of nuclear war. Similarly, psychotherapy in general, and psychoanalysis as a special form of such therapy, can be put to bad use. This is not the consequence of epistemology or the formation of knowledge, but of the way humans are and how they perceive themselves, others and the world with respect to the knowledge they have, or the way knowledge is organised. Knowledge is power because people use knowledge. However, people do not always use it in the best possible way. For a liberated society, the scrutiny of use, control of abuse and development of better technological alternatives is a sound ideal to work towards. These will indeed require fresh philosophical and scientific thinking. A science grows because of an active critical interaction in a society between its epistemology and its ethics. The questions arising at the epistemic periphery of scientific theories, about the implications of the theory for society and human dignity, and lately, for natural ecology, have assumed an all-embracing importance in modern society. We are still too romantic to give up our sense of freedom and democracy.

Any science poses sociological questions and social science has been independent enough to critically examine these questions. Often alternative sciences are developed in order to mitigate the cultural incompatibility of the prevailing science in a culture. The onus is on us, as people who use knowledge, to optimally capitalise on the tension between epistemology and sociology of knowledge as was done in the nineteenth century. Epistemological and sociological questions appear together in history and decisions of priority by the concerned communities may be required to sort out these issues. For example, it is interesting to note that the deletion of homosexuality from the DSM Manual was effected not because of clinical considerations but because of deliberations with the concerned community (Meyer, 1985, p. 1050). Goffman's (1961) sociological analysis in his *Asylums* is particularly illuminating in this context. Studying the structure of the mental hospital, he observed the clinical considerations were often limited to a very small part of the patient's stay in the hospital. A large part of the 'treatment' in a hospital may be of an administrative nature, involving its own structures of organisation, hierarchy and politics like any other institution. Often it is difficult to decide whether the treatment is clinical or administrative in nature.

The collective nature of any science transforms it into an institution, or a social contract between people. Science is given by its epistemology, but organising and using a science is left to us. In this sense, the celebrated dehumanisation is not the fall-out of a scientific epistemology, but our own incapacity to prioritise our values *vis-à-vis* the products and glamours of science. Science does not owe us humanism. We, who use science, owe it to humanity.

BIBLIOGRAPHY

■ ■ ■

ACHINSTEIN, P. (Ed.). (1983). *The Concept of Evidence*. Oxford: Oxford University Press.

ARLOW, J.A. (1979). 'Metaphor and the Psychoanalytic Situation', *Psychoanalytic Quarterly*, Vol. 48, pp. 363–85.

BETTELHEIM, B. (1983). *Freud and Man's Soul*. New York: Random House Alfred A. Knopf Inc.

BLACK, M. (1980). 'More about Metaphor', in A. Ortony (Ed.). *Metaphor and Thought*. Cambridge: Cambridge University Press, pp. 19–43

BREWER, W.F. and LAMBERT, B.L. (1992). The Theory-ladenness of Observation: Evidence from Cognitive Psychology. Paper presented at a thematic session of the XVth International Congress of Psychology, Brussels, Belgium, July.

BREWIN, C.R. (1989). 'Cognitive Change Processes in Psychotherapy', *Psychological Review*, Vol. 96, No. 3, pp. 379–94.

BROWN, H.I. (1987). *Observation and Objectivity*. New York: Oxford University Press.

———. (1990). 'Prospective Realism', *Studies in the History and Philosophy of Science*, Vol. 21, No. 2, pp. 211–42.

CARVETH, D.L. (1982). 'Psychoanalysis and Social Theory: The Hobbesian Problem Revisited', *Psychoanalysis and Contemporary Thought*, Vol. 71, pp. 43–98.

———. (1984). 'The Analyst's Metaphors: A Deconstructionist Perspective', *Psychoanalysis and Contemporary Thought*, Vol. 7, No. 4, pp. 491–560.

———. (1987). 'Epistemological Foundations of Psychoanalysis: A Deconstructionist Perspective', *Philosophy of the Social Sciences*, Vol. 17, pp. 97–115.

CHALMERS, D. (1992). Unpublished draft on Consciousness and Cognition. Indiana: Centre for Research on Concepts and Cognition.

COHEN, J. (1989). *An Introduction to the Philosophy of Induction and Probability*. Oxford: Clarendon Press.

CREWS, F. (1980). 'Analysis Terminable', *Commentary*, Vol. 70, pp. 25–34.

CUSHING, J.T. (1990). 'Is Scientific Methodology Interestingly Atemporal?', *British Journal of Philosophy of Science*, Vol. 40, pp. 177–94.

DANZIGER, K. (1985). 'The Methodological Imperative in Psychology', *Philosophy of the Social Sciences*, Vol. 15, pp. 1–13.

DILMAN, I. (1984). *Freud and Mind*. Oxford: Basil Blackwell.

DUMMETT, M. (1975). 'What is a Theory of Meaning?', in S. Guttenplan (Ed.), *Mind and Language: Wolfson College Lectures: 1974*. London: Oxford University Press.

EAGLE, M.N. (1984). *Recent Developments in Psychoanalysis*. New York: McGraw-Hill.
————. (1986). 'Critical Notice: A. Grünbaum's "The Foundations of Psychoanalysis: A Philosophical Critique"', *Philosophy of Science*, Vol. 53, pp. 65–88.
————. (1988). 'Psychoanalysis and the Personal', in P. Clark and C. Wright (Eds.), *Mind, Psychoanalysis and Science*. London: Basil Blackwell.

EDELSON, M. (1977). 'Psychoanalysis as Science', *Journal of Nervous and Mental Disease*, Vol. 165, No. 1, pp. 1–28.
————. (1986a). 'The Evidential Value of the Psychoanalyst's Clinical Data', *Behavioural and Brain Sciences*, Vol. 9, No. 2, pp. 232–34.
————. (1986b). 'Causal Explanation in Science and in Psychoanalysis', *Psychoanalytic Study of the Child*, Vol. 41, pp. 89–127.
————. (1989). *Psychoanalysis: A Theory in Crisis*. Chicago: University of Chicago Press.

ELLENBERGER, H. (1970). *The Unconscious Before Freud*. New York: Basic Books.

EMDE, R. (1988). 'Development Terminable and Interminable 1. Innate and Motivational Factors from Infancy. Part I', *International Journal of Psychoanalysis*, Vol. 69, pp. 23–42.

EVANS, G. (1982). *The Varieties of Reference*. New York. Oxford University Press, pp. 205–66.

EYSENCK, H. and WILSON, G.D. (Eds.). (1973). *The Experimental Study of Freudian Theories*. New York: Methuen.

FERGUSON, M. (1985). 'A Critique of Grünbaum on Psychoanalysis', *Journal of the American Academy of Psychoanalysis*, Vol. 13, No. 3, pp. 329–45.

FISHER, S. and GREENBERG, R.P. (1977). *The Scientific Credibility of Freud's Theory and Therapy*. New York: Basic Books.

FLANAGAN, JR., O.J. (1984). *The Science of Mind*. Cambridge: The MIT Press.

FODOR, J.A. (1981). *Representations*. London: Harvester Press.

FOUCAULT, M. (1965). *Madness and Civilization: A History of Insanity in the Age of Reason* (tr. R. Howard). London: Tavistock.

FREUD, S. (1955–74). *The Standard Edition of the Complete Psychological Works of Sigmund Freud*. Vols. 1–24 (tr. J. Strachey). London: Hogarth Press and the Institute of Psychoanalysis.
————. (1954). *Origins of Psychoanalysis: Letters to Wilhelm Fliess, Drafts and Notes—1887–1902* (ed. M. Bonaparte, A. Freud and E. Kris). New York: Basic Books.

FRIEDMAN, M. (1985). 'Truth and Confirmation', in H. Kornblith (Ed.), *Naturalizing Epistemology*. Cambridge: The MIT Press.

GADAMER, H.P. (1976). *Truth and Method* (tr. W. Glen). London: Sheed and Ward.

GASPER, P. (1990). 'Explanation and Scientific Realism', in D. Knowles (Ed.), *Explanation and Its Limits*. Royal Institute of Philosophy Supplement, No. 27. Cambridge: Cambridge University Press.

GILL, M.M. and HOFFMAN, I.Z. (1982). *Analysis of Transference—Volume II: Studies of Nine Audio-Recorded Psychoanalytic Sessions. Psychological Issues: Monograph 54*. New York: International Universities Press, Inc.

GLYMOUR, C. (1983). 'Relevant Evidence', in P. Achinstein (Ed.), *The Concept of Evidence*. New York: Oxford University Press.

GOFFMAN, A. (1961). *Asylums*. New York: Anchor Books.

GRÜNBAUM, A. (1976). 'Is Falsifiability the Touchstone of Scientific Rationality? Karl Popper versus Induction', in R.S. Cohen, P. Feyerabend and M.W. Wartofskly

(Eds.), *Essays in Memory of Imre Lakatos: Boston Studies in the Philosophy of Science*. Vol. 39. Dordrecht: D. Reidel.

GRÜNBAUM, A. (1979). 'Is Freudian Psychoanalytic Theory Pseudo-scientific by Karl Popper's Criterion of Demarcation?', *American Philosophical Quarterly*, Vol. 16, pp. 131–41.

———. (1980). 'Epistemological Liabilities of the Clinical Appraisal of Psychoanalytic Theory', *Nous*, Vol. 14, pp. 307–85.

———. (1983a). 'Freud's Theory: The Perspective of a Philosopher of Science', *Proceedings and Addresses of the American Philosophical Association*, Vol. 57, No. 1, pp. 5–31.

———. (1983b). 'Is Object-relations Theory Better Founded than Orthodox Psychoanalysis?: A Reply to Jane Flax', *Journal of Philosophy*, Vol. 81, pp. 46–51.

———. (1983c). 'Logical Foundations of Psychoanalytic Theory', *Erkenntnis*, Vol. 19, pp. 109–52.

———. (1984). *The Foundations of Psychoanalysis: A Philosophical Critique*. Berkeley: University of California Press.

———. (1986). 'Precis of *The Foundations of Psychoanalysis: A Philosophical Critique*', *Behavioural and Brain Sciences*, Vol. 9, No. 2, pp. 217–28.

———. (1989a). 'The Degeneration of Popper's Theory of Demarcation', in I.C. Jarvie and F.D. Agostino (Eds.), *Freedom and Rationality, 'Festscrift' for John Watkins— Boston Studies in the Philosophy of Science*. Dordrecht: D. Reidel.

———. (1989b). 'The Placebo Concept in Medicine and Psychiatry', in M. Shepherd and N. Sartorius (Eds.), *Non-specific Aspects of Treatment*. Stuttgart: Hans Huber Publishers.

HABERMAS, J. (1972). *Knowledge and Human Interests* (tr. J.J. Shapiro). London: Heinemann.

———. (1978). 'Systematically Distorted Communication', in P. Connerton (Ed.), *Critical Sociology*. Harmondsworth: Penguin.

HACKING, I. (1983). *Representing and Intervening*. Cambridge: Cambridge University Press.

———. (1988). 'On the Stability of the Laboratory Sciences', *Journal of Philosophy*, Vol. 85, No. 10, pp. 507–14.

HALLER, R. (1988). 'Justification and Praxeological Foundationalism', *Inquiry*, Vol. 31, No. 3, pp. 335–45.

HARTMANN, H. (1958). *Ego Psychology and the Problem of Adaptation*. New York: International Universities Press.

HEELAN, P. (1983). 'Natural Science as Hermeneutic of Instrumentation', *Philosophy of Science*, Vol. 50, pp. 183–204.

———. (1988). 'Experiment and Theory: Constitution and Reality', *Journal of Philosophy*, Vol. 85, No. 10, pp. 515–27.

HESSE, M.B. (1974). *The Structure of Scientific Inference*. New York: MacMillan Press Ltd.

HESSE, M.B. and ARBIB, M.A. (1986). *The Construction of Reality*. Cambridge: Cambridge University Press.

HOLT, R.R. (1976). 'Freud's Theory of the Primary Process—Present Status', *Psychoanalysis and Contemporary Science*, Vol. 5, pp. 61–99.

———. (1981a). 'The Manifest and Latent Meanings of Meta-psychology', *The Annual of Psychoanalysis*, Vol. 10, pp. 233–55.

———. (1981b). 'The Death and Transfiguration of Metapsychology', *International Review of Psychoanalysis*, Vol. 8, pp. 129–43.

HOLT, R.R. (1985). 'The Current Status of Psychoanalytic Theory', *Psychoanalytic Psychology*, Vol. 2, No. 4, pp. 289–315.

IZENBERG, G.N. (1976). *The Existentialist Critique of Freud: The Critique of Autonomy.* New Jersey: Princeton University Press.

JAHNKE, H.N. (1981). 'Science as Language', in H.N. Jahnke and M. Otte (Eds.), *Epistemological and Social Problems in the Early 19th Century*. Dordrecht: D. Reidel.

JAHNKE, H.N. and OTTE, M. (Eds.). (1981). *Epistemological and Social Problems in the Early 19th Century*. Dordrecht: D. Reidel.

JOHANNESSEN, K.S. (1990). 'The Concept of Practice in Wittgenstein's Later Philosophy', *Inquiry*, Vol. 31, pp. 357–69.

JOHNSON-LAIRD, P.N. (1983). *Mental Models: Towards a Cognitive Science of Language, Inference and Consciousness*. Cambridge: Cambridge University Press.

JONES, E. (1961). *The Life and Work of S. Freud* (ed. and abridged L. Trilling and S. Marcus). New York: Basic Books.

KARAZU, T.B. (1986). 'The Specificity Versus Non-specificity Dilemma: Towards Identifying Therapeutic Change Agents', *American Journal of Psychiatry*, Vol. 14, Nos. 3–6, pp. 687–95.

KINOSHITA, J. (1990). 'How do Scientific Explanations Explain', in D. Knowles (Ed.), *Explanation and Its Limits*. Royal Institute of Philosophy Supplement, No. 27. Cambridge: Cambridge University Press.

KLINE, P. (1972). *Fact and Fantasy in Freudian Theory*. New York: Methuen.

———. (1986). 'Grünbaum's Philosophical Critique of Psychoanalysis: Or What I Don't Know Isn't Knowledge', *Behavioural and Brain Sciences*, Vol. 9, No. 2, Commentary, pp. 245–47.

LAKATOS, I. (1976). 'Falsification and the Methodology of Scientific Research Programmes', in S. Harding (Ed.), *Can Theories be Refuted? Essays on the Duhem-Quine Thesis*. Dordrecht: D. Reidel.

LAKOFF, G. and JOHNSON, M. (1980). *Metaphors We Live By*. Chicago: University of Chicago Press.

LEPLIN, J. (1984). *Scientific Realism*. Berkeley: University of California Press.

LEVY, D. (1988). 'Grünbaum's Freud', *Inquiry*, Vol. 31, No. 2, pp. 193–215.

LOCKWOOD, M. (1989). *Mind, Brain and the Quantum*. London: Basil Blackwell Ltd.

LUBORSKY, L. (1986). 'Evidence to Lessen Professor Grünbaum's Concern about Freud's Clinical Inference Method', *Behavioural and Brain Sciences*, Vol. 9, No. 2, Commentary, pp. 247–49.

MC CULLOCH, J. (1986). 'Scientism, Mind and Meaning', in P. Pettit and J. Mac Dowell (Eds.), *Subject, Thought and Context*. New York: Oxford University Press

MAC INTYRE, A. (1958). *The Unconscious: A Conceptual Analysis*. London: Routledge and Kegan Paul.

MACKLIN, R. (1983). 'Philosophical Conceptions of Rationality and Psychiatric Notions of Competency', *Synthese*, Vol. 57, pp. 205–24.

MAHER, P. (1990). 'Why Scientists Gather Evidence', *The British Journal for the Philosophy of Science*, Vol. 41, pp. 103–19.

MARCUSE, H. (1964). *One-Dimensional Man: Studies in the Ideology of Advanced Industrial Society*. London: Routledge and Kegan Paul.

MARGOLIS, J. (1986). *The Persistence of Reality I: Pragmatism Without Foundations*. London: Basil Blackwell.

MARMOR, J. (1986). 'New Directions in Psychoanalytic Theory and Therapy', in J. Marmor (Ed.), *Modern Psychoanalysis*. New York: Basic Books, Inc.

MEYER, J.K. (1985). 'Ego-dystonic Homosexuality', in H.I. Kaplan and B.J. Sadock, *Comprehensive Textbook of Psychiatry*. Vol. I, 4th Edition. Maryland: Williams and Wilkins.

MORMANN, T. (1991). 'Husserl's Philosophy of Science and the Semantic Approach', *Philosophy of Science*, Vol. 58, pp. 61–83.

NISBETT, R.E. and ROSS, L. (1980). *Human Inference: Strategies and Shortcomings of Social Judgment*. Englewood Cliffs: Prentice-Hall Inc.

OPATOW, B. (1989). 'Drive Theory and the Metapsychology of Experience', *International Journal of Psycho-Analysis*, Vol. 70, pp. 645–60.

PAPINEAU, D. (1990). 'Truth and Teleology', in D. Knowles (Ed.), *Explanation and Its Limits*. Royal Institute of Philosophy Supplement, 27. Cambridge: Cambridge University Press.

POPPER, K.R. (1965). *Conjectures and Refutations: The Growth of Scientific Knowledge*. 2nd Edition. London: Routledge and Kegan Paul.

POSENER, J.A. (1989). 'A Cognitive Perspective on Object Relations, Drive Development and Ego Structure in the Second and Third Years of Life', *International Journal of Psycho-Analysis*, Vol. 70, pp. 627–43.

PUTNAM, H. (1988). *Representation and Reality*. London: Bradford Books/Cambridge: The MIT Press.

RANGELL, L. (1985). 'The Object in Psychoanalytic Theory', *Journal of the American Psychoanalytic Association*, Vol. 33, No. 2, pp. 301–34.

———. (1988). 'The Future of Psychoanalysis: The Scientific Crossroads', *Psychoanalytic Quarterly*, Vol. 57, No. 3, pp. 313–40.

RESCHER, N. (1980). *Induction: An Essay on the Justification of Inductive Reasoning*. Oxford: Basil Blackwell.

RICOEUR, P. (1970). *Freud and Philosophy: An Essay on Interpretation* (tr. D. Savage). Cambridge: Yale University Press.

———. (1981a). 'The Task of Hermeneutics', in J.B. Thompson (Ed. and Tr.), *Hermeneutics and the Human Sciences*. Cambridge: Cambridge University Press.

———. (1981b). 'Phenomenology and Hermeneutics', in J.B. Thompson (Ed. and Tr.), *Hermeneutics and the Human Sciences*. Cambridge: Cambridge University Press.

———. (1981c). 'The Question of Proof in Freud's Psychoanalytic Writings', in J.B. Thompson (Ed. and Tr.), *Psychoanalysis and the Human Sciences*. Cambridge: Cambridge University Press.

———. (1987a). 'From Existentialism to the Philosophy of Language', *Philosophy Today*, Vol. 31, No. 1/4, pp. 88–96.

———. (1987b). 'Creativity in Language: Word, Polysemy, Metaphor', *Philosophy Today*, Vol. 31, No. 1/4, pp. 97–111.

RIPS, L.J. and CONRAD, F.G. (1989). 'Folk Psychology of Mental Activities', *Psychological Review*, Vol. 96, No. 2, pp. 187–207.

ROAZEN, P. (1975). *Freud and His Followers*. New York: Alfred A. Knopf.

RUBEN, D.H. (1990). 'Singular Explanation and the Social Sciences', in D. Knowles (Ed.), *Explanation and Its Limits*. Royal Institute of Philosophy Supplement, No. 27. Cambridge: Cambridge University Press.

RUBINSTEIN, B.B. (1983). 'Freud's Early Theories of Hysteria', in R.S. Cohen and L. Lauden (Eds.), *Physics, Philosophy and Psychoanalysis: Essays in Honour of A. Grünbaum*. Dordrecht: D. Reidel.

SACHS, D. (1989). 'In Fairness to Freud: A Critical Notice of the Foundations of Psychoanalysis', *Philosophical Review*, Vol. 98, No. 3, July, pp. 349–78.

SALMON, W.C. (1967). *The Foundations of Scientific Inference*. Pennsylvania: University of Pittsburgh Press.

———. (1971). 'Statistical Explanation', in W.C. Salmon, *Statistical Explanation and Statistical Relevance*. With Contributions by R.C. Jeffrey and J.G. Greeno. Pennsylvania: University of Pittsburgh Press.

SARTRE, J.P. (1956). *Being and Nothingness: A Phenomenological Essay on Ontology* (tr. H. Barnes). New York: Pocket Books.

SCHAFER, R. (1980). 'Narration in the Psychoanalytic Dialogue', *Critical Inquiry*, Vol. 17, No. 1, Autumn, pp. 29–53.

SEDGWICK, P. (1972). 'Mental Illness *is* Illness', *Salmagundi*, No. 20. Monograph on 'Psychological Man: Approaches to an Emergent Social Type'.

SHAPERE, D. (1977). 'Scientific Theories and Their Domains', in F. Suppe (Ed.), *The Structure of Scientific Theories*. 2nd Edition. Illinois: University of Illinois Press.

SHERWOOD, M. (1969). *The Logic of Explanation in Psychoanalysis*. New York: Academic Press.

SHOPE, R.K. (1971). 'Physical and Psychic Energy', *Philosophy of Science*, Vol. 38, No. 1, pp. 1–12.

SIEGEL, H. (1990). 'Laudan's Normative Naturalism', *Studies in the History and Philosophy of Science*, Vol. 21, No. 2, pp. 295–313.

SOBER, E. (1987). 'Wesley Salmon's *Explanation and Causation*,' Review Article, *British Journal for Philosophy of Science*, Vol. 38, pp. 243–57.

SONTAG, S. (1979). *Illness as Metaphor*. New York: Vintage.

SPENCE, D.P. (1982). 'Narrative Persuasion'. Paper presented at the mid-winter meeting of Div. 39, American Psychological Association, 6 March.

SULLOWAY, F.J. (1979). *Freud: Biologist of the Mind*. New York: Basic Books.

SUPPE, F. (1976). 'Theoretical Laws', in M. Piaclecki, K. Szaniawksi and R. Wojcicki (Eds.), *Formal Methods of the Methodology of Science*. Ossolineum: Wroclaw.

SZASZ, T. (1974). *The Myth of Mental Illness: Foundations of a Theory of Personal Conduct*. New York: Harper and Row.

TARSKI, A. (1949). 'The Semantic Conception of Truth', in H. Feigl and W. Sellars (Eds.), *Readings in Philosophical Analysis*. Connecticut: Appleton-Century Crofts Inc.

TRIPPLETT, T. (1990). 'Recent Work on Foundationalism', *American Philosophical Quarterly*, Vol. 27, No. 2, pp. 93–116.

VON ECKHARDT, B. (1982). 'The Scientific Status of Psychoanalysis', in S.L. Gilman (Ed.), *Introducing Psychoanalytic Theory*. Brunner/Mazel.

———.(1984). 'A. Grünbaum: Psychoanalytic Epistemology', in J. Reppen (Ed.), *Beyond Freud: A Study of Modern Psychoanalytic Theorists*. N.J.:Analytic Press.

WAISMANN, F. (1968). 'Verifiability', in G.H.R. Parkinson (Ed.), *The Theory of Meaning*. Oxford: Oxford University Press.

WALLERSTEIN, R.S. (1983). 'Self-Psychology and "Classical" Psychoanalytic Psychology: The Nature of their Relationship', *Psychoanalysis and Contemporary Thought*, Vol. 6, No. 4.

———. (1986a). 'Psychoanalysis as a Science: A Response to the New Challenges', *Psychoanalytic Quarterly*, Vol. LV, pp. 414–51.

———. (1986b). 'Psychoanalysis, Psychoanalytic Science and Psychoanalytic Research', *Journal of American Psychoanalytic Association*, Vol. 36, No. 1, pp. 3–30.

WALLERSTEIN, R.S. (1988). 'One Psychoanalysis or Many?', *The International Journal of Psychoanalysis*, Vol. 69, No. 1, pp. 5–22.

———. (1990). 'Psychoanalysis: The Common Ground', *International Journal of Psychoanalysis*, Vol. 71, Pt. I.

WATANABE, T. (1992). Why is the Unifying of *Psychologies* so Difficult?. Paper presented at a thematic session of the XVth International Congress of Psychology, Brussels, Belgium, July.

WECKOWICZ, T.E. and LIEBEL-WECKOWICZ, H.P. (Eds.). (1990). *A History of Great Ideas in Abnormal Psychology*. Advances in Psychology Series, No. 66. The Netherlands: Elsevier Science Publishers, B.V.

WEISS, J. (1988). 'Testing Hypotheses about Unconscious Mental Functioning', *International Journal of Psycho-Analysis*, Vol. 69, pp. 87–95.

WITTGENSTEIN, L. (1974a). *Philosophical Investigations* (Tr. G.E.M. Anscombe). Oxford: Basil Blackwell.

———. (1974b). *On Certainty* (Ed. G.E.M. Anscombe and G.H. von Wright, tr. D. Paul and G.E.M. Anscombe). Oxford: Basil Blackwell.

———. (1975). *Philosophical Remarks* (Ed. R. Rhees, tr. R. Hargreaves and R. White). Oxford: Basil Blackwell.

INDEX

■ ■ ■